IDEOLOGY AND INTERNATIO

Ideology and International Institutions

Erik Voeten

PRINCETON UNIVERSITY PRESS

PRINCETON & OXFORD

Published by Princeton University Press
41 William Street, Princeton, New Jersey 08540
6 Oxford Street, Woodstock, Oxfordshire OX20 1TR

press.princeton.edu

All Rights Reserved
ISBN 978-0-691-20731-5
ISBN (pbk.) 978-0-691-20732-2
ISBN (e-book) 978-0-691-20733-9

British Library Cataloging-in-Publication Data is available

Editorial: Bridget Flannery-McCoy and Alena Chekanov
Production Editorial: Jenny Wolkowicki
Cover design: Karl Spurzem
Production: Brigid Ackerman
Publicity: Kathryn Stevens and Kate Hensley
Copyeditor: Joseph Dahm

Cover image: Shutterstock

This book has been composed in Miller

Printed on acid-free paper. ∞

Printed in the United States of America

10 9 8 7 6 5 4 3 2 1

To Kimberly

CONTENTS

CONTENTS [ix]

ACKNOWLEDGMENTS

THIS BOOK has been much longer in the making than I would prefer to admit. I started thinking about ideological contestation and multilateral politics two decades ago during my dissertation research at Princeton University. I have published articles and book chapters that reflect some of what I am trying to say in this book. However, this book is an attempt to offer a much broader and more general statement than any article or chapter could possibly permit. Indeed, aside from the chapter on populism and international courts, all the material in this book has not been published before.

Over the years, I have accumulated a great many intellectual and personal debts. I owe a great deal to Howard Rosenthal, not just for first encouraging me to look at United Nations decision making but especially for being a mentor in the truest sense: always willing to offer honest critical feedback and support in equal measures. I am hoping to pass it forward. Michael Doyle, Tom Romer, and Ken Schultz were also extremely important sources of inspiration, support, and wisdom during the early years.

I have been extremely fortunate to work in supportive university environments, first at George Washington University and now at Georgetown University. Lee Sigelman set an outstanding example of what kind, efficient, and decisive leadership looks like. He is very much missed. My colleagues and students at Georgetown University are a continuous source of inspiration. My sincerest thanks to Georgetown University's Mortara Center and the Government Department, especially its chair Charles King, for organizing a book manuscript workshop. I am extremely grateful for comments, suggestions, and criticisms from Andy Bennett, Marc Busch, Henry Farrell, Marty Finnemore, Miles Kahler, Yonatan Lupu, Kate McNamara, Abe Newman, and Nita Rudra. Nik Khalyanpur took fantastic notes and added his own valuable insights. I am also grateful to Jim Vreeland for extremely useful feedback on the full manuscript. Mike Bailey and Anton Strezhnev were outstanding collaborators on the UN ideal point estimation component of this project. Our Wednesday political economy lunch seminars are a source of outstanding critical feedback and friendly collegiality. Thanks especially to Raj Desai, Jenny Guardado, Andreas Kern,

Diana Kim, Marko Klasnja, Kate McNamara, Abe Newman, Irfan Nooruddin, Ken Opalo, Dennis Quinn, Nita Rudra, George Shambaugh, Joel Simmons, Yuhki Tajima, Jen Tobin, and Steve Weymouth. I am very appreciative to Camille Bangug, Laura Caron, Erin Sielaff, Anton Strezhnev, Brody Vogel, and Dongpeng Xia for excellent research assistance. The Peter Krogh endowment and the Edmund Walsh School of Foreign Service have provided very necessary financial support for the research that went into this book.

Several chapters of this book were presented at conferences and seminars. The chapter on militarized conflicts greatly benefited from comments at the Annual Meeting of the American Political Science Association, Philadelphia, September 2016, University of Pennsylvania, University of Maryland, New York University, Yale University, and the University of Virginia Law School. I appreciate feedback received at those seminars and from Todd Allee, Leonardo Baccini, Bernd Beber, Paul Huth, Yonatan Lupu, Ed Mansfield, Peter Rosendorf, and Beth Simmons. I appreciate the valuable comments on the populism chapter from audiences at the University of Leiden, University of Oslo (PluriCourts annual lecture), the Conference on European Studies (Glasgow), Annual Meeting of the American Political Science Association (San Francisco), the University of Pennsylvania (Perry World House), and Stockholm University. I have also greatly benefited from conversations with and comments from Silje Aambø Langvatn, Haillie Lee, Karen Alter, Cecilia Bailliet, Yoram Haftel, Sarah de Lange, Cas Mudde, Krzysztof Pelc, Beth Simmons, Jonas Tallberg, and Daniel Thomas. In addition, I greatly appreciate feedback on presentations from material in chapters 2 and 6 at the University of Sao Paolo, the University of Belo Horizonte, and MIT. I need to especially thank the PluriCourts center at the University of Oslo, and its directors Geir Ulfstein and Andreas Follesdal, for offering me a visiting professorship and a stimulating research environment for the past five years.

I thank Cambridge University Press for allowing me to reprint part of "Populism and the Backlash against International Courts," which was published in *Perspectives on Politics*. I thank Eric Crahan and Bridget Flannery-McCoy of Princeton University Press for their patience and guidance. I thank Alena Chekanov, Jim Curtis, Joseph Dahm, and Jenny Wolkowicki for their excellent help with copyediting, indexing, and making the book look good. I also appreciate the comments of five anonymous referees, who provided extensive and detailed feedback that improved the manuscript a great deal.

My most important debt is to my family. My parents, Gerrie and Rinus, and my sister, Marieke, have always supported me in ways large and small despite living an ocean apart. My daughter, Anniek, would find this book, and my conversation in general, horribly dull. I thank her for always keeping things lively and interesting. I dedicate this book to my wife, Kimberly. She has been an unwavering source of love and support since the start.

IDEOLOGY AND INTERNATIONAL INSTITUTIONS

CHAPTER ONE

Introduction

UKRAINIAN POLITICIANS faced a stark choice in 2014. They could sign a free trade agreement with the European Union (EU) or opt for closer economic cooperation with Russia and its proposed customs union. The tensions culminated in a revolution, the ouster of then incumbent president Viktor Yanukovych, and a Russian military invasion of Crimea and eastern Ukraine. How did trade agreements turn into such a high-profile political issue? The economic stakes alone cannot explain this. Two-thirds of Russian exports to Ukraine were energy resources. A trade agreement with the EU did not threaten this market. Why couldn't Ukraine sign trade agreements with both Russia and the EU?

The most plausible answer is that the conflict was not just about trade but also about Ukraine moving closer to the "West." The West refers not to a geographic direction but to an ideological vision of how international and domestic societies should be organized and an accompanying understanding about the countries the Ukraine is likely to form closer ties with. Russia's government feared that Ukraine would adopt rules, policies, laws, and institutions that are shared by the United States and Western European countries but not by Russia. The two agreements were incompatible in their policy implications and in terms of which security, economic, and diplomatic relationships are valued more.

The politics of multilateralism have always been about ideology. Multilateralism, as John Ruggie has pointed out, is a distinct form of cooperation because it is based on general principles of appropriate conduct that apply irrespective of particularistic interests.[1] These principles are not neutral.[2] The United States promoted multilateral institutions that advanced rules, norms, and policies that constitute a desirable world order from an American vantage point. Some refer to this constellation of institutions as the "liberal international order."[3] Ideology structures multilateral cooperation and competition. During the Cold War, participation in the General Agreement on Tariffs and Trade (GATT), the International Monetary Fund (IMF), and other Western-dominated institutions signified how a government positioned itself in broader global ideological conflict between a Soviet-led communist bloc and a U.S. led capitalist bloc.

Such ideological conflict continued after the Cold War ended. Russia fought a war with Georgia in 2008 that was triggered by Georgia's desire for closer institutional ties to the West. The United States opposed the creation of the Asian Infrastructure Investment Bank (AIIB) not because it feared China's development aid, which China can and does deliver unilaterally, but because the AIIB challenges values, practices, and policies that the United States–dominated World Bank cherishes. When U.S. president Barack Obama said about the proposed Trans-Pacific Partnership (TPP) that "we can't let countries like China write the rules of the global economy,"[4] he communicated not just something about a choice between the United States and China but also something about the types of rules that the TPP would embrace versus the types of rules an agreement with China might entail. By contrast, Obama's successor, President Donald Trump, has preferred bilateral informal negotiations. This transactional approach privileges the advancement of short-term particularistic interests over the pursuit of an ideological vision of how global society should be organized.

This book contends that much, though not all, distributive conflict over multilateral institutions takes place in a low-dimensional ideological space. This low-dimensional space structures cooperation and conflict in the global arena in ways that are measurable and important but often ignored in academic studies. Most rationalist theories paint a rather apolitical picture of why international institutions are created and what they do. Institutions reduce transaction costs, coordinate policies, provide impartial information, deliver independent dispute settlement, and offer good reputations to those who conform to communal norms and standards.[5] Scholars have, of course, long recognized that institutional politics is also distributive politics. As Robert Keohane and Joseph Nye pointed out in their seminal 1977 book, "We must therefore be cautious about the prospect that rising interdependence is creating a brave new world of cooperation to replace the bad old world of international conflict. As every parent of small children knows, baking a larger pie does not stop disputes over the size of slices."[6]

This book contends that contestation over international institutions is not just about the size of slices. Institutional politics is often about moving a status quo in one's preferred direction in a relatively low-dimensional ideological space. Ideology provides much of the glue in the international order. Trade agreements are in part about the specific interests of importers and exporters. Yet multilateral trade agreements are also about advancing certain principles, such as nondiscrimination and the protection of intellectual property, that are favored more by some than by others. The politics surrounding the IMF and World Bank is about who gets what loans at what conditions. But these multilateral institutions also advance a set of economic principles that compose a contested ideology.[7] States form military alliances to protect specific assets or interests. Yet multilateral alliances often form in the pursuit of more ideological goals,[8] and multilateral military coalitions often act against ideological challengers.

The argument is not that particularistic interests are unimportant. Yet even if distributive conflict over institutions is not always about ideology, the geopolitical implications often are. The Ukrainian government may well have favored the preferential trade agreement with the EU for particularistic reasons, for instance because its domestic producers wanted access to an attractive export market. However, the broader implications of this institutional choice can be understood only in the context of global ideological conflict.

The point of this book is not just to argue that ideological contestation matters but also to offer measures, a modeling framework, and empirical illustrations. The theoretical framework helps us better understand how institutional commitments hang together and may unravel together as challenges to the liberal institutional order mount. If multilateralism is distinct because it advances general principles, then we must understand challenges to the multilateral order in terms of domestic and international challenges to those principles.

The Argument in Brief

This book's argument fits in the family of rationalist distributive theories, which understand institutions as by-products of social, economic, and political conflicts.[9] Efforts by powerful actors to constrain others with whom they interact can become more general rules for how actors should cooperate and compete in the international system. This view contrasts with a rational functionalist understanding that institutions are solutions to strategic problems that impede social welfare enhancing opportunities for cooperation.

For example, chapter 8 juxtaposes two ways to understand the contemporary regime to protect foreign investments. The functionalist understanding is that the regime allows capital-importing countries to make credible commitments to refrain from expropriating foreign investments, which in turn incentivizes socially beneficial investments. The distributive ideological understanding is that the regime arose from efforts by the United States and Western capital exporters to generalize their understanding of what proper protections for foreign investments should look like.

Institutions can serve functional and distributive purposes. As Terry Moe points out,

> Political institutions serve two very different purposes. On the one hand, they help mitigate collective-action problems, particularly the commitment and enforcement problems so debilitating to political exchange, and thus allow the various actors in politics to cooperate in the realization of gains from trade. On the other hand, political institutions are also weapons of coercion and redistribution. They are the structural means by which political winners pursue their own interests, often at the great expense of political losers. If we are to understand where political institutions come from and why they take the specific forms they do, we have to pay serious attention to both sides of their theoretical story.[10]

The TPP's aims were both to facilitate trade *and* to create rules that favor the West more than China. The UN Security Council (UNSC) helps finance public goods, such as peacekeeping missions. But the UNSC is also the means by which some states try to get what they want at the expense of others. The Treaty on the Non-Proliferation of Nuclear Weapons (NPT) facilitates exchange in peaceful nuclear energy. It also prolongs a status quo that favors certain nuclear weapon states over others. The IMF provides information that helps states cooperate on monetary policies. It also pursues policies and programs favored by the United States and other states with the largest voting shares in the institution.[11]

The basic point that distributive conflict matters is neither new nor controversial.[12] This book departs from the literature in its emphasis on ideological conflict. The international relations literature has mostly used the term "ideology" in a pejorative sense, if at all.[13] By contrast, scholars of domestic politics commonly conceptualize political competition in ideological terms. This book follows the lineage of scholarship on spatial models and ideology pioneered by Anthony Downs.[14] Much contestation over international institutions can be conceptualized as conflict over moving a status quo toward one's ideal point in a low-dimensional ideological space.

An ideology is a set of more or less cohesive ideas about how a set of issues should be resolved and who should resolve them. An ideology reflects core principles about how society should be organized, including how resources should be distributed and where power appropriately resides. An ideology is thus by definition distributive: accepting a set of principles about how domestic and international societies should be organized predictably grants advantages to some states and non-state actors.

Conflict over principles exists alongside conflict over particularistic interests. For example, voting behavior of U.S. congresspeople is driven both by ideological interests, how liberal or conservative they are, and by "pork-barrel" politics, how many specific benefits they can capture for their constituents.[15]

Table I.1 offers examples of principled and particularistic interests from the U.S. perspective. The United States has an interest in advancing the principles that private property should be protected and that foreign investors should be treated at least equally to national investors (national treatment). The United States also has particular interests in protecting corporate assets. The United States can protect its particular interests without institutions, for example by threatening to punish states that expropriate the property of U.S. firms. Institutionalized principles can advance U.S. particularistic interests, but they also have broader effects on other capital-exporting and -importing states. Moreover, there is ideological competition over what principles should spread. The Soviet Union advocated for the principle that states had the right to nationalize industries and expropriate foreign investments. Latin American countries and other former

Table I.1. Examples of principled and particularistic interests for the United States

Principled interests	Particularistic interests
Free trade, nondiscrimination	Protect U.S. textile industry, get export market access for U.S. technology firms
Private property rights, national treatment	Protect investments from specific U.S. firms
No recognition of territory acquired through force	Protect Estonia's territorial boundaries, recognize Kosovo
Freedom of religion	Protect Christian minorities in the Middle East
Free and fair elections	Advocate for free and fair elections in Venezuela, protect regime stability in Saudi Arabia

colonies favored principles that would protect their ability to regulate multinational corporations. Institutionalizing principles can be an important tool in broader geopolitical conflict.

Principled and particularistic interests sometimes clash. The United States had a principled interest in creating an international trading regime that spread free trade and nondiscrimination.[16] Yet in areas where the United States did not have a comparative advantage, deviations were often accommodated.[17] In most contexts, the United States behaves as if spreading democracy is in its interest. Yet governments have always been willing to oversee democratic failings in key strategic allies. The point of this book is not to argue that principled interests dominate particularistic interests but that contestation over principles fundamentally shapes the politics of multilateralism.

The literature conceives of institutional principles as shared norms that define standards for appropriate behavior.[18] Instead, I argue that states have relatively well-ordered preferences over the principles multilateral institutions should advance and that they act purposively in pursuit of outcomes that match those preferences. Moreover, this book shows that we can estimate the ideal points of states in a low-dimensional ideological space and that we can explain a good deal of institutional conflict and cooperation using simple spatial models. Multilateral politics is often about moving a policy status quo in a low-dimensional ideological space.

So what is ideological conflict about? The precise meaning of "liberal" in liberal international system is contested and dynamic. There is broadbased consensus on some general liberal principles, such as free and fair elections as the appropriate way to compete over leadership, private property rights, and the rule of law. Yet there are considerable differences across time and space over what exactly liberalism means or what principles liberal institutions should spread. Left-wing and right-wing parties differ substantially in their views on how resources should be distributed or how conflicting principles, such as liberty and equality, should be weighted and realized. There are stark ideological differences within and between liberal democracies about how domestic societies should be organized that also have consequences for how international society should be organized.

During the Cold War, communism was liberalism's preeminent ideological contender. Communism rejects liberal principles on all dimensions. It envisages a society based on common ownership of property and an equal distribution of resources achieved through central planning. Some left-wing governments and parties in capitalist societies advanced socialist or social-democratic policy platforms that were closer to communism than the platforms of right-wing parties. Moreover, a large number of developing countries, especially newly independent countries, did not endorse communism but did wish to assign a much greater role for the state in their economies and societies. Especially in the 1970s, these countries sought to overhaul the principles that underpinned the post–World War II economic order, challenging that these principles embedded a favorable treatment for Western states, including former colonial powers. State and non-state actors also contested the racism embedded in the liberal order or that its exclusionary character favored Christian countries over those with other majority religions.

Both liberalism and communism are explicitly internationalist ideology: liberalism in its emphasis on universal individual rights and open markets and communism in its focus on a class struggle that should unite workers of all countries. Interdependence has led to a "deterritorialization of ideological conflict" in which ideological contestation that was once tied to a specific place and society has taken on relevance at a global level.[19] Interdependence means that the effects of one country's policies are conditional on the policies and actions pursued by other countries. One country's policies toward private property rights affect other countries if there is foreign direct investment (FDI). An example from the security realm is the well-known liberal peace theory, which asserts that countries that embrace essential liberal principles such as democracy, free trade, and the rule of law can form a separate peaceful community of states.[20] Of course, as Michael Doyle pointed out in his second (and much less cited) seminal article on the Kantian peace, liberal states may well be more prone to go to war with illiberal states for liberal reasons.[21] The post–World War II era offers ample examples of such wars.[22] States have pursued ideological objectives in their foreign policies.

The collapse of the Soviet Union removed communism as a viable global competitor for liberalism.[23] While this void has not been filled, this has not led to the end of ideological contestation. First, the character of the liberal order itself has changed in a way that is heavily contested. The order has moved from embedded liberalism,[24] which allowed states considerable leeway to ameliorate the domestic effects of globalization, to neoliberalism on economic issues[25] and a much greater interventionism on other issues.[26] The 1990s and early 2000s were a radical time for institutional development. Membership in both global and regional institutions became more inclusive, the policy scope of institutions increased drastically, and institutions became more legalized and less concerned with principles of nonintervention into domestic affairs. Thus, we are left with a set of more ideologically heterogeneous institutions that have more authority than before. This increases the probability that these institutions take actions that clash with domestically favored principles. Much of the current backlash against international institutions respond to these institutional innovations rather than the post–World War II order per se. There is considerable domestic and international ideological contestation over the principles that international institutions advance and how intrusive this interventionism should be.

Second, nationalism, Islamism, populism, authoritarianism, and state-led capitalism all challenge important aspects of liberalism. At first glance, these ideologies have little in common other than their rejection of liberalism. Chapter 2 argues that there is nonetheless a thin ideological alternative to liberalism, which does not set forth a full-fledged normative vision of how global society should be organized but does have some agreement on principles of noninterventionism and strict adherence to related principles that defend sovereignty. This thin ideology can be an insufficient basis to form deep multilateral coalitions and institutions, although the creation of the AIIB illustrates that a multilateral bank that outlines statist and noninterventionist principles can have appeal. More generally, agreement on opposition to liberal international institutions can be consequential even in the absence of a cohesive alternative. If we want to understand potential changes to the institutional system, we must understand domestic and international ideological changes.

The theoretical framework accepts the criticism from constructivist scholars that rationalist institutional scholars have ignored ideational sources of competition and cooperation. Nevertheless, the framework itself is rationalist. Ideology can be understood as a rational response to the costliness of political information.[27] Governments do not always know what citizens or interest groups want, and citizens do not always know what politicians have done or plan to do. Internationally, governments are unsure what other governments want and how they will act. The information needed to overcome this ignorance is costly, often prohibitively so. In the context of interdependence and institutionalized cooperation, this information is also valuable. Suppose a government wishes to propose an institution that promotes economic or security cooperation. How does that government know whom to invite to join the institution? And how do other governments know whether they should join? What should a government infer if another government joins that institution?

Ideologies are an imperfect way to cope with this lack of information. Governments often market institutions as fitting within a well-understood set of internally consistent propositions about what is good, who should win, and how power should be allocated. This allows others to predict, albeit imperfectly, how they might be affected by the institution. The EU as a multilateral organization is based on well-understood principles. The Ukrainian government's decision to create institutional ties with the EU informs others about the position that government intends to take on a range of policy issues, its internal institutional development, and the countries it wishes to build closer ties with. This information matters in the context of distributive conflict. The Russian government inferred that the Ukrainian decision to choose an FTA with the EU could have a range of consequences that the Russians deemed undesirable. Institutions allow and sometimes compel governments to commit to ideological directions.

The label "ideology" does not prejudge whether actors act out of normative convictions or their economic or security interests. Ideological conflict is about ideas but not about ideas that are divorced from material interests or power. To continue the domestic analogy, a candidate for election can self-identify as a socialist because she is a union worker who believes that a socialist (or social-democratic) party will advance her interests. A candidate can also identify as a socialist from the comforts of Park Avenue in New York City. It makes little sense to label only the second candidate as a "genuine socialist" because she identifies with the ideology out of moral conviction rather than self-interest. In the context of competition, the label "socialism" matters because it conveys information about the likely policy positions of candidates on a broad range of issues.

The value added of ideology over simply studying preferences or interests is that it highlights the connections across issues. Ideologies are sets of interconnected propositions. The same states often stare at each other from opposite sides of the fence in very different issue areas. This structures institutional politics considerably. This book develops a spatial modeling framework that is as simple as the prisoner's dilemma, coordination dilemma, battle of the sexes, and other two-by-two games that have served as mental models for rationalist analyses of cooperation.[28] The spatial model is the "common methodological base"[29] of the political economy literature outside of international relations. The spatial model starts from the assumption that actors have ideal points in a common low-dimensional ideological space. For example, the ideal points of members of Congress reflect how liberal or conservative they are, which proxies for their preferred outcomes on a range of policy issues.

There are two primary reasons why international relations (IR) scholars have not embraced the spatial modeling framework to the same extent as other rational choice scholars.[30] First, as pointed out earlier, the justification for analyzing distributive politics in a low-dimensional policy space is that ideology structures policy positions. Ideology, as conceptualized here, has not been a major focus of study in IR. Second, cooperation in the international arena differs from collective decision making in legislative politics. Collective agreements are only one of many possible ways to change the status quo in the international system. Powerful states may get what they want unilaterally, which is usually not an option for legislators in democracies.[31] Legislators have a compelling institutional reason to cooperate: no legislation passes unless a majority (or supermajority) vote in favor of a proposal. Majority voting rules do not structure interactions among states in the same way. Instead, the most compelling reason to cooperate is interdependence: payoffs depend not just on a state's own policies but also on the policies of the states with whom they interact.[32]

This book develops a spatial modeling framework that explicitly models the (asymmetric) interdependencies between states. This is new both for spatial models but also in IR more generally. The more familiar models assume an interdependent strategic problem structure in which two parties have an incentive to cooperate but there are (also) equilibria in which no or suboptimal cooperation occurs. Coordination dilemmas are those were actors benefit from harmonizing policies (or actions), but they may fail to do so, either because they have different preferences or because there is some other feature that prevents them from coordination, such as high transaction costs, lack of information, or a preexisting suboptimal coordination equilibrium that is difficult to change. Collaboration dilemmas are those where it would be socially optimal to cooperate but actors have individual incentives to cheat.

In the spatial modeling framework, these strategic dilemmas arise from different configurations of ideological conflict and interdependencies. This creates a number of new insights that have implications for empirical studies of international institutions. For example, collaboration dilemmas arise when ideological conflict is large enough and interdependencies small enough such that agreements are not self-enforcing. This suggests that the most extensive institutional enforcement structures are needed only where the benefits of institutional cooperation are relatively modest and ideological contestation is strong. This may explain why deeper institutions are not always correlated with more cooperation. Moreover, it may explain why institutional backlash is sometimes targeted at seemingly low-stakes issues.

The spatial modeling framework illustrates how cooperative arrangements between some states may adversely affect other states. If liberal institutions move the status quo in a liberal direction, then governments less enamored of liberalism are going to be negatively affected by these institutions, especially if interdependencies are strong. This can lead to conflict. Chapter 7 shows that the Ukraine anecdote fits a broader pattern: militarized conflicts frequently arise between states that have ideologically different institutional commitments.

The analysis also sheds a different light on problems of incomplete information and uncertainty. In the classic understanding, international organizations and transnational experts may acquire authority because they have information that states do not have. However, in the context of ideological conflict states may distrust experts. This may induce them to invest in their own expertise. Expertise is inherently political. Institutions may still matter but often for different reasons than commonly assumed. For example, expert organizations, like the Intergovernmental Panel on Climate Change (IPCC) matter not so much because they have expertise that states do not have. After all, many of the panel members are state employees and the knowledge is often in the public domain. However, the organization matters in that it restricts the supply of expert advice by offering a focal understanding of expertise. Institutions also play an important role in incentivizing states to communicate their private information rather than in acquiring new information about the world.

The modeling framework develops a range of other theoretical insights, some of which are then tested in the empirical chapters. I do not claim that all of these insights are new. The book relies extensively on previous scholarship. Instead, the goal of this book is to present a cohesive framework that puts ideological contestation at the heart of our understanding of how the international institutional order hangs together. That is a new contribution, which also helps to illuminate the current crisis of this institutional order.

A Brief Illustration: The WTO

Trade politics is traditionally analyzed through the lens of particularistic interests. Domestic producers push governments for protection when they fear foreign competition and for access to foreign markets when they enjoy comparative advantages.[33] Multilateral trade institutions are voluntarist contracts that improve opportunities for exchange. For example, fear of cheating may prevent states from lifting tariffs. Institutions can help by providing information that identifies cheaters or by creating dispute settlement mechanisms that facilitate tit-for-tat punishment, like the World

Trade Organization's (WTO) Dispute Settlement Understanding. Institutions solve problems. States join and create the WTO because they want these problems solved. The WTO's effects depend on the extent to which it effectively provides information and facilitates tit-for-tat punishments. The WTO's design can be understood as an attempt to best solve the collective problem that inhibits trade.

This conventional understanding isn't necessarily wrong, but it highlights only one side of the institutional story. In this book's framework, multilateral trade institutions originate not as an effort to improve collective well-being but as an attempt by powerful states to constrain the trade policies of those with whom they interact.[34] Like other multilateral regimes, the WTO is based on a set of principles that had long dominated U.S. trade policies: most notably limits on government interventionism and nondiscrimination.[35] To be sure, the WTO embeds protectionism for particular sectors where the United States and other major economies do not have a comparative advantage, such as agriculture. Nonetheless, these principles matter and are contested. For example, the WTO's general principles push for a limited role of the state in the economy. Specific agreements, like the Agreement on Trade-Related Aspects of Intellectual Property Rights (TRIPS), further embedded principles favored by the United States into the trading regime, which led to more ideological contestation.[36]

Global ideology matters for sorting into the WTO. For example, Christina Davis and Meredith Wilf have shown that geopolitical alignments are a much stronger correlate of GATT/WTO accession than expected gains in trade.[37] Political leaders are (rightly or wrongly) at least partially motivated by these broader ideological implications of institutions. There is at least anecdotal evidence for this in the WTO context. For example, U.S. president Bill Clinton remarked as the U.S. Congress voted on the agreement regarding China's WTO accession, "By joining the WTO, China is not simply agreeing to import more of our products; it is agreeing to import one of democracy's most cherished values: economic freedom."[38] Or as U.S. Trade Representative Charlene Barshefsky put it, "Would it go in a direction antithetical to Western norms? Or could it be encouraged to go in a direction that was compatible to Western norms?"[39]

In other words, the purpose of inviting China into the WTO was not just to increase trade but also to move Chinese policies in a direction that the United States desired. Today the U.S. government considers this aspect of the WTO a failure. Instead, the Trump administration has moved away from principled multilateralism and toward a transactional approach aimed at specific concessions that satisfy particularistic interests.[40] The Trump administration's refusal to approve appellate body panelists, rejection of the TPP agreement, and renegotiation of NAFTA fit this strategy. The United States no longer pursues general principled interests but seeks to negotiate bilateral agreements that best advance particularistic interests.[41] This is a significant departure from earlier administrations.

The point of this book is not that all international politics is ideological. Yet multilateral politics often is. For example, developing countries rejected reforms in the 2000 Doha Round because the modest concessions the United States and the EU were willing to make on agriculture were not worth the loss of domestic policy space, that is, less room for state intervention, they would have to give up in exchange.[42] This suggests that contestation over the appropriate role of the state in the economy continues to be important for understanding multilateral trade politics, even if trade policy (especially) is always also about particularistic benefits.

This perspective challenges the strong voluntarist interpretation that underlies most rationalist institutionalist understandings of international institutions and law.[43] Voluntarism implies that international law affects only those who of their own volition commit to be bound by international law, most commonly by ratifying a treaty. If the WTO harmonizes state policies in an ideological space, then states with preferences far removed from the WTO's creators are harmed by the institution as these states will find fewer partners with whom they can trade based on their preferred principles. The outlier states can either adjust their policies and join the institution or stay outside and become marginalized as trading powers. That is, institutions may affect the welfare of states that do not voluntarily commit. This basic insight matters for empirical studies, which typically seek evidence of institutional effects by contrasting cooperative behavior among ratifiers and non-ratifiers.

Moreover, the perspective implies that institutions may increase cooperation between some states while creating conflict with others. Chapter 7 will illustrate this point by showing that it is not the number of shared institutional memberships but the distance in the ideological portfolio of institutional memberships that correlates with the presence and absence of militarized disputes between states. There are militarized disputes over borders or other issues that have nothing to do with ideology. Yet there are also disputes that do concern the main global ideological divisions. Those disputes tend to draw in multiple states and multilateral institutions. It is not necessarily clear that more transactional trade politics will result in more conflict, but it may lead to different types of conflicts that are more about specific assets than the principles that govern the world.

A Road Map

Chapter 2 defines ideology more precisely and discusses related concepts. The chapter then outlines an approach to estimate the ideological positions of states from votes in the United Nations General Assembly (UNGA). The chapter assesses the validity of this measure. For example, changes in UNGA ideal points correlate strongly with various indicators of liberalism: such as changes in government ideology, regime type, and capital openness.

Chapter 3 discusses the relationship of the distributive ideological perspective to other theoretical approaches in the literature. The chapter discusses conceptually how attention to ideological conflict interplays with the insights from the neofunctionalist, rational institutionalist, liberal internationalist, and constructivist literatures. Readers who are less interested in how this book fits with the academic literature could skip this chapter.

Chapters 4 and 5 embed functionalist cooperation within a political economy framework. Chapter 4 proposes a simple spatial modeling framework that is as simple as the two-by-two games typically used as mental models in functionalist approaches, with the prisoner's dilemma as its most famous example. Actors have ideal points in a low-dimensional ideological space, but their payoffs are also interdependent. Actors would prefer to adopt policies close to their ideal points, but they also have incentives to adopt policies closer to the ideal points of the states they depend upon. The model (presented with little math) illustrates that there are rationales for delegating authority to institutions not because these have informational advantages but because they help address indeterminacy in collective decision making. These institutions need not be neutral and can have distributive effects even if they do not have enforcement capabilities. The model also shows how excluded actors may be affected by cooperation.

Chapter 5 extends that framework to examine the most common arguments for delegation to international institutions: information. The chapter distinguishes two rationales: delegation to acquire expertise that states do not individually have and delegation to share expertise and achieve common interpretations of expertise. While the literature emphasizes the former, the latter type of delegation is likely much more common. Moreover, it can be understood only in the context of ideological conflict between states when states have incentives not to share information truthfully. The chapter examines the conditions under which transnational and international actors can exploit such ideological conflict to gain influence.

The theoretical framework offers a way to think about institutionalization rather than a specific theory of any specific institution. The next four chapters examine empirical implications from the framework to specific questions. These are meant as illustrations of the kind of questions the framework could shed light on rather than as a set of definitive tests that discriminate the distributive ideological perspective from the rational functionalist framework.

Chapter 6 shows that ideological divisions shape how states sort into intergovernmental organizations (IGOs). During the Cold War, communist states for the most part stayed out of the core IGOs that defined the liberal order. Since the end of the Cold War, states all over the ideological spectrum have joined IGOs, but there has been considerable ideological sorting into IGOs and alliances. If we want to understand the Western liberal institutional order and its implications, we need to understand systematic ideological variation in the extent to which governments have bought into that order.

Chapter 7 examines if and how IGO memberships shape participation in militarized interstate disputes. Theorists have argued that IGOs solve informational problems, socialize states, or constitute democratic communities that prevent a resort to violence. The distributive ideological approach suggests that IGOs institutionalize ideologically cohesive coalitions that ameliorate conflicts with insiders but can exacerbate conflict with outsiders. The effect of IGOs on militarized disputes should be present only if the distributional stakes have global ideological implications as opposed to when disputes are purely over particularistic stakes, such as territory. Regression analyses support this insight. Both ideological differences and IGO membership patterns affect dispute participation in dyads that include a major power but not among neighboring states or states involved in a territorial dispute. One implication is that IGO memberships affect the distribution of militarized disputes, but it is unclear whether IGOs in the aggregate reduce militarized conflict.

Chapter 8 offers a case study of the regime that seeks to protect foreign investments from expropriation. This regime was created not just to protect firms, which could be protected through other means, but also to advance a specific vision of what rules should govern private investments over alternative visions that grant greater leeway to states. The analysis shows how ideology shapes sorting into the regime and how ideological changes help explain which states renegotiate or opt out of investment treaties.

Chapter 9 examines the rise of populism as an ideological shift that can be orthogonal to the main ideological dimension of contestation. The chapter advances two main points. First, populist leaders have incentives to contest expert-based international institutions that interpret liberal rules when these interpretations interact with preexisting populist mobilization. Moreover, populism offers an ideology to challenge the authority of these institutions. Second, populists are diverse in their positions on the main dimension of contestation, which complicates their ability to form effective multilateral reform coalitions.

The conclusion wraps up what these insights mean for international relations theory as well as for debates about the future of the present institutional order. The purpose of this book is not to persuade the reader that this distributive ideological theory is always a superior theory to alternatives. Rather, I establish that it is a plausible way to think about institutions that should be on the table in theoretical and empirical studies. Moreover, the theory offers a useful way to think through substantive questions, such as the alleged "collapse" or "twilight" of the liberal world order or whether we are moving toward a "world without the West."[44]

CHAPTER TWO

Global Ideological Conflict

CONCEPT AND MEASUREMENT

THIS CHAPTER argues that ideology is a useful analytical construct to help us understand global distributive institutional politics. The chapter first discusses the definition of institutions and then of ideology. Ideology is a set of widely understood more or less cohesive and stable ideas about how a set of issues should be resolved and who should resolve them. Ideology is a vehicle not just for spreading values but also for transmitting information. If a government proclaims to be liberal, then this tells us something about the position that government will likely take on a range of policy issues. This information is especially valuable in contexts where actors care deeply about the future intentions of others, including international institutional politics. Institutions allow and sometimes compel governments to commit to ideological directions. The chapter discusses how this definition differs from other treatments in the international relations literature, how ideology constrains policy positions, and what global ideological debates are about.

The second part of this chapter shows that the ideological positions of states can plausibly be measured in a low-dimensional space. The dimensionality of the policy space is an important source of structure in theoretical models of collective decision making. Indeed, the spatial models introduced in chapters 4 and 5 assume a low-dimensional space. This chapter uses empirical spatial models on votes in the UN General Assembly (UNGA) to estimate state ideal points on a dimension that captures support for or opposition to the Western liberal order. The validity of this measure is assessed in a variety of ways, including by regressing changes in ideal points with various indicators of liberalism: such as changes in government ideology, regime type, and capital openness. The book's empirical chapters then employ this measure.

What Are International Institutions?

John Mearsheimer defined international institutions as "formal and informal rules that prescribe the way actors should cooperate and compete in the international system."[1] This definition rightly leaves open the question whether institutions actually matter. Moreover, it includes a broad array of institutions ranging from formal intergovernmental organizations (IGOs) like the United Nations to informal arrangements like customary international law, soft law, clubs (like the G20), multistakeholder initiatives, and regulatory networks. This is important given that traditional treaty-based institutions are becoming a less central element of the institutional order.

I accept this definition with one addition: those to whom the rule pertains must share an understanding that this is so.[2] The rule that states should consult the Delphi oracle before using force would fit Mearsheimer's definition. Yet no one would acknowledge that the rule pertains to them. The modified working definition is that institutions are "widely acknowledged formal and informal rules that prescribe the way actors should cooperate and compete in the international system."

This definition still leaves open the question whether institutions actually matter. Unlike the Delphi oracle, states do acknowledge that the United Nations Security Council (UNSC) should authorize uses of force other than for self-defense. Acknowledgment is not agreement, nor is it internalization or compliance. States may well disagree that the UNSC should authorize uses of force, and they sometimes disregard the rule. Indeed, this rule barely affected international affairs between 1951 and 1989, and it remains an open question whether and why it has influenced global politics since.[3]

This definition is descriptive in that it tells us how we might recognize an institution when we see one. Conceptually, institutions are consequentialist devices that aim to steer social interactions in the context of interdependence. Institutions are attempts to specify equilibrium behavior. The definition of an equilibrium is that no actor can gain from changing only her strategy, although some (or even all) actors might have something to gain from changing the strategies of others.[4] This leaves open the question of success. The rule that states should not grab each other's territory through conquest can matter only if it successfully shapes expectations. But it can still be an institution if actors acknowledge the rule as international law even though it does not successfully specify equilibrium behavior. Actors may have unilateral incentives to deviate from rules that are nonetheless understood to define proper behavior. Other institutions attempt to construct equilibria that did not exist before, for instance by changing the informational structure, options, or payoffs. There is no guarantee that these efforts succeed in actually influencing equilibrium behavior or equilibrium selection.

IGOs are organizations whose members are three or more governments. IGOs have a headquarters and staff and meet on a regular basis under fixed procedural rules. IGOs are typically based on treaties, which define the formal rules under which states compete and cooperate inside an IGO. Yet there are also informal rules that shape how IGOs operate.[5] IGOs are thus themselves institutions, but their existence and operation are also defined by other institutions. IGOs can be more or less independent agencies charged with monitoring, implementing, interpreting, and settling disputes over rules. They are also the arenas in which much distributive politics over institutions play out.

This book focuses on global distributive conflict. Regional institutions sometimes play a role in global conflicts, as the Ukraine-EU example illustrates. Yet I am not analyzing how regional institutions address regional conflict, even if the framework may well be relevant for that context.

What Is Ideology?

IDEOLOGY IN THE IR LITERATURE

Ideology does not feature prominently in international relations (IR) scholarship. Contemporary IR scholarship on ideational factors emphasizes how norms[6] and ideas[7] foster cooperation and sometimes competition. Alexander Wendt's magnum opus lacks an entry for ideology in its index, as do Robert Keohane's, John Mearsheimer's, and Kenneth Waltz's most cited books.[8] When IR scholarship does mention ideology it is often in a pejorative way.[9]

I examined all articles published in the journal *International Organization* between 1990 and 2016 that mentioned "ideology" or "ideological" anywhere in the text. The vast majority used ideology in passing rather than as a key theoretical concept. Others distinguished liberal ideology from liberal theory[10] or discussed ideology as a utopian opposite from more reasoned analysis of international affairs.[11] Where ideology played an important and explicit role it was mostly as a foundation for claims to moral authority or legitimation rather than as a feature of distributive politics.[12]

There are a few notable exceptions in the realist, liberal, and constructivist traditions. First, Robert Gilpin recognized the importance of Marxism, liberalism, and nationalism as three contrasting ideologies about how both national economies and the international economy should be organized.[13] Moreover, Gilpin understood that clashes between these visions constituted a major challenge for the possibility of governing the global economy. However, most realists have continued to downplay the role of ideology, even in the Cold War.[14] Moreover, realists have shown little interest in explaining multilateralism, other than to emphasize its impotence.[15]

Second, Mark Haas and John Owen both examine ideology as part of the structure of the international system.[16] They argue that ideology helps states draw conclusions about the intentions of others and that the ideological distance between states matters.[17] This is compatible with the argument advanced in this book. One difference is that they equate ideology with identity and domestic legitimation institutions (especially liberal democracy). While these scholars are not primarily focused on explaining multilateral institutions, their arguments do overlap with mine.

Third, critical IR theorists have long highlighted the role of ideology in IR and related scholarship.[18] For example, Gramscian approaches have emphasized that the institutional order is shaped by a hegemonic ideology, which justifies existing arrangements of power, authority, and status in international society.[19] This order is subject to contestation from counter-hegemonic narratives. Others point to racism as an ideology that has justified international institutional arrangements and policies.[20] For example, scholars have argued that racism may help explain why the United States formed a multilateral alliance with European countries but took a more transactional, bilateral approach with Asian countries.[21] This book concurs that understanding ideological contestation is key for analyzing global institutional politics but stays within a rationalist framework and does not adopt the postpositivist perspectives of critical theorists. The goal in this book is to develop measures and models for analyzing how ideological contestation affects institutionalized cooperation and conflict in international affairs.

DEFINITION

Most social science theories outside IR offer value-neutral definitions of ideology.[22] Ideology refers to any "configuration of ideas and attitudes in which the elements are bound together by some form of constraint or functional interdependence."[23] I define an ideology as a widely understood set of interconnected propositions about how a set of issues should be resolved and who should resolve them. Ideologies have implications for what is (1) ethically good, (2) how resources should be distributed, and (3) where power appropriately resides.[24]

A few remarks about this definition are in order. First, ideologies do not just exist in the minds of individuals. They are social constructs. The political and informational value of ideologies depends on others understanding what it means for a group or individual to espouse a conservative, liberal, leftist, or communist ideology. If a politician announces that she is a conservative, then others in a society will draw inferences about that politician's positions on a wide range of issues, including taxation, health care policy, LGBT rights, abortion, and so on. The point is not that every conservative has precisely the same views on all these issues but that an ideological label nevertheless raises expectations about an actor's likely views on a bundle of issues. Similarly, if the Georgian government announces its intention to form closer ties with the West, observers will understand that this will likely have implications for policies on trade, property rights, civil liberties, and capital constraints even if we do not know precisely what position the Georgian government will take on specific issues. Ideological commitments provide imprecise information about a wide array of issues.

Second, an ideology contains what Anthony Downs called "a verbal image of the good society."[25] An ideology includes normative propositions about what is good, how resources should be distributed, and who should have power. An ideology is not a laundry list of "stuff we like." Ideologies must contain abstract interdependent principles that contain prescriptions about what actors should do in new situations. In its crudest sense, liberalism in international affairs implies a commitment to the market as the appropriate mechanism to allocate resources (albeit embedded in political and social institutions), that the government should protect certain individual rights, and that power should be determined through free and fair elections. These are general principles that have implications for how an actor should behave in a wide range of practical cases in both domestic and international affairs.

Ideology differs from regime type. Democratically elected governments vary greatly in their economic ideologies and often compete domestically with political adversaries on ideological grounds. Yet regime type influences foreign policy ideology. For example, democracies may be more likely to commit to the ideological proposition that democracy should be the organizing principle for domestic societies. International institutions dominated by democracies spread that ideology through election monitoring, tying aid to democratization, and other policies.[26]

Third, ideologies have distributive implications and are thus contentious. Stronger protections of private property make it more difficult for states to control the means of production. Property rights allow the already privileged to have continued control over land and resources, which may conflict with other distributional ideals. Such ideological divisions over property manifest themselves domestically in class struggles, ethnic struggles (if one ethnic group dominates land ownership), and/or clashes between the state and private actors. Internationally, there have long been ideological divides over just how much a state should protect the property of foreigners or whether expropriation is justified by past injustices, such as colonialism.

The broader point is that there has always been and continues to be a variety of views on what the Western liberal institutional order should look like and whether it is desirable in the first place.[27] The "end of history" was never really there.[28] The end of the Cold War did not result in a convergence on liberalism. Moreover, there continue to be important divisions within liberalism about the role of the state in the domestic economy and other issues. The next section delves deeper into the content of these ideological debates.

Fourth, ideological contestation concerns both the principles of global governance and who the governors should be. These debates are connected. Concerns about the demise of the Western liberal order are typically motivated in part by concerns that non-Western states might advance different principles and values if they were to control international institutions.[29] Western liberal democracies have promoted a verbal image of what a good global society is that is tied into Western liberal democracies taking a prominent place in that society. This is one source of contestation in the current liberal order.[30]

WHAT ARE GLOBAL IDEOLOGICAL DIVISIONS ABOUT?

The Cold War cannot be understood without acknowledging that the major players had fundamentally different views on how domestic societ-

ies and international society should be organized.[31] This book does not
seek to intervene in debates among historians about just how important
ideology was as a motivating force for U.S. or Soviet behavior. The point
here is simply that the content of the principles that many multilateral
institutions sought to advance reflects ideological principles that were favored by the United States and its allies but not by the Soviet Union. These
included principles such as that individual liberties and protections of
property rights are ethically good, that market forces should govern the
allocation of resources, and that democracy and the rule of law should
determine the allocation of power domestically.[32] Internationally, this has
implications for how investments should be protected, how trade should
be regulated, how human rights ought to be protected, and many other
issues. The manifestation of these principles into institutions has varied
over time, for instance moving from embedded liberalism toward a more
neoliberal economic ideology.[33]

Communism envisages a society based on common ownership of property and an equal distribution of resources achieved through central planning. As chapter 1 pointed out, communism is also explicitly international
but clashes with liberalism. Chapter 6 shows that governments that identified more with the communist side of the ideological spectrum joined
many fewer international organizations during the Cold War, especially
the organizations that were devoted to promoting market forces and
democratization.

Moreover, former colonies became quite successful in embedding principles, such as self-determination and the illegality of colonialism, in multilateral organizations.[34] In the 1970s, developing countries started advo-
cating for a New International Economic Order (NIEO), which advocated
for state-led industrial policies, increased control over multinational corporations, and redistribution of resources from North to South.[35] These
countries were not necessarily adopting communism but did seek a more
interventionist role for the state in the economy and were weary of the
influence of Western countries. Chapter 8 has more on the NIEO and its
influence.

It is more difficult to assign clear content to ideological contestation in
the post–Cold War period.[36] Francis Fukuyama famously claimed that the
end of the Cold War represented a decisive victory for liberalism over its
rivals: fascism and communism.[37] He argued that there are no competing
ideologies left, at least not at the global level. Fundamental Islamism has
no appeal outside of Muslim nations. Nationalism is too limited to offer a
compelling counternarrative. As Fukuyama puts it, "Most of the world's
nationalist movements do not have a political program beyond the nega-

tive desire of independence from some other group or people, and do not offer anything like a comprehensive agenda for socio-economic organization."[38] While nationalism may not offer a thick ideological vision of how international society should be organized in the way that communism did, there is an emerging thinner ideological statist vision that opposes Western liberalism. Statism as a thin ideology does not have detailed prescriptions for how domestic societies should be organized,[39] but it does have a vision on where the Western liberal orthodoxy is wrong, not just on one issue but also on many seemingly unrelated issues. Opposition to the liberal order is motivated by a set of collective ideas that emphasize self-determination as ethically good, reserve a prominent role for the state in domestic political economy, favor redistributing resources away from the West, and advocate for the restoration of noninterference into the domestic affairs of states.

China has been particularly active in organizing states on this basis. China has emerged as the leader in the Group of 77, a party-like organization of developing states in the United Nations and other multilateral organizations, including climate negotiations.[40] China's president Xi Jinping summarized this stance concisely during his September 2015 speech to the UNGA: "The principle of sovereignty not only means that the sovereignty and territorial integrity of all countries are inviolable and their internal affairs are not subjected to interference. It also means that all countries' right to independently choose social systems and development paths should be upheld."[41]

Unlike liberalism and Marxism, this ideological position does not include an agenda for socioeconomic organization nor a desire to spread a domestic political, social, or economic system to other countries. Yet this position contains considerable informational value for how states should behave vis-à-vis multilateral institutions. In the Doha Round, developing countries rallied around these principles despite greatly varying particularistic interests.[42] The newly created Asian Infrastructure Investment Bank (AIIB) promises that it will not seek to influence domestic governance or rule of law in exchange for development lending. Opposition to humanitarian interventions is typically framed in terms of more general principles of noninterference. States are increasingly trying to redefine core liberal international principles, such as Responsibility to Protect (R2P), in a way to make them more consistent with a statist ideology.[43] Thus, coalitions in different issue areas are forming around this thin statist ideology.

This ideology appeals to numerous classic schools of thought, including realism, nationalism, and anticolonialism, which are united in their resistance to liberal international interventionism even if they vary in their prescriptions for how domestic and international society should organize core social, economic, and political dimensions. Moreover, ideological contestation over the role of the state also continues to be important in the domestic politics of many countries, including traditional socioeconomic left-right conflict.

There is a fair bit of consistency on what left-right divides mean across countries even if there are also countries,[44] especially in Africa and Asia, where this left-right divide is less important.[45] Leftist parties are typically more favorably disposed toward state intervention in the economy. There is already an extensive literature that establishes that the ideology of domestic political actors, especially parties, can influence foreign economic[46] and security policies in predictable ways.[47] If left-wing and right-wing governments systematically pursue distinct trade, capital mobility, exchange rate, and foreign intervention policies, then governments compete and cooperate along a well-understood ideological dimension on these policy areas. This continues to be relevant after the end of the Cold War as multilateral institutions have pushed for these principles.

Since the end of the Cold War, globalization has transformed existing cleavages and emphasized new ones, including contestation over culture and identity.[48] In many European countries, this new transnational cleavage has become the dominant ideological division. Especially populist right-wing authoritarian parties and governments have rallied against multilateral institutions. In Latin America, left-wing populist governments have done the same, albeit for different reasons. Cas Mudde has defined populism as a thin ideology that opposes liberalism.[49] Populists take diverse views on the organization of domestic political economy but are united in their objection to the countermajoritarian implications of international law and institutions, especially if these produce substantive results that populists do not like.[50] Although there are some temporary international coalitions of populists, overall populism is not a strong force underlying coalition formation in international affairs. It is, however, a driving force for why some states are withdrawing from (parts of) the liberal international order.[51] Chapter 9 has more on populism and how it transforms support for international institutions.

Ideology and Constraint

Ideology can fulfil its informational role only if it actually constrains policy positions. It must mean something to "move toward the West" for that label to signal something. Ideological rigor is not always a virtue. There is always some flexibility on how abstract principles translate into precise positions on actual issues. Governments often find it in their interest to use this wiggle room. Yet there are at least three reasons why ideologies may constrain at least somewhat.

First, actors may genuinely believe that policy positions that are consistent with an ideological worldview are better or more appropriate. Or governments may depend on the support of actors who insist on ideological purity. Moreover, these actors may attempt to convince others of their worldview and believe that inconsistency would detract from their purposes. The core argument in this book is that ideologies shape international politics *not just* because actors seek to persuade each other but also because they seek to inform each other. Persuasion and socialization surely happen some of the time. Moreover, moral convictions may have strategic implications.

For example, the human rights literature documents convincingly that nongovernmental actors sometimes successfully sway governments to pursue a human rights agenda even if this conflicts with particularistic foreign policy objectives.[52] This book adds the idea that ideologies *also* inform. Governments understand that if they wish to trade with the EU then their human rights records will face scrutiny.[53] Governments also understand that trade with China (or the Soviet Union during the Cold War) does not come with this baggage,[54] although it may come with different ideological demands. These expectations help sort states into institutional arrangements. A government may prefer a loan from AIIB to one from the World Bank or the European Bank for Reconstruction and Development (EBRD) because it comes with fewer expectations about interference with domestic human rights. Ideology may structure international conflict and cooperation partially because some politically relevant actors are genuinely persuaded by ideological values and wish to spread these values. Governments may have feared Soviet domination for reasoned unrelated to communist ideology, but there were surely also governments that resisted communism itself. As John Lewis Gaddis put it,

> When President Harry S. Truman told the Congress of the United States on 12 March 1947 that the world faced a struggle between two ways of life, one based on the will of the majority and the other based on the will of a minority imposed upon the majority, he had more than one purpose in mind. The immediate aim, of course, was to prod parsimonious legislators into approving economic and military assistance to Greece and Turkey, and a certain amount of rhetorical dramatization served that end. But President Truman also probably believed what he

said, and most Americans and Europeans, at the time, probably agreed with him. Otherwise, the United States would hardly have been able to abandon its historic policy of peacetime isolationism and commit itself, not only to the Truman Doctrine, but to the much more ambitious Marshall plan and eventually the North Atlantic Treaty Organization as well.[55]

Second, ideological consistency may help actors communicate private preferences amid distributive conflict. Misperceptions over preferences are an important source of bargaining failures. Actors sometimes have incentives to misrepresent their own preferences, which in turn makes it more difficult to truthfully reveal them. Ideological consistency may be strategically desirable if others expect states to act in a consistent manner.

Standard reputational accounts focus on past records of compliance. Ideologues can also build up reputational credibility.[56] Governments use ideology to market policies or institutions to both domestic and international audiences. This creates expectations over what likely bargaining positions will be. It may be easier to commit to bargaining positions that fit these expectations than to commit to positions that do not. Institutions offer incentives to provide ideologies as well as to stick with them. For example, China may value its ability to credibly communicate that it reliably stands for noninterference in domestic affairs. If China proposes a new institution, like the AIIB, then other states may believe that the promise of noninterference in domestic affairs over human rights (or corruption) is credible.

This argument implies that states may sometimes have reputational incentives for noncompliance. Suppose, for instance, that an international organization issues an edict that goes against a government's ideological commitments. Noncompliance would diminish a government's reputation for compliance. Yet noncompliance might strengthen perceptions of ideological consistency. It is notoriously difficult to disentangle the influence of reputation when one decision can have countervailing implications on different kinds of reputations.[57] Yet theoretically, governments may be able to more credibly communicate their bargaining positions on new issues if the position follows from a well-understood set of interconnected propositions (ideology). This is especially true in multilateral contexts that depend on adherence to general principles.[58]

Third, ideology constrains through policy interdependence. The attractiveness of policy options depends on what other policies are in place. Once a state moves some policies in a market-oriented or open trade direction, then the incentives to change other policies changes. This makes ideological consistency more attractive. It will also change incentives to join inter-national institutions.

There is ample empirical evidence that liberal economic, social, and political policies have diffused in similar patterns.[59] The same is true for institutional relationships. Strengthening institutional trade ties with a country creates incentives to strengthen investment ties. There are strong correlations between memberships in bilateral investment treaties (BITs) and in preferential trade agreements (PTAs).[60] Strengthening institu-tional economic ties with a country may also create incentives to form in-stitutional security ties (and vice versa), as evidenced by the strong correla-tion between membership in trade pacts and alliances.[61] So Ukraine's desire to create a PTA with the EU may also signal something about its future security alliances. IGO memberships send signals to markets about a range of future policies.[62] There is a common logic underlying many institutional arrangements that creates real interdependence in many (though not all) institutional choices.

There is nothing inherently new about this claim. Still, few scholars examine how this common logic structures cooperation and conflict over international institutions. One exception is the budding literature that ex-amines IGO memberships as networks.[63] Network approaches helpfully expose the structure underlying state portfolios of institutional member-ships. The theoretical underpinnings of those relationships derive not from ideology but from the idea that joint institutional memberships cre-ate social ties among states. This literature has little to say about why there is variation in institutional portfolios, but it does suggest that the resulting patterns of social ties shape consequential behavior in international affairs. To network theorists, the choices by states to join similar IGOs stem not from a shared ideology but from similarities in their preexisting IGO membership portfolios. Chapters 6 and 7 have more to say about similari-ties and differences between the spatial and network approaches to model-ing interdependencies.

Measuring Ideological Positions

If political contention is ideological in the way that I use the term here, then it takes place in a policy space of limited dimensionality. The dimensionality of the policy space is an important assumption theorists must make when they analyze collective choice, coalition formation, or crisis bargaining, es-pecially with more than two actors. The spatial modeling literature is lit-tered with results showing that equilibrium formation is much more straightforward in a unidimensional policy space.[64] Unidimensionality does not always make things easier. For example, sometimes cooperative outcomes can emerge because actors can link issues across different dimensions, each valued differently by different actors.[65] But unidimensionality structures coalition formation and simplifies theoretical models.

I first illustrate how ideal points in a one-dimensional ideological space can be estimated from votes in the UNGA. I then show how these ideal points correlate with domestic variables before turning to how they help structure membership in international institutions. Much of the discussion here offers a nontechnical review of research published elsewhere.[66] That research also goes into more depth on the dimensionality question. There are some periods in post-1945 conflict that were multidimensional, especially North-South conflict that intersected with East-West conflict in the 1970s and early 1980s.[67] Chapter 9 returns to the question of orthogonal ideological dimensions, but most of this book focuses on unidimensional politics.

USING UN VOTES TO ESTIMATE STATE IDEAL POINTS

Scholars have long used roll-call votes in the US Congress to estimate legislator ideal points.[68] Congresspeople vote on a range of policy issues. Liberalism-conservatism is a latent dimension that underlies many of these choices. Congressional voting is not purely one-dimensional. In some periods of U.S. history, a second dimension, for example racial issues, has been important.[69] Moreover, congresspeople sometimes vote over non-ideological interests, such as to protect military bases in their districts. Yet a stable single dimension explains about 90 percent of congressional voting choices during a large portion of its history. Ideology imposes considerable structure on congressional voting. Scholars have found that one or two ideological dimensions dominate most legislatures.[70]

Scholars have also long used roll-call votes in the UNGA to compute indicators of state interests. This is not because the UNGA is by itself that important.[71] Instead, the UNGA is the only place in which states have since 1946 regularly expressed policy positions on human rights, (nuclear) disarmament, colonialism, the Middle East, economic development, and other contentious global issues. UNGA resolutions are nonbinding. This gives more incentives for sincere expressions of policy preferences than for strategic voting, although there is evidence of vote buying on some issues.[72]

Similarity in UN voting patterns correlates with numerous consequential outcomes, including the likelihood of interstate militarized disputes,[73]

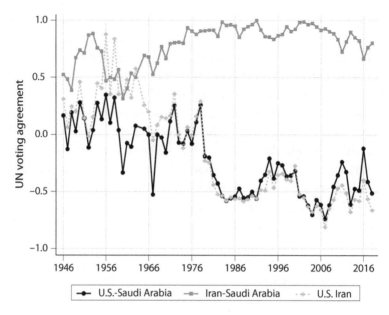

FIGURE 2.1. Vote similarity between United States, Iran, and Saudi Arabia.

the severity of those disputes,[74] the formation of military coalitions,[75] the location of terrorism,[76] the distribution of foreign aid,[77] the lending behavior of the World Bank and International Monetary Fund,[78] compliance with aid agreements,[79] the probability of signing treaties,[80] the provision of troops to UN peacekeeping missions,[81] the distribution of diplomatic missions,[82] and whether countries adopt the Chinese renminbi to their basket of reserve currencies.[83]

Scholars typically interpret these correlations as evidence for the importance of "common foreign policy interests" without specifying what this means. There are two problems with this type of interpretation. First, UNGA votes provide information over whether states have a shared ideology about how the global institutional system should work but not necessarily about shared particularistic interests. Figure 2.1 illustrates this by examining the dyadic vote agreement scores between three states: Saudi Arabia, the United States, and Iran. The agreement score (or S-score) equals –1 if states never vote together and 1 if they always vote together. The score reflects the average agreement between two states among all roll-call votes.[84] This is the most common way UN votes have been used in the study of IR.

The United States and Saudi Arabia, despite their common strategic interests, rarely vote together. By contrast, Iran and Saudi Arabia, fierce rivals, vote with each other a lot. The U.S.-Iran dyad looks more like we would expect: there is a fair bit of shared voting until the Iranian Revolu-

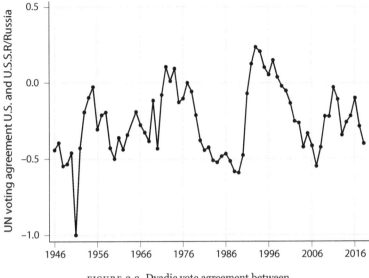

FIGURE 2.2. Dyadic vote agreement between
United States and Russia / Soviet Union.

tion. These results make little sense if voting agreement is an indicator of
"common interests" writ large. But they do make sense in ideological terms.
The conflict between Iran and the United States since the revolution is
about global ideology. As mentioned earlier, Saudi Arabia and the United
States have common strategic interests but not a shared ideology. Saudi
Arabia and Iran have a lot of disagreements, but they are typically not about
issues like the end of colonialism, human rights, or the adoption of new
global treaties.[85] Saudi Arabia and Iran share an aversion to the liberal
order even as they are fierce rivals on other issues. It is important to specify
what we mean when we write about "common interests."

Second, and related, UN votes are not expressions of how much one
state agrees with another state. UN votes are not relational. UN votes reflect whether a state agrees with a resolution that advocates for a particular
way to address an issue of global interest. This means that measures based
on UN votes are highly vulnerable to changes in the agenda.

Figure 2.2 illustrates this point using the example of vote similarity
between the United States and Russia / the Soviet Union. Voting agreement between the United States and the Soviet Union has been extremely
volatile. There are large yearly shocks to voting agreement in a period of
the Cold War where relations were stable. Moreover, intertemporal com-
parisons have limited external validity. For example, the figure suggests
that the Cold War briefly ended in the early 1970s when the S-score reached
positive territory. Moreover, the figure implies that by 2007 the relationship between Russia and the United States had soured to Cold War levels

but that things have gotten much more harmonious since. Neither of these interpretations withstands a basic face validity test. The next section shows that these irregularities disappear once we estimated a model that controls for changes in the kind of resolutions that the UNGA votes on.

Moreover, the dyadic vote agreement indicator cannot distinguish between changes in U.S. voting behavior and shifts in Russian or Soviet behavior. That is, did the Cold War end because the Soviet Union changed its voting behavior or because the United States did so? This can be important more generally, especially if we would like to understand whether changes in government ideology correspond to foreign policy changes.

IDEAL POINT ESTIMATION

This book follows in the footsteps of domestic politics scholars in estimating an empirical spatial model on a set of observed roll-call vote choices.[86] The conceptual idea is that states have an ideal point in a latent low-dimensional ideological space. States are more likely to favor a resolution if it more closely reflects their preferred ideology. In a one-dimensional space, each roll call is characterized by two parameters. The first is a cut-point.[87] States with ideal points on one side of the cut-point are expected to favor a resolution, whereas states on the other side are expected to vote against (probabilistically). The further a state is from the cut-point, the more likely it will vote with its ideological side.

The second is a discrimination parameter. Not all resolutions divide states according to how they position themselves vis-à-vis the Western liberal order. For example, there were many resolutions in the 1970s that reflected North-South conflict.[88] On these resolutions, the United States and the Soviet Union typically voted together. This explains why the U.S. and Soviet Union appear so close together in figure 2.2 in that period. Since these resolutions provide no information about the main dimension of contestation, they should not be weighted heavily for explaining differentiation along the first dimension.

Ideal-point models simultaneously estimate ideal points and roll-call parameters. Michael Bailey, Anton Strezhnev, and I estimated a dynamic model that separates shifts in the UN's agenda from shifts in ideological positions by holding constant the roll-call parameters of identical resolutions.[89] This helps separate agenda changes from preference changes. The large fluctuations in voting agreement with the United States in figure 2.2 presumably stem from variation in what the UN votes on rather than how much the United States and the Soviet Union agree. If we

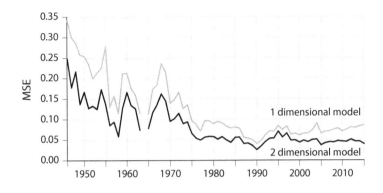

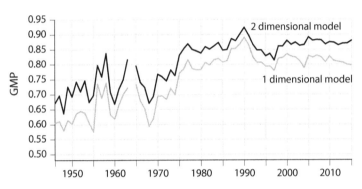

FIGURE 2.3. Fit of one- and two-dimensional models. GMP = geometric mean probability; MSE = mean squared error.

know that two resolutions are identical, then we can detect true preference changes.

For example, in 2016 U.S. president Barack Obama decided to abstain rather than vote against a long-standing UN resolution on the U.S. embargo on Cuba. This reflected a change in position from previous years, a move that coincided with other foreign policy changes toward Cuba. Yet in 2017, newly elected president Donald Trump reversed the UN vote.[90] Because we know that the resolutions are identical, we can fix the roll-call parameters across these years, which will help us identify preference change. Moreover, providing this type of glue to our estimates helps us hold constant the interpretation of the underlying ideological space from 1946 to 2017.

Figure 2.3 compares the fit of one- and two-dimensional models.[91] The mean squared error is the average squared distance between the expected vote (based on a one- or two-dimensional model) and actual votes. The geometric mean probability (GMP) is the model-estimated probability

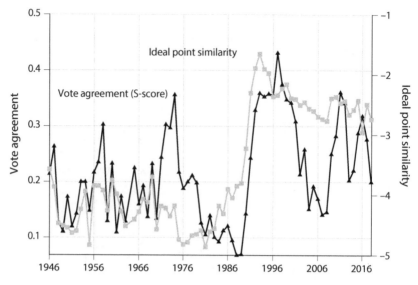

FIGURE 2.4. Voting agreement and ideal point similarity between the United States and Russia / Soviet Union.

that the country voted as it actually did for each vote. The overall levels of GMP are comparable to those for the U.S. Congress.[92] The larger the gap in explanatory power between the first and second dimensions, the more the second dimension contributes to the model's explanatory value.

While there are some periods in which the second dimension adds considerable explanatory power, including in recent years, the second dimension's importance is inconsistent. Moreover, while intertemporal correlations between first-dimension ideal points are consistently .95 or higher, correlations between second-dimension ideal points are typically modest and sometimes close to zero.[93] This suggests that there is no consistent interpretation of the second dimension. Consequentially, this book focuses on the first dimension.

Figure 2.4 plots the ideal point similarity[94] between the U.S. and Russian/Soviet ideal point in the same figure as the dyadic vote agreement from figure 2.2. We can see that ideal point similarity is much more stable than vote agreement. Moreover, the ideal point similarity changes dramatically only with the end of the Cold War. After 1990, the ideal point distance never returns to the acrimonious levels of the Cold War but does notice a souring of relations in the mid-1990s.

Nevertheless, figure 2.4 still paints a dyadic picture. It does not tell us whether or when the United States shifted its voting behavior or whether the Soviet Union / Russia did. Figure 2.5 plots the ideal points of the five

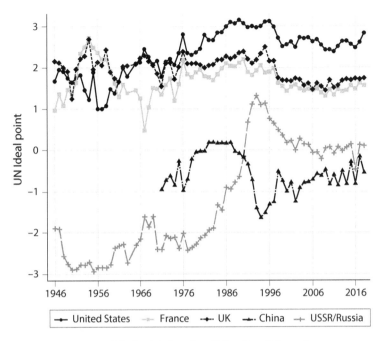

FIGURE 2.5. Ideal points based on UN voting, P-5 members.

permanent members of the UN Security Council over a seventy-year period. It now becomes clear that the Soviet Union shifted its position after
Mikhail Gorbachev came to power in 1985. Moreover, Russia shifted its
position away from the United States when Vladimir Putin came to power
in 1999 but has been relatively consistent since the mid-2000s. More recent fluctuations in ideal point similarity with the United States are due to
changes on the U.S., not the Russian, side. The graph clearly depicts that
the Trump administration has moved away from the center.

Overall, the positions of these powerful states are fairly stable over
time. Yet there are some notable shifts that correspond with well-known
events. For instance, China moves toward the non-Western side of the
spectrum following Tiananmen Square and its subsequent shift back toward the West as it started angling for WTO membership and economic
integration.

Figures 2.6 and 2.7 repeat this exercise for Latin American states. Figure 2.6, which plots dyadic voting agreement with the United States, shows
that Latin American states have become more hostile toward the United
States over time and that Cuba shifted earlier than the other Latin American states. But it is otherwise difficult to distinguish countries. In terms of
voting agreement, it seems like all Latin American countries are the same!

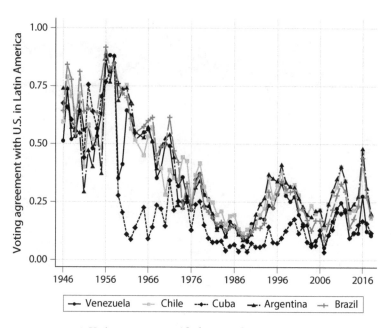

FIGURE 2.6. Voting agreement with the United States in Latin America.

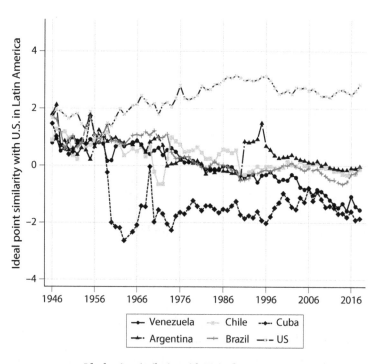

FIGURE 2.7. Ideal point similarity with United States in Latin America.

The ideal points in figure 2.7 display much clearer differences between the various states and within states over time in a way that lends face validity to the interpretation that the first dimension captures conflict over the Western liberal order. For example, Chile moved away from the West during the brief Allende government and then toward the United States under Pinochet. Venezuela's outlook changed noticeably after Hugo Chávez came to power. Chile and Argentina are currently closer to the U.S. ideal point than the other Latin American countries. This figure better represents ideological shifts that are consequential for international affairs.

THE CORRELATES OF UN IDEAL POINTS

The preceding figures show that ideal point estimates based on UN voting have some face validity as measures of the degree to which states oppose or support the Western liberal order. This section shows that the measure also has some external validity in that it correlates with changes in the factors that scholars think are associated with supporting a liberal order.

I focus on the three factors highlighted earlier. First is democracy. The literature that links shared democracy to shared cooperation is voluminous.[95] Most of this literature is not about the link between democracy and liberal ideology. Instead, the effect of democracy runs through institutional factors, such as the constraint democracy imposes on executives or the information provided by transparent democratic institutions. Yet democracies may also reliably favor principles embedded in institutions that promote human rights and the spread of democracy. The UN regularly votes on resolutions related to these issues. I use the Polity measure for democracy, which is the most widely used measure in the literature.[96]

Second, liberals emphasize the role of open markets.[97] While many democracies have open market economies, there are also democracies that lean toward a more socialist domestic political economy and nondemocracies that have embraced open market economics. Given that the liberal institutional order focuses heavily on instilling free trade, capital movement, and other principles of market economics, countries with more market-oriented economies should be more favorably disposed toward the Western liberal order. I follow Erik Gartzke in using the Chinn-Ito measure of capital openness to measure market orientation.[98]

Third, as argued in the introduction, the ideology of domestic governments should be correlated with foreign policy ideology. For example, left-wing governments systematically pursue different trade, welfare, and capital mobility policies from right-wing governments.[99] Both left- and

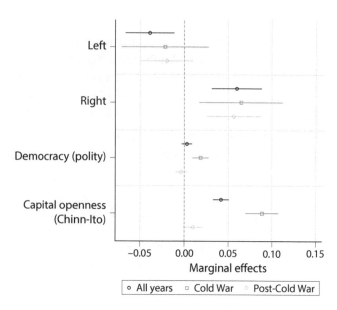

FIGURE 2.8. Fixed effects regression coefficients on UN ideal points.

right-wing governments in advanced Western democracies typically accept the general premises of liberal internationalism. But they still vary slightly in their foreign policy orientation and, consequentially, their ideal points.[100] For instance, a recent study found that left-wing (liberal) governments in Anglophone democracies were more inclined to vote with the rest of the world than were right-wing (conservative) governments.[101]

Figure 2.8 summarizes the evidence.[102] The figure plots the coefficients from a regression analysis. The regression model includes country and year fixed effects. This means that the model estimates whether changes in the characteristics of states (or governments) correlate with ideal point changes. All independent variables are lagged one year. The estimates are for the 1975 to 2016 period (due to data availability), but similar results hold when I examine the Cold War and post–Cold War periods separately. The full results are in the online appendix at https:// press.princeton.edu/books/paperback/9780691207322/ideology-and -international-institutions

First, countries that become more democratic (measured by their Polity scores) shift toward the U.S. ideal point during the Cold War but not thereafter. Second, countries that loosen their capital controls also shift toward the United States.[103] This effect was much larger during the Cold War but it persists. Third, shifts in domestic ideology matter. Governments whose executive belongs to the political left shift away from the United States compared to governments that are on the political right.[104]

These findings are consistent with those of other studies of the domestic correlates of UN ideal points.[105] The goal here is not to offer an exhaustive analysis of the correlates of why states alter their ideal points other than to communicate the basic point that a country's ideological perspective is not independent from factors that other liberal scholars have identified as important for institutional politics, such as democracy, economic openness, and left-right ideology. Nor is ideology the same thing. A country's ideological position encapsulates how all these factors contribute to a country's position on a range of issues regarding the U.S.-led liberal international order.

Conclusion

This chapter has defined and operationalized ideology in a way that is common in the literature on domestic politics but not in IR. The core argument is that much, though not all, institutional politics in the international arena takes place in a low-dimensional ideological space. Since 1946, there has been a dominant dimension of contestation that separates states with differing ideas about how a wide variety of issues should be resolved and who should resolve them. On the one side, there are states who are more comfortable with U.S. leadership, whose preferred image of society is one in which democratic elections allocate political power, where markets allocate resources, and where courts protect individual rights. On the other side, governments advocate for a greater role of the state in domestic and international economies, emphasize self-determination as ethically good, and favor redistributing resources and authority away from the West and the restoration of noninterference into the domestic affairs of states.

This is obviously a simplification of actual ideological differences. The key point is not that we must label states as belonging to one of two monolithic camps. There are many different manifestations of liberal internationalism over time[106] as well as disagreements among liberal internationalists.[107] Governments vary in both the degree to which they embrace liberal internationalism and the means to achieve a liberal international society. Communists during the Cold War were quite different from the post–Cold War opponents of the liberal international order. The essence of the spatial approach is that we are able to order states along an ideological dimension that captures conflict over many policy issues reasonably well. The same states often glare at each other from opposite sides of the fence. Moreover, some states are more likely than others to jump the fence.

The next chapters show that this simplification is useful both theoretically and empirically. Chapter 3 explains how conceptualizing competition and cooperation in a low-dimensional ideological space adds to existing theories of international institutions. Chapters 4 and 5 use a spatial modeling framework to gain theoretical insights about institutional politics. Chapters 6, 7, and 8 examine whether the measure developed in this chapter helps explain institutional participation and effects.

CHAPTER THREE

Ideology and Theories of International Institutions

THIS CHAPTER explains how this book's theoretical framework contrasts with and complements existing theories of international institutions. The chapter discusses four families of theories: functionalism, rational institutionalism, liberal internationalism, and constructivism. These theoretical frameworks yield meaningful insights about important aspects of the post–World War II multilateral order. Yet they can be enriched by conceptualizing multilateralism in terms of cooperation and competition in a low-dimensional ideological space. This chapter sets the stage for the next two chapters, which develop a more explicit theoretical framework based on spatial models. This chapter connects that framework to broader debates in the literature.

Functionalists and their intellectual descendants understand institutionalization as an incremental process driven by interdependencies and the spillover effects from previous institutionalization. Transnational and supranational bureaucrats, judges, scientists, and other experts are important driving forces. Yet expertise and technical cooperation are rarely ideologically neutral. This book's framework can help us understand the conditions under which such ideological contestation obstructs or creates opportunities for transnational actors.

Rational institutionalists argue that states delegate authority to international institutions in order to solve strategic problems that prevent states from reaping collective gains. This book's framework builds on this approach by embedding strategic problems in a spatial model. This helps us understand how institutions need not be social welfare improving, how states may be affected by institutions even if they do not participate in them, and how selection into institutions may be determined by ideology rather than a functional need for problem solving. Moreover, the framework shows how imperfect information and interdependence result in inequities of influence. If information is costly and valuable, then more powerful actors have disproportionate opportunities to gather and disseminate information that helps move the status quo toward their ideal points.

Like this book's framework, liberal internationalist theorists argue that the post–World War II multilateral order reflects the values and priorities of the United States. John Ikenberry argues that the multilateral order binds the United States to not exploit its immediate relative power advantage in exchange for locking in durable institutional advantages.[1] The spatial ideological framework can shed light on two key critiques to liberal internationalism: first, the critique from especially constructivists that liberal internationalist theories have failed to conceptualize the contentious nature of the liberal order and, second, realist criticisms that institutions cannot truly restrain powerful states. Competition in a low-dimensional ideological space constrains and informs. Ideology provides a form of glue that made the U.S. commitment institutions more credible. The flip side is that when a U.S. government came to power with an alternate ideological vision, people started questioning the U.S. commitment to the liberal order even before actual actions to undermine that order had taken place.

Finally, constructivists have long emphasized the ideational foundations of multilateral institutions. However, they have focused on norms, culture, and identities rather than ideology as the basis for doing so. I discuss why a focus on ideological contestation helps further this research program, especially if we are interested in understanding the strategic implications of the assumption that actors have varying ideas about how domestic and international societies should be organized.

Functionalism and Its Descendants

Functionalism is premised on the idea that forming an ever-spreading web of international institutional relationships that meet specific technical and nonpolitical needs can spur broader international cooperation.[2] This is an old and influential idea. In the early nineteenth century visionaries like the French count Saint-Simon argued that increasing authority for scientists, bureaucrats, and lawyers would undermine the power of statesmen with the ability to wage wars. Saint-Simon proposed that direct governance by a "union of commercial and manufacturing industry with literary and scientific industry" was the only viable alternative that would help overcome "destructive conflicts."[3] He and his followers were internationalists who believed, or hoped, that science and industry had the power to unite people toward a common enterprise. As Ernst Haas put it, they believed that peace would follow only if the "government of men" were replaced by the "administration of things."[4]

The second half of the nineteenth century saw some movement in that direction. The first formal international organizations were neither high-minded attempts to subject war to the rule of law nor elaborate collective security schemes. They were functional agencies designed to tackle confined problems of interdependence. The oldest extant intergovernmental organization (IGO) is the Central Commission for the Navigation of the Rhine (1815). Later, governments created organizations to manage new forms of communication, such as the International Telegraph Union (1865; now the International Telecommunications Union) and the General Postal Union (now the Universal Postal Union). Other organizations addressed coordination problems in the development of technology, such as the International Bureau of Weights and Measures (1875).

This continued in the early part of the twentieth century. Most remember the League of Nations for its failed attempts at collective security,[5] but most of its employees were located in its specialized agencies charged with specific problems such as health, drugs (especially opium), economic stability, and refugees.[6] Several of the league's most influential international bureaucrats moved to the United States during World War II and helped shape the new United Nations and its specialized agencies, many of which continue to play an important role in international affairs.[7]

In the immediate aftermath of World War II, functionalism again became prominent among theorists such as David Mitrany but also statesmen, like Jean Monnet, whose League of Nations experience had made him skeptical of grand schemes to achieve collective security.[8] Monnet described the aim of the European Coal and Steel Community (ECSC) as follows: "Through the consolidation of basic production and the institution of a new High Authority, whose decisions will bind France, Germany and the other countries that join, this proposal represents the first concrete step towards a European federation, imperative for the preservation of peace." Monnet's phrase "petits pas, grands effets" captures the spirit of the argument.[9] The small step of creating a functional agency that addresses a particular problem also creates actors at the international level who may use their authority to push for further integration. This is how the story of the European Community (now European Union) is sometimes told. The

ECSC created spillover effects that led to the creation of the Atomic Energy Community (EURATOM) and the European Economic Community (EEC), which gradually evolved into a single market and then a more profound political union.[10]

The long-standing critique of functionalism is that it is too mechanical in its reliance on collective interests and technocracy as the driving forces for integration. Even the nineteenth-century internationalist scientists could not agree on whose standards to adopt.[11] Ernst Haas's neofunctionalism offered a restatement that continues to be influential.[12] Haas dispenses with the notion that states act in pursuit of the common good, even in areas that appear technical. In the context of interdependence, organized economic interests pressure governments to harmonize specific policies. These narrow areas of cooperation can have broader unanticipated effects if governments learn that their interests are best served by further institutionalized cooperation.[13] Functional spillovers occur when cooperation in one sector results in pressures for cooperation in adjoining sectors. Eventually, these may yield political spillovers where supranational technocrats obtain political authority and loyalties gradually transfer to international organizations.

Even if neofunctionalism appeared to describe some aspects of European integration,[14] its processes were not replicated elsewhere. Moreover, in Europe the theory seemed unable to explain why regional integration stalled after its early successes. Haas was so disillusioned that he declared functionalism "obsolescent" in the mid-1970s.[15] European integration became dominated by broader issue linkages with more at stake, thus endangering the incrementalism at the root of functionalist theories.[16]

Contestation over European integration was driven more by diverging socioeconomic ideological visions of what European integration should become than by narrowly conceived national interests.[17] More leftist parties and governments advocated for more closely regulated capitalism. More right-wing governments advocated for a vision in which European institutions cement and spread free market ideals across the continent. In recent years, identity-based conflict has become the more prominent ideological dimension of contestation over European integration issues.[18] The labels for this dimension vary, but they generally contrast more socially liberal and cosmopolitan values versus traditional and authoritarian values.[19]

More generally, distributive conflict over functional cooperation is not just over whose producers benefit more[20] but also over the aims of institutionalized cooperation. The International Monetary Fund (IMF) does more than just solving informational problems; it solves them in particular ways. The literature has long (and rightly) pointed out that the IMF favors the particularistic strategic interests of its main stakeholders, most notably the United States.[21] The IMF also pursues policies and practices that seek to advance a particular vision about how global and domestic economies should be organized. This vision is much more in line with U.S. than Chinese or Russian ideological commitments. The distributive effects of the IMF go beyond "who gets what loans at what conditions." They are also about what rules the IMF bureaucracy gets to enforce and the information it chooses to collect. For example, IMF regulations and recommendations about capital controls reflect a general vision about how the global economy should work that is not universally shared.[22]

Modern neofunctionalist theories explain how transnational or supranational bureaucrats, experts, and judges affect international outcomes. The largest body of evidence comes from the European Court of Justice, which has used its authority and alliances with domestic actors to help construct the European internal market.[23] There is also evidence from various regulatory areas extending beyond Europe, such as privacy,[24] securities markets,[25] and bribery.[26] Others highlight the importance of "epistemic communities" of scientists who have acquired authority independent of states.[27] Anne-Marie Slaughter argues that we have witnessed the emergence of a "new world order" in which transnational networks of judges, bureaucrats, and scientists have peeled away power from central governments.[28]

These authors are united by the claim that loose alliances or networks involving international and domestic (non)governmental actors shape policy outcomes in ways that are not entirely within the control of governments. Building on historical institutionalism, they highlight that initial acts of delegation have unintended consequences that governments cannot perfectly foresee.[29] Yet modern neofunctionalists rarely venture into more ambitious terrain—that this process deepens political integration, removes issues from distributive politics, and ultimately makes wars between nation-states less likely.

The influence of such transnational and supranational experts can be studied in the context of ideological distributive conflict. For example, neofunctionalist theorists insist that international judges are "trustees": independent decision makers who gain authority through their expertise and who make their decisions largely independently from political pressures by governments.[30] Yet there is ample empirical evidence that international judicial behavior reflects the ideology of the governments that appointed them and is responsive to government interests.[31] Chapter 5 argues that supranational and transnational bureaucrats and judges rarely have expertise that at least some powerful states do not already possess. Yet in the context of ideological conflict, delegation to such agents may nonetheless occur for a different reason: governments have difficulty credibly sharing their information if they have divergent ideological interests. This creates room for these agents to shape outcomes. Thus, the political nature of the principal-agent interaction may help explain how agents exercise authority independent of states.

Finally, postfunctionalist theories emphasize the interplay between social forces and the functional needs for institutions.[32] This perspective recognizes that international institutions need continued social support (legitimacy) from their constituent communities and that providing material benefits may not suffice. Postfunctionalists share an interest in social cleavages and politicization,[33] but they do not highlight ideology or develop spatial models and measures.

Rational Institutionalism

In the early 1980s, a new theoretical literature emerged on international institutions that took its inspiration from the "new institutional economics," "transaction cost economics," or "contract theory."[34] This branch of economics asks why, when, and how authority relations emerge in a specific type of anarchical environment: markets.[35] Uncertainty, hidden information, or, more broadly, "transaction costs" prevent otherwise beneficial cooperation (trade) from occurring. Actors create institutions to reduce these transaction costs and allow mutually beneficial trades.

This framework offers a way to think about institutions without the need to dispense with the anarchy assumption that underlies so much theorizing about international relations. Institutions make transactions between states more efficient, help monitor state behavior, reduce cheating, and provide a way for states to make credible commitments. States remain the primary actors. If there is meaningful delegation to institutions, then this is the consequence of voluntary and reversible state acts. The aspirations of the rationalist institutionalism literature are less transformative than those of the functionalism literature. Yet the two bodies of literature also have much in common, most notably the presumption that institutions emerge from a desire to improve social efficiency in the context of interdependence.

The rational institutionalist literature starts from the premise that interdependence creates strategic situations that are not zero sum. Of particular interest are mixed-motive games, in which there is some incentive to cooperate but also incentives to defect. Fear of cheating inhibits cooperation. Institutions can help, for example by providing information that identifies cheaters or by creating dispute settlement mechanisms that facilitate tit-for-tat punishment.[36]

Rational institutionalists incorporate distributive issues in one of three ways. First, the classical functionalist approach is to acknowledge that states have diverse interests but that institutions address those issue areas where states do have common interests.

Second, the rational design literature views distribution as a problem that institutions can solve.[37] For example, Barbara Koremenos codes a random sample of international legal agreements.[38] She found that 27 percent of international agreements address distributive issues.[39] The theory expects this latter set of agreements to have design features that optimally solve distributive issues. So the design of voting rules or dispute settlement procedures can be explained by a common desire to resolve distributive problems.

A related approach is that preinstitutional bargaining addresses the issue of heterogeneity, allowing institutions to focus on enforcement problems.[40] The intergovernmentalist two-step approach is an example.[41] The first step is to determine the domestic actors and institutions that define state preferences. The second step is to take those preferences as given for international interactions and explain bargaining outcomes as a function of the constellation of interests and capabilities. Institutions cement and help enforce the bargaining deal.

This approach usefully acknowledges the role of distributive conflict in the creation of international institutions. The framework builds on this by modeling a specific kind of distributive conflict: ideological conflict. Yet institutions don't *solve* distributive problems but *structure* distributive politics. For example, bilateral investment treaties (BITs) allow multinational corporations to bring a breach of contract claim to an investment arbitration panel.[42] Such institutions shape how distributive conflict is conducted but do not depoliticize the issue.[43] In practice, governments reserve ways to influence even seemingly independent bodies, including legalized dispute settlement mechanisms.[44]

Similarly, knowing that the United Nations Security Council (UNSC) permanently assigns veto power to five states creates expectations about how that institution will act. These expectations are partially driven by understandings about the ideologies of the five permanent members (the P-5). The UNSC does not solve the distributive problems between the P-5 or between the P-5 and other states. But the UNSC's voting rules shape the conduct of distributive politics on conflictual issues.[45]

A third approach builds on principal-agent models, which suggest that principals (governments) could sometimes collectively benefit if they delegated some tasks to agents (international institutions).[46] This can be because international bureaucrats have informational (or expertise) advantages or because delegation reduces the transaction cost of policy making. In order to profit from delegation, agents typically have some leeway to implement policies that reflect their preferences. This means that international institutions may well do things differently from how their principals would have. Principals can limit this discretion through contractually defined routes, for example by influencing appointments, budgets, and so on. There is increasing attention to how the delegation of this authority is shaped by ideological contestation.[47] Chapter 5 builds on spatial models of delegation to provide theoretical foundations for such an analysis.[48]

Liberal Internationalism

Liberal internationalists argue that the post–World War II multilateral institutional order reflects both the asymmetric power and the values of the United States. For example, John Ikenberry argues that the United States voluntarily agreed to restrain itself in the post–World War II order in exchange for promises by others to bind themselves to a liberal institutional infrastructure that would have favorable long-term consequences for the United States. States voluntarily accept limits on their own behavior as part of an exchange for reciprocally extended restrictions on the behavior of others.[49] Ikenberry, like Ruggie, recognizes that multilateral institutions created by the United States advance quite distinct principles than what alternative institutional orders may have looked like. In terms of this book's framework, the liberal institutional order is designed to move outcomes toward the U.S. ideal point.

The main challenge for Ikenberry is to explain how the liberal constitutional order sticks once conflicts of interest become apparent.[50] Why would a state feel bound to honor an agreement it no longer values? And why would states that took no part at all in negotiating the UN Charter feel bound by it? Why wouldn't states challenge the order after their power increases? Ikenberry and others explain this by arguing that institutions are sticky, for example because they generate increasing returns.[51]

Ideology provides an additional source of constraint that can help explain the durability of the order. First, unlike ad hoc cooperation, institutionalized cooperation typically aims to define the terms of interactions for a relatively long time. All of this creates a lot of ex ante uncertainty over the cost and benefits of institutionalized cooperation. Actors cannot perfectly foresee how a cooperative agreement will affect them. The willingness of rational actors to make costly policy adjustments and/or invest in institutional resources depends on their expectations about how their institutional partners will act down the road on issues and conflicts that are not yet fully defined. Organizing institutions around a set of ideological principles that credibly reflect U.S. long-term interests helps inform other states what a commitment to the liberal order might entail.

Some realists claim that it is impossible to be sure about intentions and thus it is best to assume the worst, prohibiting stable institutionalized cooperation.[52] This is not a persuasive argument. It is trivially true that states can never be fully confident about the intentions of others. But the conclusion that states are therefore better off not cooperating does not follow.[53] In strategic settings, outcomes always depend on how others will act. Uncertainty about intentions affects not just multilateral cooperation but also unilateral actions.

For example, as Thomas Schelling pointed out a long time ago, Germany can never be confident that the United States will protect its security.[54] Does this mean that Germany should not rely on NATO and the U.S. nuclear umbrella and instead develop nuclear weapons of its own?[55] Not necessarily. Germany can also not be confident that the United States or Russia would not act during the process of acquiring nuclear weapons, or that having nuclear weapons would not draw it into costly conflicts with other states. Security, by definition, depends on the actions of others. States have no choice but to devote inordinate amounts of time and effort forming *expectations* about what others are *likely* to do.[56]

States have to form expectations not just about each other's proclivity for compliance but also about the future preferences of their partner states. Cooperation with like-minded states requires fewer policy concessions and allows for deeper cooperation.[57] If a state cooperates with others that have relatively similar ideologies, then it is less likely to find itself locked into an institution it no longer favors. Moreover, preferences and compliance are logically related.[58] Incentives to defect increase with the cost of policy adjustments. If a state can reasonably assume that its institutional partners have similar preferences on future issues, then the expected cost of policy adjustments will be lower and the probability of cooperation higher. One important role of ideology is that it is a shortcut for forming expectations about future preferences of states on a wide range of issues.

To return to the NATO example, the credibility of the U.S. commitment to defend Germany hinges not just on the U.S. reputation for honoring its commitments but also on beliefs that the United States will find that it is in its interest to defend Germany. Germany's likely adversaries have geopolitical interests opposite from those of the United States. That was most obviously true during the Cold War. But it is still true today. If Russia, China, or Iran were to attack Germany, then it is reasonable to guess that the United States would have a strong interest in defending Germany. We can make these assessments only because we have some reasonable idea that U.S. interests will be more closely aligned with those of Germany than those of Iran, Russia, or China on a future conflict. Beliefs about preferences and interests shape expectations about both future conflict and cooperation.

Second, this book argues not just that states have diverse preferences over the liberal institutional order but also that low-dimensional ideological conflict has structured global politics at least since 1945. Social choice theorists and scholars of collective decision making have long pointed out that low-dimensional ideological spaces structure collective decision making.[59] Strategic decision making relies heavily on the beliefs actors have about the strategies of others. Ideology helps organize beliefs about the interests of the many actors involved in multilateralism. Institutions help create expectations about the rules and processes that shape strategic interactions.

An example illustrates both points. Suppose China and the United States have opposing but interdependent interests over trade rules. That is, they prefer cooperation over noncooperation but much prefer to cooperate at their own ideal points and prefer some noncooperative arrangements over some forms of cooperation. Suppose these two states would each like to convince other states to pursue a common policy as close to their own preferred policy as possible. A consequence of interdependence is that the more states they can get to move closer to their side the more attractive it becomes for others to also move.

To give an example, if Vietnam shifts its policies toward the United States, then it becomes more attractive for Cambodia to do the same because Cambodia has some dependency on both countries. An institutional arrangement, like the Trans-Pacific Partnership (TPP), is a way for Vietnam to credibly announce that it is changing policies. Ideology helps others form beliefs about what other policy or relationship changes might follow from this institutional membership. Does it make Vietnam more likely to shift other economic policies or engage in other types of political and security relationships with the United States? Ideology and institutions help structure distributive politics even in the context of great power competition.

Asymmetries in interdependence are not always large enough to pre-determine outcomes. Even the United States cannot always get what it wants without compromises. The IMF was largely designed according to U.S. wishes, even if it had to compromise a bit with some European states. The World Trade Organization's (WTO) rules are certainly closer to the U.S. ideal point than China's (at least in 1994 and in 2000), but the WTO also constrains the United States. Smaller states influenced core legal principles that underpin the global institutional order.[60] When asymmetric interdependencies are insufficiently large, we might also see multiple institutions organized around ideologically different principles. Development banks are a good example. The Asian Infrastructure Investment Bank (AIIB) espouses an ideology that is much closer to China's ideal point compared to the World Bank.

Institutions like voting rules, agenda setting authority, and dispute settlement processes can structure outcomes toward particular solutions.[61] The next chapters show that institutions can play this role even if they have no enforcement power or independent expertise. The theoretical conundrum that follows is how institutions with distributive consequences but without expertise or enforcement advantages survive. One set of answers is functional: institutions have transaction cost advantages. Or it could be that actors expect to benefit from an institution in the long run even if in the short run decisions go against them. Other answers stress path dependency: actors may invest in institutions that they will later adhere to even if they occasionally return disadvantageous decisions. But it could also be that actors are caught in an expectations trap. Everyone expects everyone else to adhere to the institution. In the context of strong interdependence (and thus strong coordination benefits) it may be difficult for either actor to change these beliefs. Shared understandings of what happened the last time shape beliefs of how everyone will act in similar situations in the future. This highlights the importance of sequences in ways that are similar to (but based on a different theoretical logic from) historical institutionalist scholars.[62] Ideology structures the available alternatives for institutional formation.

Constructivism

Constructivist theories emphasize the social and ideational foundations and effects of international institutions.[63] This book builds on constructivist theories in important ways. The framework follows Ruggie's insights that the U.S.-led international order after 1945 is based on multilateralism, which is a distinctive form of organizing international cooperation around a set of general principles.[64] As explained in previous chapters, Ruggie labeled the key overarching principle "embedded liberalism," which was displaced by more neoliberalist principles after the end of the Cold War.[65] Moreover, like Ruggie and most constructivists, I argue that it makes little sense to distinguish ideas from interests. After World War II, American policy makers created institutions that embedded ideological principles in an effort to construct a world order that was conducive to the spread of democratic capitalism and that was able to contain the power and ideological appeal of the Soviet Union.[66] The relevant distinction is not between ideas and interests but between a multilateral approach that advances ideas that are in the U.S. interests and a transactional approach that seeks to resolve strategic exigencies in ways that favor the United States.

Despite these communalities, this book's framework is explicitly rationalist. Rationalism is based on a fundamentally different set of assumptions than constructivism and can be used to answer different kinds of questions.[67] In constructivist approaches, the preferences of actors are socially constructed and can change through socialization, persuasion, or social interactions. By contrast, rationalist approaches require assumptions about the distribution of preferences. The advantage is that rationalist approaches can answer questions about the strategic implications of the configuration of preferences. Thus, rationalists and constructivists tend to answer different kinds of questions. If we assume that actors have ideal points along a single ideological dimension, how will these actors address problems of strategic interdependence? What role do international institutions play in this? Those are the types of questions that the framework developed in the next two sections is designed to answer. These are quite different questions than those typically asked by constructivists.

Perhaps surprisingly, the positivist constructivist literature has placed very little emphasis on ideology.[68] Yet this literature sometimes uses identity in ways that appear similar to ideology. For example, Alexander Wendt famously pondered why "500 British nuclear weapons are less threatening to the United States than 5 North Korean nuclear weapons."[69] Wendt understood the Cold War as being about clashing intersubjective social identities rather than clashing ideologies:

> The intersubjective basis of social identities can be cooperative or conflictual. What matters is how deeply the social structures they instantiate penetrate conceptions of self, not whether self and other are normatively integrated. The Cold War was a social structure in virtue of which

the United States and the USSR had certain identities. These were embodied in "national security world- views" (in terms of which each defined self and other) and in role positions in a social structure. . . . The content of national interests was in part a function of these structurally constituted identities (as well as of domestic ones). The United States had an interest in resisting Soviet influence in Angola because the Soviets were an enemy and enmity is a social relation.[70]

To Wendt, the end of the Cold War involved changes in "deeply penetrated conceptions of self" and enemy relations. Ideology and identity can be related but are conceptually distinct. An ideology is a set of beliefs about how the world should hang together. A social identity is an image of oneself vis-à-vis others. Aggregate actors, such as governments or political parties, often proclaim their ideologies in party manifestoes or other documents. Thus, if a new government or leader (like Gorbachev) comes to power who espouses a different ideology than a predecessor, then we can naturally expect that government to have different preferences over foreign policy. Once the Soviet government ended its adherence to communism, this signaled a dramatic departure in ideology, which had foreign policy consequences.

It is much more complex to think through what it means for an aggregate actor, like a state, to have an identity. Moreover, we typically do not think that a state's identity suddenly changes when a new government comes to power. Over time, "deep conceptions of self" may well change as a country becomes democratic and capitalist. But identity is usually slow to change.

Conclusion

The purpose of this chapter was to place this book's theoretical framework in the context of four theoretical families: (neo)functionalism, rational institutionalism, liberal internationalism, and constructivism. This book builds on insights from these perspectives but also deviates from them in important places. The next two chapters develop the framework in much greater detail.

CHAPTER FOUR

A Spatial Modeling Framework

THIS CHAPTER introduces a simple spatial modeling framework to analyze how variations in interdependence and ideology shape incentives for cooperation and competition. The goal is to present a framework that is as simple as the prisoner's dilemma, coordination dilemma, battle of the sexes, and other two-by-two games that have served as mental models for rationalist analyses of cooperation.[1] The spatial model easily accommodates multiple actors and distributive conflict and allows for analyses of how institutions structure choices. The spatial model starts from the assumption that actors have ideal points in a common low-dimensional ideological space. Yet their utilities are determined not just by their own policies but also by the policies of other actors. This interdependence creates incentives for cooperation. In this context, institutions may help actors achieve mutually beneficial outcomes, but they also have distributive implications. Institutions help shift policy status quos in particular directions.

This chapter lays out the main intuitions with very little math. Moreover, I deliberately impose very little structure on the models. Like with the two-by-two games, the point is to see how institutions could structure outcomes rather than analyze the effect of particular institutions.

A Simple Spatial Model with Interdependence

Consider a set of $2,...N$ actors. Each actor i has a unique ideal point θ_i in a K-dimensional Euclidean outcome space. Each actor also adopts a policy, a vector p_i, that maps into the outcome space. In this chapter, this mapping is direct. The next chapter considers models where uncertainty about the world affects the translation of policies into outcomes. The interpretation of the outcome space as ideological means that a space of few dimensions (low K) can incorporate preference divergence over a large number of issues.

Actor i's utility is a common, continuous, and decreasing function of the distance between p_i (the policy) and θ_i (the ideal point). Without interdependence, a rational actor should adopt its ideal point as policy. Yet interdependence means that utilities are also partially a function of the policies that others adopt. Robert Keohane and Joseph Nye defined interdependence as "situations characterized by reciprocal effects among countries or among actors in different countries."[2] Keohane and Nye distinguished between *interconnectedness* and *interdependence*. Interconnectedness refers to the flow of money, goods, people, and messages across international boundaries. Interdependence refers to the fact that much of international life is characterized by situations in which actors, even powerful ones, cannot independently achieve what they want. The actions of other actors affect their payoffs and thus their optimal strategies.

Interdependencies are ubiquitous in the international system, although they vary across policy areas and relationships. A small open market like the Netherlands would much prefer that Germany have similar regulations to it. It cares a lot less about Bolivia's regulatory framework. Germany's regulations are more important to the Netherlands for products it wishes to export to Germany (like agricultural products) than for products it does not (like solar panels). Germany's payoffs are generally much less dependent on Dutch regulations than vice versa.

Interdependencies are also omnipresent in security. The expected payoff of military aggression depends not just on the strength of the immediate opponent but also on if and how the rest of the international community will respond. Military interventions are cheaper and less controversial if they are done with a large coalition. Indeed security is inherently an interdependent concept: it depends fundamentally on the actions of others. For example, data travel across borders and thus cannot be adequately protected by national laws. If societal preferences lean strongly toward privacy, then a society may be harmed if other countries do not adopt similarly high standards. The reverse is also true. A government that wants to give its security apparatus easier access to personal data could be harmed by foreign barriers to data access. There could also be efficiency benefits to harmonization. Companies operate across borders and pay a steep price for adjusting to multiple regulatory regimes. Individuals and security agencies each benefit from a predictable regime with clear rules, although each might want different rules.[3]

None of this goes beyond what Keohane and Nye pointed out in their seminal study of power and interdependence.[4] Yet the two-by-two games that dominated much of the follow-up literature rarely explicitly modeled asymmetric interdependencies. The approach in this chapter modifies the basic spatial model by assuming that utility is a function of not just how far a policy is from a state's ideal point but also how far it is from the policies of other states. The distance between actor i's and actor j's policies is $D_{ij} = f(p_i - p_j)$, where f is a Euclidean distance function. The assumption is that coordination yields benefits to both states if policies move closer.[5] The importance of coordination benefits depends on the sensitivity of actor i to actor j's policies defined by weights $w_{i,j}$. These weights can be asymmetric. That is, if actor i depends more on i than vice versa, then $w_{i,j} > w_{j,i}$.

In the simplest case where there is a single-dimensional policy space, no switching cost[6] or other nonspatial considerations, and a linear utility function, then actor i's utility is a function of how far its policy is removed from its ideal policy and the interdependence weighted distance from other states' policies:

$$U_i = -|\theta_i - p_i| - \sum_{j \neq i}^{N}((w_{i,j})^* D_{ij}) \qquad \text{(eq. 4.1)}$$

The first part of the equation $(-|\theta_i - p_i|)$ captures that utility decreases the further its actual policy is from its preferred domestic ideal point. The literature sometimes discusses this "sovereignty cost," although this is not the procedural cost of delegating authority but the cost of adjusting policies to deal with the effects of interdependence. A state may have incentives to pay this cost regardless of any institution because there are benefits of coordination, especially for states with high interdependence $(\sum_{j \neq i}^{N}((w_{i,j})^* D_{ij}))$. This second term resembles the spatial weight term in empirical studies of diffusion, which is not always well motivated theoretically.[7] Together, the utility function captures the idea that interdependence creates pressures for harmonization and may undermine the ability of citizens to steer their government to implement domestically preferred policies.[8]

A clear implication is that the more other countries with whom state i interacts have already adopted a set of policies, the greater the incentives for state i to adopt a similar policy. The main decision-theoretic idea behind this equation is thus that countries minimize their sovereignty cost subject to interdependency constraints. If interdependencies increase or ideological congruence increases, the incentives to coordinate also increase (and vice versa). The next subsection examines the strategic implications of this utility function.

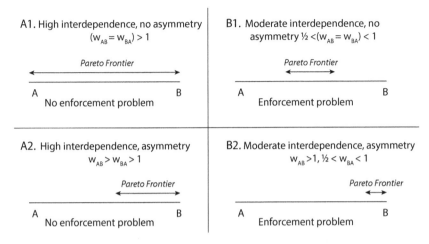

FIGURE 4.1. Ideological conflicts, interdependence, and enforcement problems.

An Example with Two States

Suppose there are just two states: A and B. Without loss of generality we set ideal points at opposite sides of the ideological spectrum: $\theta_A = 0$ and $\theta_B = 1$. The simplest linear utility function that encapsulates both benefits to coordination and autonomy costs is:

$$U_A = -p_A - w_{AB}{}^*|p_B - p_A|$$

$$U_B = -(1 - p_B) - w_{BA}{}^*|p_B - p_A|$$

The first term captures that utility for states A and B is declining in how far the new policies take them from their respective ideal points. The second part captures the benefits to coordination, where w_{AB} and w_{BA} reflect the degree to which the benefits of coordination matter relative to moving from the ideal point.[9] If the benefits to coordination are relatively small (w_{AB}, $w_{BA} < \frac{1}{2}$), then there is no possibility for a Pareto improvement. Each state continues its domestically preferred policy.

Figure 4.1 illustrates four sets of parameter values where the interdependence weights are sufficiently large such that there are incentives to coordinate. In quadrants A1 and A2, interdependence is so high that once a coordinated solution is achieved, there are no incentives to cheat. The quadrants differ in the degree of asymmetry in the interdependence. In quadrants B1 and B2 the incentives for coordination are more modest such that concerns about cheating exist after reaching agreements.

The analysis below examines the role institutions can play in these different strategic settings and what the impediments to their creation are.

These strategic dilemmas have important similarities to the familiar coordination and collaboration dilemmas from the rationalist institutionalist literature.[10] Yet looking at them in the context of divergent but interdependent spatial preferences yields valuable new insights.

HIGH INTERDEPENDENCE
(NO ENFORCEMENT PROBLEMS)

In quadrant A1, w_{AB} and $w_{BA} > 1$ and there is no asymmetric interdependence. The benefits to coordination are so large that each state is unilaterally better off coordinating. Yet states disagree what common policy to coordinate on. The main impediment to effective cooperation is not cheating but distribution, as in the familiar battle of the sexes game. There are multiple equilibria with vastly different distributive implications.

In order to understand what agreement out of the many possible agreements will emerge, we must impose more structure on the bargaining between A and B. The fundamental problem is what social choice theorists, most famously Kenneth Arrow, have dubbed "cycling."[11] Cycles imply instability: any outcome in a cycle can replace any other as the collective outcome. This suggests that social processes in international politics produce only transitory results. In other words, international politics would be in continuous disequilibrium.

In reality, neither legislative nor international politics are characterized by excessive cycling. Instead, institutions impose structure that steers society toward some outcomes and away from others.[12] Institutions address issues of indeterminacy, which are ubiquitous in strategic dilemmas with distributive conflict.[13] As Kenneth Shepsle and Barry Weingast put it in an overview of the literature, "Norms, structure, and agenda power . . . induce equilibrium outcomes. . . . These *political* elements of the decision setting do not rid the world of Arrow's phantom, but rather demonstrate how its effect can be restrained by institutional features."[14]

Most of the structure in domestic politics stems from ideology, which limits the dimensionality of the policy space and the institutions of government. Institutions are "structure induced equilibria."[15] Institutions induce equilibria by determining the order in which actors make proposals and the ability of actors to amend proposals, setting the rules on how proposals become laws, and so on. Examples are voting rules, the distribution of agenda setting powers, the presence of veto players, and the role of parties as legislative cartels.[16]

These institutional structures address distributive indeterminacy rather than enforcement or information problems. After an agreement is reached, no party has incentives to deviate from it. Yet in the international system, states may have incentives to ignore institutions that have unfavorable distributive consequences. For example, the UN General Assembly (UNGA) looks like a legislature. It has committees that draft proposals and amendment rules, and it adopts resolutions with majority rule. But the resolutions are nonbinding and often have no effect on state policies. Since the 1960s, the United States has known that it will lose most of the time if it accepts the UNGA as an institutional mechanism. Chapter 8 illustrates this point with regard to customary rules regarding the protection of foreign investments. Once majorities were slipping for the United States' most preferred version, the United States and other Western countries started to develop alternative institutions.

Yet institutions can still play an important role in an environment where powerful actors can influence the status quo through unilateral actions. For example, Farrell and Saloner examine coordination on incompatible standards where there are costs to delaying agreement.[17] They compare market mechanisms (unilateral moves by actors) and a committee system. A committee that regularly votes on a single standard without being able to enforce the result of its vote achieves coordination faster than the market, although the system works even better when both mechanisms operate simultaneously. That is, the committee does not need an informational advantage or exclusive jurisdiction to affect outcomes, but costly unilateral moves help shape the committee outcome.

Leslie Johns shows that an international court can help states coordinate on a resolution to a dispute even if litigation is costly, information is not a problem, and the court's decisions cannot be centrally enforced.[18] That is, the court does not need to have expertise or enforcement capabilities. The court matters simply because it proposes one out of many possible solutions to a dispute and this affects the beliefs of actors.

That international law and institutions can have a focal effect is well understood.[19] Yet sometimes this focal effect is thought to be innocuous, like coordinating on driving on the left or the right side of the road. In the context of ideological conflict, the focal effect of institutions is distributive even if it selects an equilibrium from along the Pareto frontier. Suppose that the main dimension is ideological conflict over how interventionist the government should be in the economy. If the institutions tend to pick policies that are close to zero (heavy regulation), then this makes state B worse off relative to plausible alternatives even if state B has no immediate incentive not to implement the proposals. This is exactly the kind of criticism often levied against the European Commission (rightly or wrongly). State B could leave the organization. Yet if other states on which it depends continue cooperating, then it may be costly to do so, as Brexit illustrates.

If institutions have these types of distributive effects, we must naturally ask, where do these institutions come from? There are at least three types of answers. First, principal-agent theorists think of the delegation of agenda-setting power as a constraint that actors impose upon themselves in order to also constrain others from proposing endless alternatives. Deliberately delegating authority to an agenda-setting institution is a costly act that requires actors to overcome a separate bargaining problem. As such, this is more likely in ongoing integration initiatives where an institution can address a range of issues. Suppose for example that states A and B are creating a single market and expect that many interrelated issues will arise that have high interdependence. Then they may consider delegating the task of picking a proposed common policy/regulation to an independent bureaucracy. They would still maintain the right to accept or reject the proposal. Yet the agenda-setting institution can affect outcomes by proposing the alternative on the Pareto frontier that is closest to its ideal point.

One advantage of this bureaucracy may be that it reduces transaction costs vis-à-vis negotiating each common policy separately. Yet the argument for delegation does not necessarily rely on the bureaucracy having more expertise or implementing better decisions. A bureaucracy that randomly picks a proposal that both states can then vote up or down (an agenda setter) could work just fine.[20] It may break distributive indeterminacy if both A and B believe that accepting adverse decisions is worth the long-run benefits of the institution. If there are multiple states, then the institution's decisions may carry force simply because it is difficult to collectively organize on an alternate way to coordinate.

A second, neofunctionalist, variant is that transnational actors exploit indeterminacy to develop rules that match their preferences. An example is Henry Farrell and Abe Newman's argument that informal or soft-law arrangements maintained by transnational alliances reshaped bargaining outcomes between the United States and the EU in areas with high interdependence.[21] The authority of these cross-national layering arrangements does not come from formal delegation. Yet they can alter the effective status quo for domestic institutional actors when coordination on something is more attractive than holding on to domestic regulatory status quos. By moving the status quo, the transnational actors also alter the preferred policies of domestic institutional actors. This can be interpreted as an example where transnational actors strategically exploit indeterminacy. The next chapter discusses specific examples where transnational experts can exploit their expertise in the context of distributive conflicts between states, thus embedding a neofunctionalist rationale more firmly in a distributive context.

A third possibility is distribution "all the way down": institutions emerge as by-products from distributive conflicts. That is, beliefs about the rules under which future disputes of a certain kind will be resolved can be shaped by past resolutions of specific conflicts rather than deliberate institutional invention. Any feature of the environment that makes some beliefs more prominent than others are crucial in the context of distributive indeterminacy.

As an illustration, consider the creation of the ECSC, a classic example in the functionalist literature discussed in the previous chapter. It is not so clear that the ECSC actually did all that much to solve problems in the coal and steel market.[22] An alternative perspective views the Treaty of Paris and the institutions it created as by-products from an attempt to "solve a particular historical problem": the command over resources in the Ruhr area.[23] The Schuman Plan was driven by French concerns that Germany could abuse its market power in steel amid scarcity in the market.[24] The specifics of the plan were shaped by diminishingly attractive outside options for the French.[25] Yet the institutions created by the Treaty of Paris did alter expectations and structured future bargaining in the sense that the High Authority, the Assembly, and the European Court of Justice (ECJ) shaped beliefs about how future distributive conflicts could be addressed amid high interdependence.

It is worth reemphasizing that these arguments apply only if interdependencies are strong and if the institution exercises its discretion (or biases) within the bounds identified by the Pareto frontier. Governments still reserve the right to reject proposals. Moreover, the next chapter illustrates that informational rationales are also important even in this context. Yet it is possible to construct a rationale for institutional influence even when the institution has no particular features that help solve informational or enforcement problems. Instead, institutions are consequential in picking a policy along the Pareto frontier.

This theoretical point has implications for empirical studies. For instance, empirical studies often claim that NGOs, transnational actors, or international institutions make states do things that they would not have otherwise done. But what does this mean? Do NGOs steer policies to different points along the Pareto frontier? Do they change state interests? Do they change the Pareto frontier? These are conceptually distinct outcomes that may be difficult to distinguish in real-world settings. Simply showing that an outcome is closer to an NGO's preference than a state's revealed preference does not tell us whether the NGO was able to strategically exploit indeterminacy or construct new authority or was irrelevant.

An NGO that strategically exploits indeterminacy "matters" in the sense that the outcome is closer to the NGO ideal point then it otherwise might have been. In William Riker's terms, these NGOs engage in heresthetics, or the art of political manipulation.[26] This differs from an argument in which NGOs shape the way states understand what their interests are in the first place. In the spatial framework, that would mean states shift their ideal points toward the NGO. This type of argument falls outside of the scope of rationalist explanations. This does not mean that it is empirically wrong, just that it is a different kind of theoretical claim.

This analysis also puts into context a key theoretical debate in the context of the EU between intergovernmentalists[27] and neofunctionalists.[28] The core of the debate involves the degree to which governments continue to control European integration or whether transnational processes and supranational actors have effectively taken that control from governments. No serious scholar of EU politics would argue that distributive politics among governments doesn't matter nor that supranational judges or bureaucrats have no influence. Nor should this be reduced to an empirical debate about the size of coefficients. Instead, we ought to think theoretically about just how distributive intergovernmental politics and transnational authority interact. The next chapter follows up on this point.

Panel A2 in figure 4.1 examines the situation where both states are highly dependent on each other but A's utility is affected more by B's policy than vice versa (asymmetric interdependence). The strategic situation is the same as above: institutions can help structure bargaining and help resolve problems of indeterminacy. The difference is that the bargaining range moves toward B's ideal point.

This introduces power in a way that is subtly different from Stephen Krasner and Lloyd Gruber's arguments that power asymmetries and go-it-alone power determine bargaining along a Pareto frontier or can lead to institutions that are not along that frontier.[29] As I have argued elsewhere, outside options shape the Pareto frontier but are of little use when bargaining along it.[30] Unilateralism defines the bound of the Pareto frontier. The United States' unilateral abilities to intervene militarily, to impose Section

301 sanctions, and to bail out countries skew the design and functioning of the United Nations Security Council (UNSC), World Trade Organization (WTO), and International Monetary Fund (IMF) toward U.S. interests. In order for the United States to agree to a multilateral agreement, that agreement must make the United States better off than unilateral actions. This puts other countries in a disadvantageous bargaining position compared to quadrant A1. But that does not necessarily mean that countries are worse off because of those institutions. The relevant comparison is not a world in which power asymmetries do not exist.

In this scenario the institution should be set up to structurally favor B: that is, to respect the lower bound. If there are strong asymmetries in interdependencies, we should expect weighted voting that favors the states with the stronger outside options.[31] More generally, the distributive perspective focuses attention on voting rules, participation rules, agenda-setting power, and other aspects of institutional design that guide the process of picking one solution out of many possible solutions.

MODERATE INTERDEPENDENCE

Panel B1 in figure 4.1 examines the intermediate range of values ($\frac{1}{2} < w\alpha$, $w\beta < 1$). These are situations with a collaboration and a coordination problem. There are social welfare gains if both states shift policies to any point along the Pareto frontier. The Pareto frontier is smaller than in Panel B given that the gains from coordination are smaller. Moreover, even though both states would prefer an agreement along the Pareto frontier to adopting policies that match their ideal points, both states have incentives to defect from an agreement. Each state individually would prefer to maintain the status quo while the other state moves its policy toward the agreement.

Similar to the prisoner's dilemma, this strategic situation creates a demand for enforcement institutions, such as those that monitor compliance, resolve disputes about noncompliance, and increase the shadow of the future.[32] States have problems credibly committing to a collective agreement in the absence of such institutions. A committee or court that provides a focal solution is not sufficient because its recommendations will not be self-enforcing.

A simple but important insight is that those areas where interdependencies are relatively high also require the least intrusive institutions. In other words, important gains from coordination can be achieved without much institutional structure. At some point, the low-hanging fruit has been picked. More intrusive institutions are needed in order to grasp ever smaller benefits from cooperation (even if the policy concessions aren't necessarily greater). If states care not just about policy outcomes but also about maintaining control of policy, then this institutionalization will be hardest and most controversial, which is consistent with the experience in the 1990s, especially in Europe.[33]

This simple insight helps make sense of East Asia, which has experienced important gains in economic integration despite weak institutions because it has concentrated on coordinated moves that were generally in the interest of all individual states.[34] Further gains with more intrusive institutions may be more difficult politically. Moreover, this insight matters for empirical studies, which sometimes seek in vain for correlations between high levels of legalization or institutionalization and high levels of cooperation.[35] If stronger institutionalization is necessary on those issues where interdependence is insufficient for endogenous enforcement, then we should not expect a strong correlation between levels of institutionalization and cooperation. Rather, we should expect enforcement institutions in cases where the gains from interdependence are moderate and agreements are not self-enforcing.

The anticipation of enforcement problems influences institutional design. Maggi and Morelli analyze a model with a first stage where all states can unanimously agree to resolve a range of future policy issues by voting according to a specified rule.[36] Some form of (qualified) majority rule is Pareto improving under quite general conditions. But when enforcement is a concern, then unanimity voting becomes the Pareto improving rule.[37] The implication is that states may be willing to shift policies to an outcome they did not vote for if interdependencies are strong and they expect everyone else to implement the new agreed upon policy. Yet when there are enforcement issues, the Pareto frontier becomes smaller.

Panel B2 from figure 4.1 sketches a situation with asymmetric interdependence. This moves the bargaining range toward state B's ideal point compared to panel B1. This presents a situation where state B has to ask for very large policy concessions from state A, and after making those concessions, state B still has incentives to cheat (as does state A). This is a typical situation that requires what John Ikenberry called "strategic restraint."[38] The powerful state must find a way to make its commitment to the institutional solution binding in order to induce the less powerful state to make large policy concessions for only moderate gains. Allison Carnegie shows how institutions with bite, such as the WTO, are especially useful between states with opposing policy preferences and amid large asymmetries.[39] Trade amid asymmetry may leave the weaker state concerned that the continuation of market access may be conditional on political concessions. This leads to underinvestment and less trade than would be socially optimal. The WTO addresses this issue by credibly making market access unconditional.

The spatial modeling framework highlights the fragility of such institutional solutions. Institutions that bind great powers are needed to address strategic problems that require large policy concessions in exchange for modest welfare gains. Where the welfare gains are obvious, institutions are self-enforcing. Yet realists often fail to understand that self-enforcing institutions may have very large distributive consequences.

Multiple Actors

Extending the analysis to multiple actors and multilateral cooperation makes apparent how ideology structures cooperation and competition. The bargaining game between two states, A and B, discussed in the previous subsection does not differ from a standard "divide-the-pie" game. Any gains for a third actor in a divide-the-pie game would necessarily reduce the shares of the other two. This is not true in a spatial modeling context. The unidimensional spatial model assumes that state ideal points can be ordered along a single dimension. Suppose state S's ideal point is at the midway point between states A and B. An agreement between A and B to cooperate at the midway point would be a massive win for S but would not take anything away from states A and B. By contrast, if state S were to the right of states A and B, then an agreement between states A and B would harm state S. Thus, the distributive consequences of cooperation are conditional on ideal points.

If rationalist functionalist analyses examine multiple actors, it is usually to understand if and how a larger number of actors complicates the ability to solve cooperation problems.[40] Here I focus on two different insights. First, institutions created by some actors can affect other actors' interests. Second, sequencing matters in understanding how actors are affected by the creation of institutions. I am keeping the analysis as simple as possible to give the intuition behind these basic points.

Let's consider a third state S. Suppose A and B coordinate their policies through an institution and that S is not involved at stage 1. This can be for a variety of reasons. Perhaps S was not yet part of the state system, for example because it was a colony. Another possibility is that there has been change to S's interdependencies with A and B or preferences. Regardless,

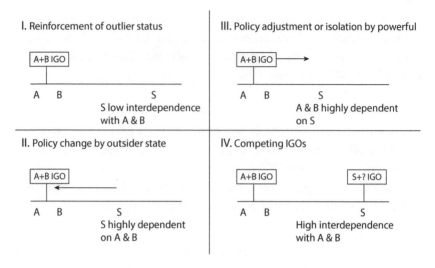

FIGURE 4.2. Impact of an IGO on outsider.

it is quite common for multilateralism to progressively include more states.[41]

Whatever the reason for its initial exclusion, A and B's cooperation affects S. Exactly how depends on the nature of its interdependencies with A and B and on S's ideal point. S's utility is a function of how far its policy is removed from its ideal point and the cost of not coordinating with A and B, which is a function of dependence and distances between the policies of S and A and B:

$$U_S = (-|\theta_S - p_S|) - (w_{SA}{}^*|p_S - p_A| - w_{SB}{}^*|p_S - p_B|)$$

Figure 4.2 sketches four scenarios. In panel I, S is a state like North Korea, a preference outlier with few interdependencies. S has little incentive to join the institution, nor would A and B want it to. Yet if A and B move closer together as a consequence of institutionalized cooperation, then state S is even more isolated from its closest counterpart than it was before. In chapter 7, I argue that liberal international institutions have had precisely this effect for what we sometimes call "rogue states": liberal institutions amplify the isolation of illiberal states. This effect becomes more pronounced if institutionalized cooperation amplifies the interdependencies between A and B: that is, if interdependencies are endogenous to institutional cooperation (which they probably often are).

In panels II and III, S has large interdependencies with A and/or B. S is not an extreme outlier, but its preferences do diverge from those of both

A and B. The analysis depends strongly on asymmetries in interdependence. If S is very dependent on A and B but not vice versa, then S may be "forced" to join A and B's institution without having much influence on it (panel II). That is, A and B's choice of a cooperative agreement becomes the de facto new status quo for S. This captures the idea that for weaker states, joining institutions with the states they depend on is sometimes only superficially voluntary. Institutional cooperation between other states changes the structure of a weaker state's decision-making environment, thus inducing these states to make large policy adjustments. Note that this effect would be larger the more of the world economy would be represented by the institution. Thus, an organization like the WTO has the theoretical ability to induce very large policy adjustments.

Consider for instance what this means for former colonies, which had no say in the creation of many institutions that regulate interactions. While these states nominally have a choice, existing institutions have already structured outcomes and rules in ways that may be quite unfavorable to them. This basic point about structural inequities is not at all novel though is rarely motivated from a rational choice perspective.[42]

If S is a preference outlier but A and B are asymmetrically dependent on it (panel III), then we could see quite different scenarios. If asymmetric interdependencies are sufficiently large, then A and B are incentivized to adjust to S's ideal point or something close to it. But if interdependencies are small relative to the ideal point gap, then A and B may decide to cooperate among themselves and leave S out of it, even though S is the more powerful state.

This may characterize the situation for the United States, which is often a preference outlier in contemporary multilateral negotiations. Its market size and military power are sometimes sufficient to make other states followers. But at other times its status as a preference outlier leaves it outside of institutions. A and B may have incentives to accept smaller gains from coordination in exchange for smaller policy adjustments. In order to attract members, the United States will have to accept compromises that make institutions more moderate than the U.S. ideal point. Sometimes the United States prefers to stay out of multilateral institutions rather than accept the ideological compromise. A powerful country like Germany is more central in the distribution of ideal points and more likely to benefit from multilateralism.

If there are relatively symmetric and high interdependencies, then the presence of S can influence the bargaining range and thus the institution.

Yet sequencing now matters. If for whatever reason A and B had already established an institution, then S would have little option but to join the original institution unless it can create outside options that are sufficiently strong to trigger a credible alternative proposal. An example may be the United Kingdom in the context of European integration. The United Kingdom was not a party to the initial treaties and did have relatively outlier preferences over regulation and high interdependencies. This induced the country to join an integration project with an institutional status quo that was relatively unfavorable to the United Kingdom.

Suppose that for exogenous reasons S's interdependencies with A and B increase over time. If S wants to become an export-based economy, then there is little choice but to do so by playing to the existing rules of the system. There are a host of institutions that developing states have joined even if the rules are not favorable for them or they do not have adequate representation in their decision-making structures. How the resulting distributive issues are resolved depends on whether the dissatisfied states can effectively create substitute institutions or successfully bargain for reforms by leveraging their outside options.[43]

The classic theoretical argument for the first mover advantage in institutionalization is that institutions have increasing returns.[44] The argument sketched in this section suggests a complementary reason: institutions structure bargaining between states and are difficult to change collectively because it would require states to overcome a new problem of indeterminacy. I am arguing not that the traditional argument about stickiness is incorrect but that it highlights only one side of institutions: their efficiency-enhancing properties.

Finally, there may be scenarios, as in panel IV, where the ideological differences are so large that the creation of a new IGO spurs state S to create its own IGO with other states. Suppose that some states with medium preferences would be attracted to join the new IGO created by A and B (as in panel B). S may now have incentives to create its own IGO to offer an attractive other option. The success of this depends on S's interdependencies with the intermediate states and its ability to offer a better deal to those states than A and B. The result would be institutional polarization. One example is the AIIB, mentioned already. Development lending is not an area with high interdependencies (for donors), so it is more attractive to form a separate institution at one's own ideal point.[45] Similarly, Poast and Urpelainen argue that democratizing states sometimes create their own IGOs because existing IGOs with established democracies do not sufficiently reflect their values.[46]

Conclusions

This chapter has offered a framework for modeling strategic dilemmas of cooperation and competition in a low-dimensional ideological space. The goal was not to produce specific models of institutions. I focused the analysis on two important points: that institutions have distributive consequences for excluded states and that sequencing matters.

This analysis only scratches the surface of how to incorporate multiple actors in a spatial modeling framework. Unfortunately, it is not possible to simply apply the insights from domestic politics, especially for those issues where enforcement issues arise. For example, in legislative bargaining, it often makes sense to reduce the analysis to pivotal actors, such as the median voter or institutional veto players, like the president in the U.S. context.[47] In the absence of majority voting, it is not always so clear whom the pivotal players are. Moreover, the framework proposed here incorporates interdependencies among the actors, which quickly complicates the analysis. Still, the framework offers a useful way to think through the strategic issues of multilateralism in a way that differs from the classic two-by-two collaboration and coordination dilemmas that have dominated this literature

Two insights are especially crucial. First, institutions that achieve the largest gains often require the least extensive institutional infrastructure. The logic is simple: if interdependencies are large, then institutions are self-enforcing. The problem is indeterminacy: how to find one of many institutions that could yield Pareto improving benefits. Importantly, this implies that institutions matter even if they are self-enforcing and if states have no incentives to deviate from the collective agreement. Institutions reflect one of many ways in which states could cooperate. However, it does not mean that more extensive institutional commitments are correlated with increased cooperation. To the contrary: intrusive institutions are needed where agreements are not self-enforcing because the benefits to coordination are only modest.

Second, the creation of institutions among some states affects the utilities of other states. If some states coordinate their policies, then others may incur policy losses because states with whom they interact move policies away from their ideal points. Thus, creating institutions and inviting states to join institutions can be a source of conflict. Chapter 7 examines the empirical implications of this point, which implies that multilateralism can induce both cooperation and conflict and that it does so along ideological lines.

CHAPTER FIVE

Expertise, Ideology, and Distributive Politics

THE MOST common theoretical argument for why politicians willingly delegate authority to committees, bureaucracies, courts, and other independent agencies is that policy making and rulemaking are complex activities that require technical, scientific, and legal expertise. Politicians could benefit if they delegated authority to specialized agencies, regulators, or committees as long as the expected gains from reduced uncertainty outweigh the expected losses from reduced control and the cost of creating the agency.[1] International relations scholars have liberally applied this argument to explain why states delegate authority to international bureaucracies, courts, expert communities, and other organizations.[2]

In this chapter, I examine these assertions in the context of distributive ideological conflict between states. I do not take issue with the claim that the role of institutions, transnational networks, and IGOs often revolves around information and expertise. Yet both the demand for and supply of expertise are affected by the context of ideological distributive conflict between states.

First, and most obviously, expertise is rarely neutral amid ideological conflict. The world's institutions primarily advance a variant of a liberal worldview. Even experts who faithfully apply and interpret those rules advance this worldview over an alternative worldview. Even neutral well-informed experts appear biased to ideological opponents of liberalism.

Second, a recurrent theme in the literature is that transnational or international experts can use informational advantages to move outcomes toward their preferred policies.[3] The literature has ignored that transnational actors can exert this distributive influence only if they solve a coordination problem among themselves. If experts and states are ideologically diverse, then experts can compete away their informational advantages. I argue that transnational networks of regulators, judges, arbitrators, and scientific experts are institutions that constrain the supply of expertise. This limits competition and helps experts exert influence over outcomes.

Third, the canonical rationalist delegation model assumes that agents (experts) have privileged information, which governments cannot easily verify. Yet situations where international or transnational experts have information that (some) governments do not have are not that common. Many international institutions are less about information acquisition as about incentivizing state and non-state actors to share information and finding a common interpretation of what information means. In the context of ideological competition, sharing information and finding common interpretations have distributive implications.

Fourth, ideological conflict among governments creates opportunities for international and transnational experts to provide interpretations that can resolve disputes. Yet this same ideological conflict also contributes to the fragility of their authority. We cannot assume that judges, regulators, or scientists are valued simply because of their expertise. Experts face strategic problems communicating that they are trustworthy given that biased or corrupt experts have incentives to mimic true experts. This trust is subject to deliberate destruction by ideological opponents to liberalism. The chapter on populism and international courts further explores this issue.

The Informational Model

This section starts with a brief discussion of the workhorse model that underlies most rationalist arguments about delegation for expertise.[4] The canonical model assumes that a political actor (the principal) has the authority to implement a policy p but the actual outcome x depends not just on the policy but also on "a state of the world" or a random shock ω.[5] Principals care about outcomes rather than policies. The principal observes only the probability distribution $F(\omega)$ from which the shock or the "true state of the world" is drawn. In addition, there is an expert, regulator, scientist, or judge (the agent) who observes ω (perfectly or imperfectly) or who can exert costly efforts to acquire information about the true state of the world.

The agent may have incentives to misrepresent her information, for example because she favors stricter environmental regulations than the politician. Nonidentical preferences prohibit completely truthful information transmission. As long as uncertainty is large relative to the preference discrepancy, then the agent can credibly transmit some information.[6] The politician benefits because the agent's signal helps her to implement a better policy.

The political actor and the expert do not need institutions to communicate. Yet institutions can improve the transmission of information. Institutions could transfer resources (a wage) to the agent and/or restrict the principal's actions in a way that incentivizes the agent to invest in expertise. For instance, Thomas Gilligan and Keith Krehbiel argue that Congress may be better off restricting its ability to amend committee proposals because this gives committees better incentives to invest in expertise.[7]

In order to incentivize an agent, a politician sometimes delegates authority to an agent with divergent preferences.[8] If the agent cares about policies close to her ideal point, then she may invest in expertise, but only if doing so actually makes it more likely that these policies are adopted. For example, suppose financial regulators have preferences for more risk-averse regulations than a politician. The politician may still find it in her interests to grant the financial regulator some autonomy. Without autonomy, the regulator would have no incentive to invest in information acquisition. Yet this transaction works for both sides only if the politician can detect that the agent actually invests in acquiring expertise and uses that expertise in her decisions. The problem is that lazy or biased agents have incentives to mimic sincere or neutral agents.

IR scholars have borrowed insights from the canonical model to motivate the authority of institutions as diverse as the UN Security Council,[9] the International Monetary Fund (IMF),[10] the World Bank,[11] the International Energy Agency,[12] and others. A much-cited edited volume on delegation in international affairs uses expertise as its primary motivating example.[13] Tana Johnson and Johannes Urpelainen find that international bureaucrats are given more discretion when the issue requires more specialized technical and scientific knowledge.[14] They interpret this as evidence that the demand for expertise indeed underlies decisions to delegate. Barbara Koremenos finds in a random sample of legal agreements that 60 percent manage uncertainty about the world, making it by far the most common problem that drives institutionalized cooperation.[15]

The appeal of this framework is that it provides an account for why states would voluntarily delegate authority to an IO that may occasionally do things that differ from what states want. The framework does not depart from the anarchy assumption nor the primacy of states. The agent structures the options and information governments have, dealing with both distributive and stochastic indeterminacy.[16] Yet the ultimate policy decision remains within the exclusive provenance of governments.

Chapter 4 already elaborated on the complications applying models developed for legislative behavior to the international arena. First, unlike legislators, states have a unilateral ability to implement policies and to create expertise using domestic agencies. Some analyses motivate the assumption of a common principal with the idea that states first need to solve a bargaining problem before they can delegate to an IGO.[17] Yet the distributive problem cannot be bracketed this easily. If states have different preferences but share a desire for more information, then multiple states could each create their own agency or form multiple multilateral agencies that better reflect their ideological preferences. Moreover, the distributive conflict does not end after the delegation has taken place. Experts must remain conscious of the varying ideological preferences of states as they signal their expertise.

A second problematic assumption is that states cannot verify the agent's message. We must ask where such information asymmetries are likely to come from in the international system. Even expert-based international institutions like the Intergovernmental Panel on Climate Change (IPCC) often consist of domestic experts. The panel pools and interprets publicly available information, but it does not have information that states do not have.

Table 5.1 classifies different strategic settings based on the informational and distributive problems. The remainder of this chapter analyzes these strategic settings informally, using examples to illustrate the insights.

Table 5.1. Intersection of informational and distributive problems

		Informational problem	
		Acquisition	Sharing and interpretation
Distributive problem	Shared interests	Flu vaccine, asteroid protection, common environmental challenges	Epidemics, systemic financial risk
	Heterogeneous interests	Nuclear or WMD inspections, development financing	UN Security Council authorizations, dispute resolution

Information Acquisition

SHARED INTERESTS

If states have shared objectives and a shared desire to acquire information about the world, then at least some important component of the needed information must be global or transnational in nature. For example, states may all benefit from more information about asteroids that could destroy the earth, what flu vaccine is most appropriate in a specific season, or where systemic risks to the international financial system are located. This gives states incentives to pool efforts to acquire the missing information.

Even in this harmonious setting, there are two distributional issues. First, even if states have harmonious preferences, it may well be that expert communities have different interests and can use their authority to advance these interests. This possibility is what often interests scholars: experts may move outcomes to what experts want over what governments want. The claim that "transnational actors matter" is a distributive claim: it means that environmental experts or transnational networks of lawyers or financial regulators or epistemic communities can move rules and regulations toward their ideal points.[18]

Suppose that environmental experts have preferences for stricter regulations than governments.[19] Principal-agent models show that governments may listen to a signal from those experts if asymmetries in information are large enough. The more uncertainty and the more the agent knows relative to the principal, the more the agent can move policy toward its ideal point.[20] Importantly, this relies on the assumption that governments are unable (at reasonable cost) to assess the veracity of expert signals.

Yet if there are multiple expert communities, then the principal chooses the expert whose preferences are most aligned with it. This is called the "ally principle."[21] If there is free competition between experts, then experts compete away their informational advantages.[22] In the absence of conflict between states, it is unlikely that experts can use their expertise to shift policy toward their ideal point unless experts manage to restrict competition among themselves or there are exogenous reasons that restrict the supply of expertise.

Scholars rarely present arguments about transnational networks, professionalization, epistemic communities, or socialization as claims about restricting competition between experts. For example, Tana Johnson and Johannes Urpelainen explain how the WHO, UNDP, UNESCO, UNFPA, UNICEF, and the World Bank were able to acquire a major role in the design of the new UNAIDS agency despite initial opposition from states.[23]

They ascribe this influence to the expertise of these agencies. This may be so, but it is equally important that these six agencies successfully coordinated to prevent each from competing away its expert advantage. Johnson and Urpelainen report that states threatened to cut off AIDS funding to individual agencies if these would not yield, suggesting that competition was credible and that the coordination dilemma was not easy to address.

Another example is the IPCC, which consists of hundreds of experts drawn from government, the private sector, and academia all over the world. These experts have varying preferences and assessments about the causes, solutions, and harms of climate change.[24] The main effect of the IPCC is to consolidate a global climate change epistemic community through issuing common reports that aggregate and interpret existing scientific evidence.[25] The availability of a consolidated signal makes it less attractive for governments to hire or rely on individual experts closer to their ideological preferences, unless these preferences are extreme (e.g., climate denial). The IPCC restricts experts with diverse preferences in their ability to sell their expertise, which in turn empowers the epistemic community of experts.

The key insight is that transnational or supranational actors can leverage their expertise to steer policy outcomes in their preferred direction if they solve the supply-side problem by coordinating among themselves. Organizational sociologists have thought a lot about how professional communities do this. Bourdieu conceives of professional fields as organizational structures that help separate insiders from outsiders.[26] For example, international commercial arbitrators have constructed a set of norms through practice that has transformed the dispute settlement regime for international commercial contracts.[27] These arbitrators need not have the same preferences, but they have constructed practices that separate them from nonprofessionals. Transnational networks and epistemic communities[28] are in part efforts to coordinate experts on a common set of practices and interpretations that set boundaries on what is and what is not professional expertise. This is a different way to understand the implications from practice theory than the common interpretation.[29]

Second, creating an agency that acquires expertise is costly. Who will pay those costs? Even if all states want the information and have identical preferences, they would still prefer that others pay for it. The resulting collective action problem has received ample attention in the literature.[30] What has received less attention is that this collective action problem may create opportunities for intrinsically motivated nongovernmental or transnational actors.

For example, scientists who care intrinsically about a policy may offer their expertise at a lower price than what it would take to create a new agency (assuming that they are able to resolve the aforementioned coordination problem). Domestic regulators who care about their policy area could take the initiative to form a network. Such a network may well be a substitute for a more formal (and costly) IGO that would have to be created through different channels than just those who are most intimately involved in a policy area.

This logic suggests a rationalist account for how intrinsically motivated transnational experts can construct their own authority. It also suggests an explanation for why technocrats and (international or domestic) bureaucrats so often take the initiative to create IGOs.[31] For example, a group of intrinsically motivated health experts may be willing to create a collective agency that governments may not be willing to invest in. Intrinsic preferences matter in the context of collective action problems.

A different type of distributive issue arises if one large state (or a few states) has the ability and incentives to produce the information alone. This would turn an "uncertainty about the world" problem into an information-sharing problem. The relevant question becomes, what incentives does the powerful state have to share the information with others? One possibility is that the powerful state will sell the information, for money or concessions. If multiple states have unilateral incentives to acquire the information and can extract rents, then we may see duplication.

HETEROGENEOUS STATE INTERESTS

The issues discussed in the previous section magnify if principals (states) have diverse ideal points. Most of the literature that considers multiple principals with diverse preferences focuses on legislatures.[32] Legislators face a different collective decision-making problem than states. Unlike legislators, states can implement their own policies and acquire their own expertise. The status quo is not the necessary reversion point if there is no cooperative action. Indeed, if creating domestic agencies were costless, then each state would and should do so. Moreover, as the previous chapter discussed, states cannot be forced to resolve the collective decision-making problem with a vote. A voting rule is itself an institution that states must first agree on and that must be enforced.[33]

The supply of experts is again an important and underappreciated issue. On the one hand, a unified group of experts may exploit heterogeneity if states share a common desire for information. The logic is not that different from before, except that the experts now face the problem that they must persuade multiple states that a signal reflects actual information rather than ideology. This is more difficult as expert and state are further apart in the ideological space.

On the other hand, heterogeneity among states may make it more difficult for experts to solve their own distributive problem. When states have homogenous interests, only one (group of) expert(s) can influence states.[34] This provides strong incentives for coordination. With heterogeneous interests, states may hire the experts with whom they align more closely (the ally principle). This may complicate coordination among experts. Individual experts can get contracts and policy influence without compromising on their policy or ideological views. States could form small like-minded coalitions that each listen to their own set of experts.

For example, states may prefer to finance more effective development projects over less effective ones. If states also have divergent preferences over where the aid should go, then they may still have incentives not to delegate to a common agent. There are about two dozen multilateral development agencies. The Asian Infrastructure Investment Bank (AIIB), Asian Development Bank (ADB), European Bank for Reconstruction and Development (EBRD), and World Bank all develop expertise about the quality of development projects, but their funding patterns also reflect their donor's ideologies.[35]

Ideology matters as a short cut about the preferences of states and experts. States that are ideologically closer to China were more likely to join the AIIB.[36] The next chapter shows that such ideological sorting shapes IGO membership patterns more generally. Governments often maintain control over the appointment of experts to international bodies. They can use this authority to appoint experts who match their ideologies.[37] Since governments have highly imperfect tools to sanction agents, selection matters a great deal. Governments do not have this opportunity in more informal transnational networks. Nevertheless, governments must make inferences about the preferences of experts when they decide whether to accept signals.

Asymmetries in outside options also affect outcomes. For example, Leslie Johns finds that when one principal can exercise an outside option, a bureaucrat who is biased toward that principal can better reveal private information than a more neutral bureaucrat. She illustrates this with a case study of UN weapons inspectors in Iraq. The broader implication is that institutions closely follow the preferences of the principals with the strongest outside options.[38]

This brings us back to an extension of Anthony Downs's core insight that incomplete information creates opportunities for the wealthy to gain influence in democratic politics.[39] Downs's argument is that if information acquisition is costly and if information can be used to move policy in a desired direction, then wealthy actors have incentives and opportunities to invest in information acquisition. The same is true in the international system. In terms of international cooperation, this turns a problem of information acquisition into a problem of information sharing. Are powerful states willing to share information? Can powerful states credibly share information given that they are likely biased toward certain policy positions? International institutions frequently address issues of information sharing as well as interpreting information.

Information Sharing and Interpretation

A crucial assumption in most of the rationalist delegation literature is that there are experts or institutions that possess information that governments do not have and cannot easily verify. Transnational experts gain distributive authority through strategic deception. By contrast, in constructivist accounts respect for expert authority stems from societal inclinations to defer to rational-legal authority.[40] In the rationalist model, expert signals cannot be verified easily because states lack information. In the constructivist model, expert signals cannot be challenged easily because doing so would violate a sense that experts appropriately exercise authority.

It is not clear how widespread situations are where IGOs or transnational actors gather or possess information that states do not have. For example, much of the literature on transnational actors focuses on how domestic governmental actors form networks that influence international cooperation.[41] These actors may well have preferences, interests, and/or information that other parts of the government do not have. Such networks primarily solve problems of information sharing and coordination rather than the acquisition of new information. Similarly, IGOs frequently aid information sharing in the context of interdependence. For example, IGOs like the IMF gather national statistics from governments that they then standardize and disseminate to other states. International courts have expertise,[42] but states also have lawyers and scholars with international legal expertise. International courts typically do not have information that states do not have. An international judge reveals not a private signal about the truth but an expert interpretation based on public information, given the limited investigative capacities of most international courts with the possible exception of the International Criminal Court (ICC).

This matters because it suggests that the workhorse model on which so much of the rationalist literature relies may not be the appropriate model for a large number of international or transnational institutions. Instead, we need to think about the role institutions play in incentivizing states to reveal private information and to coordinate states on a common interpretation of that information.

For example, Alexander Thompson applies Keith Krehbiel's informational model of legislative delegation to the UN Security Council (UNSC).[43] This model presumes that the UNSC has agency because it develops expertise on matters of peace and security that states do not have. It is not really clear what that information would be. The UNSC is an arena in which states discuss and vote on matters of international peace and security under preexisting procedures. The UNSC's informational role is that it forces states to reveal their preferences through voting and that it potentially coordinates states on a common interpretation (or fails to do so).[44]

Similarly, the UN Human Rights Council (UNHRC) does not reveal new information about human rights violations. Instead, its voting procedures force states to reveal whether they believe that a target state should be publicly shamed for its rights violations.[45] These votes reflect ideology as much as actual assessments of rights records.[46] The votes reveal new information about the extent to which the international community is willing to protect an alleged rights violator rather than information about what countries violated rights.[47]

Neither the UNHRC nor the UNSC is an expert organization. The members are states, who are not always elected because they have expertise or even a good track record on peacekeeping or human rights.[48] Yet many expert organizations are also less about acquiring new expertise rather than coordinating existing expertise on a common interpretation. I have already mentioned international courts and the IPCC as examples. Even many formal IGO bureaucracies are often more about incentivizing states to share information and standardizing that information than acquiring new information. For example, the IMF has standardized financial statistics. The IMF also develops some new expertise in the process. But it is not clear that the IMF has much expertise or information that the United States does not have or could not easily get access to. If this is so, then in a rationalist accounting its authority must come from another source than informational asymmetries.

If states have homogenous preferences, then nothing stands in the way of truthful information transmission as long as the information does not have competitive implications and cannot be protected and sold. Interdependence can mean that states have incentives to share information about health emergencies, financial contagion, and so on. If interdependence overwhelms heterogeneity, then states don't have incentives to keep their private information secret and thus, like in the previous chapter, there is no great need for strong interventionist institutions. Institutions may reduce transaction costs. But institutions need not have informational advantages over states: they just need to facilitate the collection and dissemination of information that states provide. As in the previous chapter, the low-hanging fruit of international cooperation can be plucked without a great deal of institutional structure.

Information sharing is a lot more complex when heterogeneity is large enough that governments have incentives to not truthfully share information and to dispute attempts at coordinating disparate signals into a common interpretation. In this context, information transmission and coordination are distributive problems. This helps explain the finding from chapter 6 that even sorting into functionalist IGOs is ideological. If IGOs are more about sharing information and agreeing on coordinated interpretations than information acquisition, then the payoffs to the IGO should be higher as the government expects that the IGO's members are closer to a state's ideal point.

Even quite minimal institutional structures could help actors reveal private information and coordinate on similar interpretations. Consider standard setting organizations. Farrell and Simcoe discuss a model in which two actors bargain over a standard.[49] Each agent has private information over the quality of her preferred standard but also private preferences such that each prefers her own standard. There is also a third party who does not have information over either proposal's quality and has no private preference. The third party's utility function is increasing in the quality of the standard and decreasing in delay. Ex ante it is in the interest of both private parties to allow the third party to intervene at any time and randomly pick either proposal.

The intuition is that the war of attrition does not screen very well when the quality of both proposals is high and/or vested interests are strong. This leads to long and inefficient delays. The neutral agent may watch the initial stages of the bargaining to uncover if it selects out the poorer proposal, but she will be less patient than the parties with vested interests. This captures the decision-making process in standard-setting organizations, where the pivotal voter is often someone who does not have a private stake in the success or failure of a particular standard. Impartiality is a more important feature than expertise. This means not that the third party should be ignorant but that there is no reason to presume that the third party is somehow wiser than either of the parties bargaining over the standard.

The standard-setting committee has no enforcement power. Its decision is more likely to be self-enforcing as there are more parties that don't have a high private stake. All of these parties would have an interest to adopt the chosen standard. This makes holding out less attractive for the party that lost the lottery if utility depends on how many parties have accepted a standard (see the previous chapter). This provides a rationale for delegation that has distributional consequences and is welfare improving (in expectation), even if it does not always select the highest quality standard. The standard-setting organization does not need to have enforcement capabilities or superior information to influence outcomes.

The committee structure works better when the committee is not forced to take an immediate decision. There are circumstances where acting outside of the institutional setting quickly selects the best proposal. The logic is thus based on a combination of market and nonmarket strategies, which often turns out more efficient than either fully market-based or fully centralized solutions.[50]

Leslie Johns considers a similar model in which an international court can have distributive implications by simply breaking a tie.[51] Christina Schneider and Branislav Slantchev analyze a model where states have diverse preferences over collective action.[52] In the model, states have incentives to delegate authority to an IGO (agent) that helps states reveal private information through voting and that then uses the information to coordinate states on collective action.

What these models have in common is that an agent without enforcement power or informational advantages can nonetheless influence outcomes by creating incentives for states to reveal private information and by coordinating behavior. As I suggested earlier, these types of organizations are very common in international affairs. For example, citizens, businesses, and governments file cases with international courts. In this process, these actors reveal private information about the effects of international law. International courts also help those actors converge on a common interpretation (coordination). The IMF and World Bank gather and standardize economic data that are private information, which states may sometimes not be inclined to share.[53] Standard-setting organizations receive information about possible standards and then choose among them. Disputes before investment tribunals reveal private information about claims and coordinate on an interpretation of investment law.

All of these tasks are political. They also require expertise. Yet they do not depend on the international actor having access to privileged information or even on them having enforcement power. The key requirement is that governments trust that the international actor is indeed interested in advancing the best standard or legal interpretation or at least is not biased toward some interpretation for reasons other than the quality of the information. Such trust is by no means a given. The next section discusses this issue in more detail.

The discussion so far has sidestepped instances in which states have an interest in information that another state would desperately like to keep private. Such strategic dilemmas require stronger and more interventionist institutions. For example, states have delegated authority to the International Atomic Energy Agency (IAEA) to inspect facilities and verify whether states are meeting their obligations to refrain from developing nuclear weapons.[54] IAEA inspectors have incentives to truthfully reveal their findings and may recommend enforcement actions to the Board of Governors, which can refer a case to the UNSC. Enforcement thus still depends on whether states with diverse ideologies agree that sanctions or other measures should be imposed on norm violators. Such centralized attempts at uncovering private information are important but rare in the international system.

Institutions sometimes create opportunities for states to send costly signals. Andrew Kydd shows how states, through costly signals, can reassure each other that they are trustworthy.[55] Signing treaties that are costly to implement is an example.[56] As argued earlier, these signals may be not just about trustworthiness but also about ideology. For example, when Georgia opted for a trade treaty with the EU but not with Russia, it meaningfully signaled its ideological preferences. This is a distributive story where Georgia becomes more trustworthy to some states but less so to another (Russia).

Susan Hyde argues that the norm to invite international election monitors emerged through a diffusely motivated signaling process in which such invitations came to be expected of "true democrats."[57] Election monitoring is organized through a bewildering array of international governmental and nongovernmental organizations, each with its own processes, biases, and varying arrays of credibility.[58] This allows committed liberals to separate themselves at least somewhat from others through their choice of monitors.

A crucial additional issue is that information is typically asymmetrically distributed among principals. While it may sometimes be reasonable to presume that an IGO has an informational advantage over a smaller country, this does not necessarily mean that it can use its expertise to its advantage when dealing with a major power, such as the United States. For example, the United States was long reluctant to share satellite technology because it wanted to enjoy the benefits of its relative advantages. When the United States lost its relative technological advantage, then a common regime emerged.[59] Asymmetries in information may prevent coordination for competitive reasons.

I am not aware of any theoretical discussion of such informational asymmetries, but their significance should be clear. First, we must ask why the United States or another major power can't just communicate its technical information to other states. If interests are homogenous, then many governments may prefer to simply copy the policies of states with greater capacities rather than invest in their own expertise or an IGO. Indeed, we observe a great deal of policy diffusion that is not centralized through IGOs.[60]

Second, if there is an IGO, it suggests another source through which some states can better influence the IGO's direction than others: asymmetric information. If both the agent and some but not other principals are informed and the informed principal has veto rights (as the United States effectively has in the IMF), then the agent's agenda-setting power should be severely curtailed toward the ideal point of the informed principal. The institution can practice strategic deception against some states but not others. These are issues that deserve further study.

Trust and Distrust in Experts amid Ideological Conflict

The preceding discussion focused mostly on the incentives for governments to delegate authority to institutions even if governments are ideologically divided and the institution has no strong informational asymmetric advantages. Instead, the institution helps governments share private information and coordinate on a common interpretation of this information. The leverage of transnational and international experts over governments thus often stems less from asymmetric access to information than from features, such as their perceived impartiality,[61] that help them collect and translate this information into a collective decision.

Perceptions of impartiality are vulnerable. People tend to interpret expert information through ideological lenses, even when it comes from reputable international agencies.[62] An impartial agent who interprets liberal rules expertly may still not be trusted by actors with different ideologies. Principal-agent models offer limited answers on how agents can maintain trust. Principals (governments) give agents a conditional grant of authority that they can exercise within bounds defined by a contract (treaty). Once agents exceed those bounds principals can use a variety of control mechanisms, including firing agents, noncompliance, overriding decisions, reducing budgets, and withdrawing from an institution. The threat of such actions should keep agents from excessively overstepping their delegated authority. This reassures principals that in the long run agents cannot affect their interests negatively without punishment.

There is some evidence that agents, such as international judges, respond to these incentives.[63] Yet other scholars argue that control mechanisms are typically weak and difficult to exercise by individual governments.[64] Instead, these scholars argue, the relationship between experts and states is fiduciary rather than contractual. That is, political actors accept the signal because they trust the sender. Yet the literature on trusteeship tends to take trust for granted. I advance three points in this section. First, if the relationship between political actors and experts is fiduciary, then we must ask how actors build up and maintain trust. Much of the literature on trusteeship assumes away this problem by pointing to expertise as the grounds for trust. Second, trust becomes a much more central property if experts do not have privileged access to information. Third, trust in experts is vulnerable to deliberate destruction in the context of ideological conflict.

THE TRUSTEE IDEAL

Karen Alter identifies three characteristics of trustees.[65] First, they are selected because they have expertise and because they are "disinterested actors."[66] Second, trustees are entrusted to make decisions according to their own best judgment and without interference from other interested parties. These two criteria characterize the paradigmatic trustee as an impartial professional actor who expertly interprets preexisting rules and precedents and who is immune to external pressures.

The third characteristic appears at odds with this characterization. The trustee has a putative beneficiary that differs from the principal (the government). These beneficiaries include national courts, nongovernmental organizations (NGOs), firms, banks, and more broadly "the general public." Importantly, these beneficiaries have some leverage over the principal, for example because they vote in elections or hold independent judicial or administrative authority. This limits the ability of governments to control agents. As Karen Alter puts it, "The Trustee cannot put the interests of the Principal over that of the beneficiary without engendering legitimacy problems for itself. The Principal also cannot only care about controlling the Trustee because the Trustee may in fact be deemed a superior decision-maker, and efforts cast as 'political interference' or exceeding state or Principal authority can alienate the Trustee's constituency and members of the Principal whose support is needed for recontracting."[67] This is an important and valid critique of the principal-agent approach, which focuses too narrowly on government-IGO (or expert) relationships. Surely, regulators, judges, and other experts typically have to think about their relationships with businesses, NGOs, and domestic judges and regulators.

But the assumption that the beneficiary values the court because it is a superior decision maker is unsustainable in the context of distributive ideological conflict. Domestic publics, interest groups, NGOs, and firms have their own interests. Presumably, they value the expert because they believe that delegation to an expert will yield more favorable substantive outcomes to them than alternatives. Introducing additional beneficiaries creates more potential sources of influence. For example, international criminal tribunals are sometimes accused of currying too much favor to NGOs,[68] and international investment tribunals are frequently charged with favoring multinationals. Such charges could undermine the trust (some) governments put in these institutions.

More generally, it is not automatic that if trustees faithfully abide by their fiduciary duties, then they will gain trust and thereby legitimacy. There are three issues. First, expert decisions, like rulings in arbitral tribunals, have distributive consequences. There are winners and losers. It is not clear why the losers should always respect these decisions just because they were made by experts. Second, in the context of ideological conflict, there is no guarantee that actors less enamored of the rules will value the expertise. Someone who opposes liberalism may not value an expert interpretation of liberal rules. Third, trustees need to balance the desire to appear knowledgeable and impartial with imperatives to give their varied beneficiaries what they want.[69] Finally, the authority of the trustee relies not just on the trustee applying preexisting rules in a disinterested and professional fashion but also on her ability to ensure that its beneficiaries observe that this is the case. As Diego Gambetta and Heather Hamill put it, "The trustee is a strategic player, not inert matter passively waiting to be appraised by the truster."[70] Self-interested or biased trustees can mimic impartial experts. This leaves trustees open to challenges in the context of ideological conflict.

TRUST, INSTITUTIONS, AND VERIFIABILITY

Diego Gambetta defines trust as a coping device for dealing with the freedom of others.[71] Trust matters precisely because experts have the opportunity to disappoint expectations. Trust is especially important when there is no possibility for outsiders to verify (perhaps at a cost) whether the trustee acted in a trustworthy manner.

Consider the example of secondhand car salesmen, who work in one of the least trusted professions in the United States (only above lobbyists and congresspeople).[72] The reason why many people distrust car salesmen is that they have incentives to lie: a good car without problems fetches a higher price than a lemon.[73] Institutions can manage the distrust. Examples are CARFAX reports, warranties, and online feedback. These institutional mechanisms work reasonably well because even if the consumer cannot observe the quality of the car at the time of purchase, the quality of cars is ultimately observable. Or, more accurately, outcomes that are closely correlated with the quality of cars are observable. This allows institutions to price warranties and to create records of historical performance. It also helps individual car dealers to build up reputations for honesty even if we do not trust car salesmen more generally. So the market for secondhand cars works pretty well even if people do not trust car salesmen.

If international institutions are like used car salesmen, then the principal-agent approach works reasonably well. Remember, the problem is asymmetric information about something that can ultimately be observed (or at least we can observe something that is closely correlated with that information, such as the longevity of a car). Governments could create a fire alarm or police patrol that oversees agent performance.[74] For example, an agency empowered to eliminate polio may be evaluated on the occurrence of new polio cases or the distribution of vaccines. Neither of these outcomes is wholly within the control of the agency, but both are correlated with agent performance.

Yet if the strategic problem for the expert is not revealing private information but convincing beneficiaries of a particular interpretation, then institutions to manage distrust become more complicated, especially when the beneficiaries have diverse ideological beliefs.

Consider another analogy. A priest has no private information about the quality of promises regarding the afterlife.[75] Potential beneficiaries cannot at reasonable expense discover the quality of such promises or whether one priest is a more superior decision maker than another. Producers of inscrutable goods create symbols or practices that are costly to imitate by imposters.[76] Celibacy is an obvious example. Some priests may more accurately or eloquently invoke biblical verses. Yet while such symbols may allow individuals to recognize "real" priests, these symbols are at best weakly correlated with the quality of the promises priests make. When overall trust in clergy declines,[77] this poses a problem not just for individual churches but for a religion as a whole. Unlike for the market in secondhand cars, trust is essential for religious exchanges.

International trustees may not be exactly like priests, but the quality of their output is often inscrutable—not in the sense that we can never assess the rightness or wrongness of a decision but in the sense that there is no objective way to determine what answer among those that surpass a plausibility standard is of the highest quality. For example, an international human rights judge provides interpretations of international human rights law in concrete cases. How do we know if the judge is performing this task well? Human rights cases are often contentious. Domestic legal experts or law professors may well have interpretations that run counter to the international human rights judge. It is not clear how a court's beneficiaries would navigate between such diverse interpretations other than to prefer the one that most closely resembles their private interests.

Moreover, if the international institutional system is by and large liberal, then the rules, laws, and regulations that trustees apply and interpret are typically also liberal. This gives opponents of liberalism reasons to challenge trustees even if these are impartial and professional. Inscrutability means that trustees may not have a basis to prove their superiority as decision makers. They may not be able to build up a reputation for quality or expertise that could form the basis of trust and that may shield them from attacks.

For example, studies suggest that large majorities of the general public in most countries say that they trust international courts (compared to many other legal and political institutions).[78] Yet these same studies also find that very few people are willing to accept international court decisions that they disagree with.[79] Moreover, people barely know anything about international courts. Trust in international courts is often a byproduct of things over which they have little control, such as respect for legal values and trust in the international institutions most closely associated with a court.[80]

International courts may benefit from their relative obscurity. In countries where trust for domestic courts and international institutions is high, international courts are also generally trusted.[81] This "trust by association" may yield legitimacy in the sense that it makes it more likely that actors perceive that a court's judgments should be obeyed. This may leave international judges free to exercise their fiduciary duties, even if trust bears little relation to knowledge about whether judges accurately exercised their responsibilities. Yet this is a double-edged sword. As Diego Gambetta puts it, "Trust is a peculiar belief predicated not on evidence but on the lack of contrary evidence—a feature that . . . makes it vulnerable to deliberate destruction."[82] Chapter 9 examines how salient ideological conflict over the desirability of liberal international court has spurred backlashes against these courts. In the context of ideological conflict, appeals to expertise and impartiality may be insufficient to preserve institutional authority.

Conclusion

Many IGOs and other transnational actors are experts with high degrees of professionalism. Their primary task is sometimes to acquire new information that governments do not have. If this is so, then they can use this asymmetric information as a form of leverage to move policy in their preferred directions.

Yet on most issue areas (powerful) governments employ their own experts. The international actors may not have information that governments do not have. Instead, their primary tasks are to encourage governmental and nongovernmental actors to share information and to coordinate on a shared interpretation of that information. I argue that this better describes the core activities of organizations as diverse as the IMF, standard setting organizations, transnational financial regulators, the IPCC, and international courts.

Sharing private information amid ideological conflict involves distributive conflict. So does coordinating on a common interpretation. Putting disinterested experts in charge does not solve the problem. If the rules of the international system primarily advance liberal objectives, then opponents of these objectives are likely to challenge interpretations, regardless of how expertly or neutrally the opinion was arrived at. Interpretations are typically at least somewhat inscrutable: it is often not possible to objectively verify whether the interpretation was accurate. Chapter 9 will illustrate empirically how ideological challenges to liberalism can result in backlash against international experts.

CHAPTER SIX

Ideological Structure
and Membership in
International Institutions

THIS BOOK'S core argument is that global institutional politics reflects cooperation and competition in a low-dimensional ideological space. Institutions result from efforts by some states to shift the status quo toward their ideal points. A basic observable implication is that ideology shapes decisions to join international institutions. States should be more likely to join institutions with similarly minded states. Moreover, membership in international institutions should reflect the ideological structure of world politics.

This chapter examines these implications empirically. The first part focuses on intergovernmental organizations (IGOs). An IGO is an organization with three or more states that holds plenary meetings at least once every ten years and that has a permanent secretariat or headquarters.[1] There are already numerous studies that show that UN ideal point differences (or UN voting similarities) correlate with membership in treaties and IGOs,[2] as well as specific institutions such as defense cooperation agreements,[3] the General Agreement on Tariffs and Trade (GATT) or World Trade Organization (WTO),[4] and the Asian Infrastructure Investment Bank (AIIB).[5]

This chapter adds to this evidence but also shows that there is a low-dimensional structure underlying IGO memberships that closely matches the ideological structure that emerges from UN voting patterns. That is, both UN voting and IGO membership patterns appear to operate in a similar low-dimensional ideological space. Moreover, ideological changes help us understand the changing nature of the global institutional system. The evidence includes regression analyses with country fixed effects, showing that changes in ideological positions are associated with changes in membership patterns.

The latter part of the chapter shows that similar patterns apply to ratifications of global treaties as well as alliances. As chapter 2 argued, global ideological orientations have implications for economic, cultural, human rights, security, and other issues. Thus, positioning on an ideological dimension can shape sorting into a wide variety of institutions. The final section compares the implications of the spatial approach to an alternative way of conceptualizing and measuring the structure underlying IGO memberships: network analysis.

Ideology and IGO Memberships

At least since 1945, the creation of IGOs has reflected a purposive attempt to create a Western (or U.S.-led) liberal international order.[6] The goal of many IGOs during the Cold War was to forge multilateral institutionalized ties among democracies, capitalist countries, or countries otherwise preferring to align themselves with the United States and other Western states. During the Cold War, the Soviet Union and its ideological allies stayed out of many of these IGOs.

Figure 6.1 illustrates this point. The figure plots the number of IGO memberships on the vertical axis and distance from the U.S. ideal point on the horizontal axis in 1985, as the Cold War was nearing its end. Countries more sympathetic to communism and the Soviet Union joined many fewer IGOs than those sympathetic to capitalism and the United States.[7] Communist countries initially joined the general UN-related institutions but did not join IGOs with a more explicit liberal internationalist agenda. They did not create many formal institutions of their own. During the Cold War, joining international institutions for the most part meant joining a club that was friendly to U.S. interests.

The post–Cold War situation is strikingly different. Figure 6.2 shows that by 2010 states on the opposite side of the ideological spectrum from the United States had joined roughly as many IGOs as those more closely aligned with the United States. By 2010, there is no longer a correlation between IGO memberships and ideal point distance from the United States.

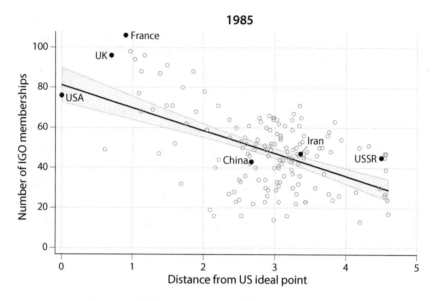

FIGURE 6.1. Number of IGO memberships and distance from U.S. UN ideal point.

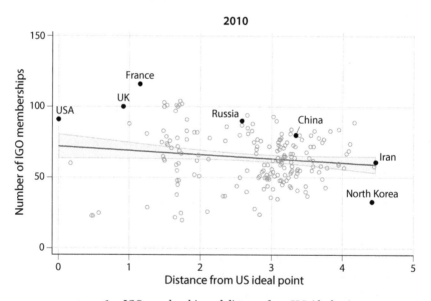

FIGURE 6.2. IGO membership and distance from U.S. ideal point.

One interpretation is that this provides evidence for the "end of ideology," as Francis Fukuyama famously predicted in 1989.[8] After liberalism's ideological victory, there are no longer large groups of states that deliberately want to exclude themselves from IGOs. China, Brazil, India, and other rising states are not opting out of the main global institutions. Instead, they are seeking to reform these institutions.[9] Even Iran would like to become a WTO member.[10] Other than North Korea, few countries explicitly want out.

Yet even if most states have embraced some aspects of liberal internationalism, there remains considerable ideological controversy over the extent to which international institutions should promote other aspects of the liberal agenda, such as political and civil liberties, the rule of law, democracy, and a diminished role for the state in domestic economies and societies. An important implication is that the core global IGOs have become more heterogeneous and that they now include more powerful member states with ideological preferences that diverge from those of the United States. The United States has an increasingly difficult time shaping the policies of the WTO, International Monetary Fund (IMF), World Bank, and other formal institutions. States press for institutional reforms to change voting weights and/or create new institutions that may rival the existing ones.[11] The latest example is the AIIB, which the U.S. fears could undermine the World Bank. Other organizations, especially the WTO, have institutional rules that produce stalemates. It is much harder to get agreement in these institutions with more states with diverse preferences.

From the U.S. perspective, it has gotten more difficult to get IGOs to do the things that the United States wants them to, even holding constant institutional rules that it favors. The United States has a harder time shaping the decisions of existing institutions as well as the design of new institutions. Many new IGOs do not include the United States at all. Figure 6.3 demonstrates this. Before World War II, the United States joined few IGOs. However, by 1950, the country was a member of almost all existing IGOs, excluding a few regional ones. Between 1970 and 1990 the rest of the world created more IGOs, but the U.S. line remained flat. The gap between the number of IGOs the United States is and is not a part of has never been larger and continues to grow with the announced U.S. departure from the World Health Organization (WHO) in 2020.

An example is the International Criminal Court (ICC). In the 1990s, the United States took the initiative to promote international criminal justice and was highly instrumental in creating the tribunals for the former Yugoslavia and Rwanda. The country was a willing participant in the negotiations for an ICC with limited jurisdiction, essentially preserving U.S. veto power over investigations involving Americans. Yet the United States lost in the battle over institutional design and stayed outside of the institution.[12]

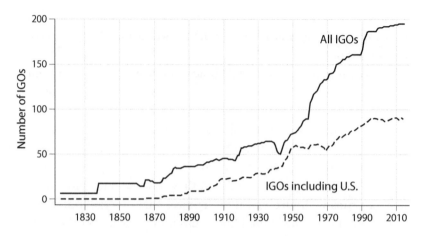

FIGURE 6.3. Creation of intergovernmental organizations with and without the United States. Source: Correlates of War IGO data 3.0.

There are similar trends for treaties. The United States has refused to ratify major legal agreements on climate change (e.g., the Kyoto Protocol), human rights (e.g., the UN disabilities treaty), arms control (e.g., the Nuclear Test Ban Treaty), and use of the oceans (the Law of the Sea Convention). This outcome has coincided with the growing ideological gap between the United States and most other countries, including Western countries (see also chapter 2).[13] A new multilateral IGO must appeal to a broad range of countries. If the IGO is too close to the U.S. ideal point, then that IGO may not be very attractive to many states. If the IGO is too far from the U.S. ideal point, then the United States may opt to stay out. As a consequence, the current multilateral system is "U.S. led" only in a perfunctory way. The United States remains a highly influential player in the core global institutions but has become much less influential in shaping the future direction of multilateralism.

IDEOLOGICAL SORTING INTO IGOS

The relationship between UN ideal point and the number of IGO memberships does not necessarily reveal evidence for or against ideological sorting. Figure 6.2 could mean that ideology has become irrelevant for sorting into IGOs or that China, Russia, and other powerful states have forged new institutional ties with states that are more skeptical of the Western liberal international order.

To get at ideological sorting in a more systematic way, I use an empirical spatial model to estimate state ideal points from the matrix of IGO

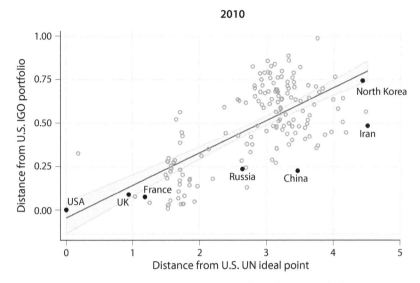

FIGURE 6.4. Distance from U.S. IGO portfolio and U.S. UN ideal point.

memberships. This model treats the decision to become a member of an IGO as a vote on that IGO. The model includes only IGOs with an intercontinental reach, thus excluding purely regional integration efforts. The closer two states are in the resulting low-dimensional space, the more similar their portfolio of IGO memberships. Yonatan Lupu has similarly estimated state ideal points from the matrix of treaty memberships.[14]

I used W-NOMINATE in R to estimate ideal points from the IGO membership matrix.[15] W-NOMINATE is a static model, which presumes that the underlying ideological structure is consistent. I assume that this is true for the post-1946 period. I include only states that are in the Polity data. This provides a size cutoff and ensures that very small states that join few IGOs do not influence the estimation. Examination of the scree plots suggests that a one-dimensional model fits the data well. A simple model that assumes that IGOs can be characterized by a fixed cut-point along a single stable dimension helps classify 83 percent of state memberships correctly.[16]

Figure 6.4 shows that the correlation between a country's distance with the U.S. ideal point in UN voting and the U.S. ideal point in IGO membership is still very high in 2010. What this tells us is that the closer (further) states are to the United States in their revealed ideological perspective, the closer (further) their IGO membership portfolio is to that of the United States. Thus, even if the number of IGO memberships no longer correlates with U.S. ideal point, states that often vote with the United States still join

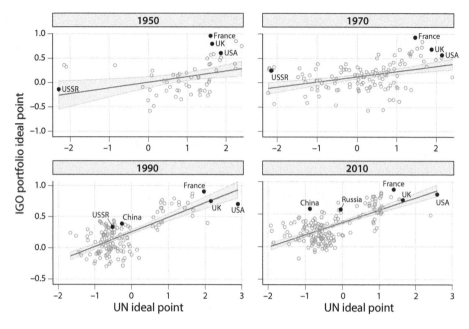

FIGURE 6.5. The relationship between UN ideal point and
IGO ideal point in 1950, 1970, 1990, and 2010.

many of the same IGOs as the United States. There is still considerable
ideological sorting.

Figure 6.5 plots the UN ideal points against the first dimension coordinate from the IGO portfolio W-NOMINATE estimation at four points in
time: 1950, 1970, 1990, and 2010. Unlike figure 6.4, figure 6.5 measures not
distances but the estimated ideal points. Spatial models are not inherently
relational. Each state has its own ideal point that can be represented in a
common space. The plot shows that the ideal points underlying UN General Assembly vote choices and membership patterns in IGOs are strongly
correlated with each other. This suggests that a considerable ideological
structure underlies both sets of choices.

Figure 6.5 also shows that the correlation between UN ideal points and
the IGO portfolio ideal points has increased over time. This is at least suggestive that there is a self-reinforcing mechanism at play, as suggested in
chapter 4. There is some evidence that states start voting more with each
other when they join many of the same IGOs.[17] Scholars interpret this as
evidence of socialization.[18] It is not clear how mid-level diplomats who
meet each other in diverse IGOs would socialize states into voting alike in
the UN. Indeed, there is very little evidence that diplomats get socialized
into an IGO's norms,[19] and it is not clear how this might translate into

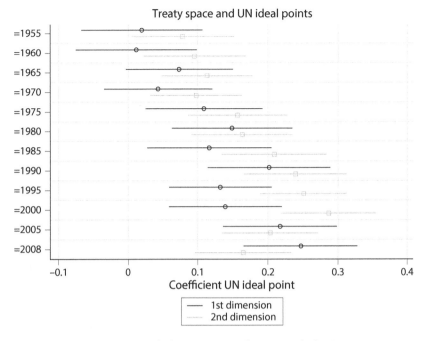

FIGURE 6.6. UN ideal points regressed on treaty ideal points.

state socialization. Another interpretation is the policy interdependence argument from chapter 4: Policy movement in one ideological direction often gives incentives for further movement into that direction. Once a state starts adjusting its trade, investment, and human rights policies in accordance with IGO standards, its ideal point may shift, and this may give renewed incentives for joining more similar IGOs.

Yonatan Lupu estimated two-dimensional W-NOMINATE ideal points on a matrix of ratification of global treaties.[20] Figure 6.6 plots the bivariate regression coefficients of UN ideal points on the first and second dimensions at five-year intervals.[21] The point of the exercise is purely descriptive: does the structure underlying treaty membership resemble the ideological structure as revealed through UN votes?

As in figure 6.5, the correlation between UN ideal point and treaty-based ideal points strengthens over time. Since the mid-1970s, UN ideal points have correlated with both first- and second-dimension treaty ideal points. In the treaty space, neither the first nor the second dimension purely reflects Cold War conflict. Two-dimensional models are rotationally invariant, meaning that we can arbitrarily rotate all ideal points without changing distances between them. The Cold War axis runs diagonally through the two-dimensional space. Still, there is a high correlation between the ideal point underlying UN vote choices and treaty ratification choices.

A REGRESSION ANALYSIS

The preceding section showed that there are similarities between the low-dimensional structure underlying UN votes and the IGO and treaty space. This section uses more conventional regression analysis to examine whether individual states indeed sort ideologically into IGOs.

The unit of analysis is the state-IGO-year, focusing on the forty-eight IGOs that are coded as interventionist by Boehmer, Gartzke, and Nordstrom.[22] These are organizations that "contain mechanisms for mediation, arbitration, and adjudication, and/or other means to coerce state decisions (such as withholding loans or aid), as well as means to enforce organizational decisions and norms."[23] The analysis focuses on these IGOs as decisions to join them could be costly. They include organizations across issue areas. Similar results obtain on the sample of all IGOs.

The dependent variable takes the value one in the year a state joins an IGO and zero otherwise. The main estimation is a logit model where observations drop after a state joins the IGO. Exiting an IGO is sufficiently rare to warrant this approach.[24] The analysis includes a third-degree Hermite (orthogonal) polynomial of time to reflect that any state should become more likely to join an IGO as time progresses.

The main independent variable is the average ideal point distance between a state and the IGO's members. The smaller the ideal point distance, the more likely it is that a state will join. I also look just at the ideal point distance with an IGO's most powerful member, identified by its CINC score, which is an aggregate measure of capabilities from the Correlates of War project based on military, population, and economic output.[25]

The analysis includes fixed effects for both states and IGOs. These control for unobserved time-invariant characteristics of states that may make them more likely to join IGOs as well as unobservable characteristics of the IGO that may make the IGO more attractive to any state. This analysis thus focuses on the extent to which changes in ideal points help explain sorting into IGOs.

The models include the proportion of IGO members from the same region[26] and the number of border states that are already part of the IGO,[27] reflecting that states are often attracted to IGOs that include nearby states or other states in the region. These neighborhood patterns could confound the correlation between ideal point and IGO membership as ideal points are also regionally clustered.

Democracies join more intergovernmental organizations and are particularly attracted to IGOs that already include many democracies.[28] The model includes both a country's level of democracy, measured by its Polity score,[29] and the distance between the state's and the IGO's average level of democracy.[30] Chapter 2 already demonstrated the relationship between ideal points and democracy, thus suggesting that democracy could be a confounding variable.

Finally, the model includes measures of economic and security interdependence. Chapter 4's framework implies that states should be more likely to join organizations that contain other states on which they depend. First, the models include the proportion of a state's exports that go to states that are already IGO members.[31] The idea is that states should be more attracted to IGOs that already include trade partners. Second is the proportion of the IGO's members with which a state has a defense alliance.[32] This reflects the idea that even non-security IGOs become more attractive when they consist of states with which one has a secure relationship.[33]

The full table is available as part of the online appendix. Figure 6.7 gives estimates of the marginal effects for the key substantive variables. Membership of contiguous states and regional membership had large positive effects but are omitted from the graph. Polity scores are transformed to run from −1 to 1 to make the estimates more comparable to the other coefficients (although these are not standardized coefficients, so they are not directly comparable). All independent variables are lagged by one year. The figure presents three models: one that includes both the ideal point distance with the average member and the most powerful member and models that include one of these variables.

Even after including country fixed effects, neighborhood effects, democracy, as well as security and economic relationships with IGO members, ideological differences with IGO members still correlate substantially and significantly with joining new interventionist IGOs. Both the distance with the average member and that with the most powerful IGO member exhibit this pattern, although the coefficient for distance with the average member is larger. Moreover, the coefficients are large relative to the other variables. A one-standard-deviation increase in ideal point distance with the average IGO member is correlated with a decrease in the probability of joining an IGO about twice the size as a one-standard-deviation decrease in the Polity score. This comparison is important because democracy is the

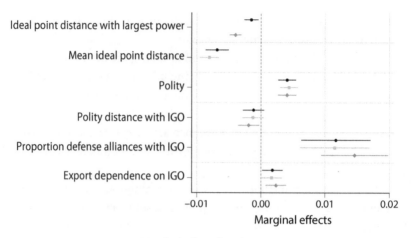

FIGURE 6.7. Marginal effects from logit regression on
interventionist IGO memberships.

most persistent focus of the literature.[34] As chapter 2 illustrated, democracy is correlated with global ideology, but the two are not the same thing.
It is thus important to show that changes in ideology correlate with IGO
membership even after controlling for democracy.

The other variables correlate with IGO membership in the directions
we expect. Greater export dependence and more allies in an IGO correlate
with a greater probability of joining in a given year. Democracies are more
likely to join regardless of the IGO's membership. But the evidence is less
conclusive on whether states are likely to join IGOs that are similar to
them in their democratic composition. The confidence interval for that
coefficient includes zero in two specifications.

Overall, the evidence strongly suggests that ideology shapes membership patterns of IGOs, although we cannot tell whether this is because
states apply to those IGOs whose members they have more in common
with or whether this reflects decisions on the part of existing members to
allow in countries that are closer to them ideologically (or both).

Alliances

A military alliance is a formal agreement among independent states to
cooperate militarily in the face of potential or realized military conflict.[35]
Unlike most, but not all, global treaties and IGOs, states cannot unilaterally opt into alliances. Alliances are relational. They reflect specific reciprocal obligations to assist others in the defense of their country's security.

The dominant explanation for why states sign formal alliance treaties is that these allow governments to convey credible information about their future intentions.[36] This book argues that such commitments are easier if states share similar ideologies. A shared ideology helps states predict that they will likely be on the same side of a future military conflict.

Scholars have long used the similarity between countries' alliance portfolios as a measure of their shared interests.[37] The presumption is that if countries A and B have alliances with many of the same countries, then their global security interests must be similar. By contrast, if two countries have divergent alliance patterns, then they may be in opposing camps. The most popular measure of alliance similarity is the S-score, which in its most common application is identical to the distance in a K-dimensional space between the alliance portfolios of two states, where K is the number of states in the global system.[38] This distance may be weighted, for example, to grant alliances with states that are more powerful a higher weight.

While the use of this measure is widespread in dyadic analyses of conflict, few (if any) scholars have asked whether there is an ideological structure underlying alliance portfolios. Multidimensional scaling analysis (MDS) can uncover state ideal points from dyadic distance measures. MDS is an old technique that represents objects in a low-dimensional space such that the interpoint distances correspond as closely as possible to the dyadic distances.[39] For example, MDS can accurately reproduce a two-dimensional map from a matrix of as-the-crow-flies distances between cities. In this case, the fit is perfect because the intercity distances reflect a two-dimensional space.

I estimated a classical MDS based on the weighted S-scores provided by Daina Chiba, Jesse Johnson, and Ashley Leeds.[40] There is considerable structure underlying alliance portfolios. In 1970, a one-dimensional solution classifies 65 percent of the distances in alliance portfolios correctly.[41] A two-dimensional solution captures 76 percent. By 1990, the first dimension captures only 48 percent but the two-dimensional solution still classifies 74 percent of the variation. In 2010, the two-dimensional solution classifies 65 percent of the variation. In other words, much of the variation in alliance portfolios can be represented by plotting states as points in a two-dimensional space.

Figure 6.8 plots these points for 1950, 1970, 1990, and 2010, identifying the P-5 UNSC members by name. Both the Cold War and its end are easily discernable. During the Cold War, the first dimension clearly distinguishes

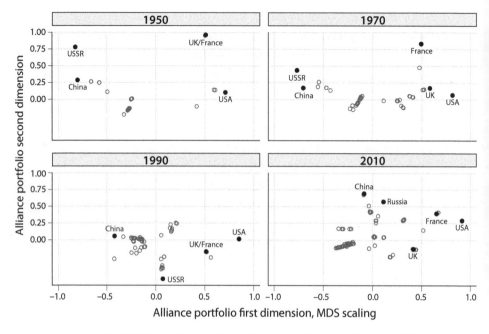

FIGURE 6.8. Multidimensional scaling solution from S-scores alliance portfolios.

the Soviet Union and its allies from the United States and its allies. Russia moved toward the center of the space as the Cold War ended in a similar way to the patterns for UN voting observed in chapter 2. The United States still occupies the most extreme position on the first dimension and has grown increasingly isolated. This means that its patterns of alliances are quite different from those of other states.

Figure 6.9 plots the correlation between the first-dimension estimate from the MDS scaling and the first-dimension UN ideal point in 1950, 1970, 1990, and 2010. The correlation is strong in all years. There is considerable similarity in the ideological structure underlying UN voting and alliance portfolios.

The scatterplots offer suggestive evidence that the structure underlying the choice of alliance portfolios resembles the ideological structure underlying UN voting. Yet ideology is itself a function of other factors that could also be related to alliance formation. Most notably, there is a large literature that finds that democracies are more likely to form alliances with each other.[42] This may be for reasons that are unrelated to ideology, such as that democracies are better able to make credible commitments to each other. But it could also be that at least in the post-1945 world many democracies have shared a set of objectives about how global society should be orga-

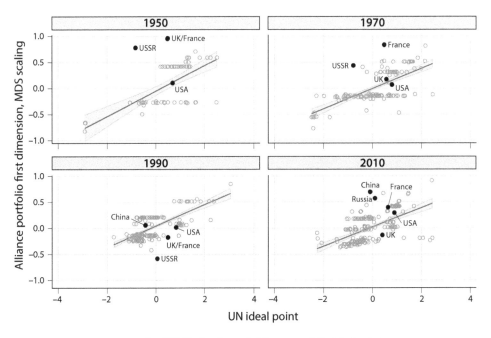

FIGURE 6.9. UN ideal point and alliance portfolio ideal point.

nized (see chapter 2). Indeed, the correlation between shared democracy and alliance commitments holds only after World War II.[43]

Figure 6.10 presents the results from a linear regression model with alliance portfolio similarity as the dependent variable. The unit of analysis is the state dyad-year from 1946 to 2016. The model includes fixed dyad effects and a third-degree time polynomial. This means that we can assess only the extent to which changes in ideal point similarity and shared democracy correlate with changes in alliance portfolio. The model also includes the ratio of maximum military capabilities to total dyad capabilities (measured by CINC scores), as we know that asymmetrically capable states join fewer alliances. The appendix includes the full table of results.

Figure 6.10 shows that the correlation between ideal point distance and alliance portfolio similarity remains large and statistically significant even after controlling for joint democracy, capabilities, and fixed dyad effects. The same findings hold after introducing the difference between democracy levels and alternative ways of conceptualizing capabilities (see the appendix). The standardized coefficients suggest that the coefficient for ideal point distance is about twice as large as the coefficient on joint democracy. When ideal point distance increases by 1 between a pair of states, the weighted alliance similarity on average drops by around 0.03. The

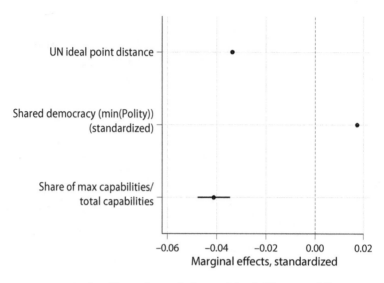

FIGURE 6.10. Regression analysis on weighted alliance portfolio similarity (S-scores) with dyad fixed effects.

point is not to make a causal argument but simply to demonstrate that the patterns described in this section are not fully due to the correlation between regime type and alliance commitments.

Network Analysis and Ideological Structure

Network analysis is an alternative way to analyze the structure of institutional memberships.[44] Network analysts consider states as nodes that form ties of different strength. These ties can be channels for the transmission of material goods but also channels for the spread of ideas and information. A node's position in the network shapes its power and its subsequent behavior. Network theories typically draw from areas outside of international relations, most notably the sociology of friendship and authority ties. Network analysts have developed tools to measure characteristics of the network and its nodes, such as the degree to which nodes are central or fulfill a brokerage function by linking different parts of the network together.

There are important commonalities between the network and the spatial approach. Both approaches highlight that state decisions to enter institutions depend both on past decisions and on other states' decisions. More importantly, the structure that underlies membership patterns is important in both approaches. Indeed, some of the measurements of network concepts closely resemble spatial approaches.

Network analyses typically start with converting an IGO membership matrix into a matrix that expresses the strength or similarity of ties between states. For example, Brandon Kinne measures the structural similarity of membership portfolios by computing the Pearson correlation between memberships of two states.[45] This is an alternative measure of similarity than the more familiar tau-b or S-scores widely used in the literature for alliance patterns (although these measures are typically strongly correlated). Kinne visualizes IGO membership patterns with multidimensional scaling, as in figure 6.7. There are other network concepts that do not have a spatial analog, such as brokerage roles,[46] but core network concepts like structural equivalence or similarity are hard to distinguish empirically from spatial approaches.

While network theorists use multidimensional scaling for visual representation, the reduced dimensionality plays no specific role in network theory. In the network approach, state attributes are relatively unimportant. Instead, the structural position that a state occupies in the network shapes its behavior.[47] To understand the conceptual differences, consider an outlier state like North Korea. In a network approach, an outlier state has few connections to the network. This isolated position itself determines what power North Korea has and how it will behave. By contrast, in a spatial model, an outlier state has extreme ideological preferences. Outlier states choose not to join institutions because the goals of these institutions clash with their ideological outlook. Concurrently, institutions may not want outlier states for the same reason.

The difference becomes clear when we compare theoretical expectations regarding changes of government. The spatial model expects quick changes if a new government with a different ideology comes to power. For example, Eastern Europe quickly integrated into the world's institutional structure once they rid themselves of communist governments. Attributes matter. The network position itself does not constrain a change in behavior. Yet the ideological structure does constrain what options states have. Newly elected governments in Eastern European states understood (in a broad sense) the policy consequences of joining the specific set of available institutions. This structured their choices in the post–Cold War environment.

The next chapter introduces some empirical tests of network and spatial approaches in the context of the relationship between institutional memberships and militarized disputes. The point is certainly not to suggest that spatial approaches always offer a superior understanding to network approaches. Yet sometimes the network literature is too quick to apply network concepts to IR or to interpret correlations between network measures and outcomes as evidence for network theories. Network theory is expressly relational. Yet there are many network analyses that analyze data that is not necessarily an expression of ties between states.

For example, scholars have analyzed co-voting in the UN General Assembly as a network.[48] Yet a vote is not an expression of the closeness of the relations of two states but an expression that both states agree on the desired fate of a UN resolution (see chapter 2). A vote reveals information about that state's ideological position not about its relationship with a specific other state. Belgium never gets to vote on how much it likes Bolivia.

IGO memberships are also not obviously relational. That two states are members of the same IGO does not necessarily reflect that they engage in more extensive bilateral diplomacy or that they can pass more information to each other, as is often assumed in network analyses.[49] State representatives in IGOs are usually mid-level bureaucrats with relatively little capacity to influence a state's broader foreign policy goals. We ought to be somewhat skeptical that this type of interaction has large socialization effects, as network theorists often presume.[50] Alliance treaties and PTAs are more explicitly relational. Network concepts have more potential in such contexts.

Network approaches and spatial approaches can sometimes offer different but complementary interpretations of the same data. For example, in a recent article, Brian Greenhill and Yon Lupu find that the IGO network has become less fragmented over time.[51] Their analysis identified distinct regional clusters. The clustering approach identifies groups of states with similar patterns of IGO membership and thus depends less on the idea that IGO memberships reflect ties between states. Greenhill and Lupu find that states within clusters increasingly have ties through IGO memberships with states in other clusters. This may well be an insight that can accompany the earlier finding in this chapter that there has been an increased amount of ideological sorting into IGOs even as the number of IGO memberships is no longer correlated with ideology.

Conclusion

This chapter has presented considerable evidence that membership in IGOs, global treaties, and alliance treaties reflects ideological sorting. States typically prefer to join institutions with other states that have similar ideal points. Moreover, the low-dimensional latent structure underlying IGO, treaty, and alliance memberships strongly resembles the main dimension of contestation in the UN. This is so both during and after the Cold War.

These are descriptive findings. We cannot conclusively demonstrate that ideological orientations cause states to sort into certain IGOs rather than others just as we cannot conclusively demonstrate that democracy or interdependence has such effects. Yet the descriptive findings about the common structure underlying institutional memberships are important by themselves. Institutional politics takes place in a low-dimensional space. This structures competition and cooperation considerably and validates the core assumptions in the previous chapters. This does not mean that ideology is the only thing that matters. Actors have (dis)interests on issues that may lead them to form coalitions with unusual allies on specific cases. Yet there is a lot more structure underlying patterns of cooperation and competition than we typically acknowledge. Ideology, understood as an organizing device, deserves a prominent place in our theoretical and empirical toolkits. The next chapter develops how this shapes state participation in militarized interstate disputes.

CHAPTER SEVEN

Ideology, Institutions, Power, and Militarized Disputes

THIS CHAPTER applies the theoretical framework to analyze the ultimate, and most elusive, promise of international organizations: that they make the world a more peaceful place. About two dozen empirical studies provide support for a version of this idea: there is a negative and significant correlation between joint membership in intergovernmental organizations (IGOs) or preferential trade agreements (PTAs) and militarized conflict between pairs of states.[1] Some studies find that this correlation depends on the democratic nature of IGO membership,[2] institutional characteristics of IGOs,[3] or the positions states have in the network of IGOs or PTAs.[4] Scholars have also offered theoretical foundations for a causal interpretation. Rational institutionalists posit that IGOs help states find peaceful bargaining solutions by resolving informational and commitment problems. Others argue that IGOs help states cooperate or even socialize states into more cooperative arrangements that prevent uses of force.

These rationales emphasize one side of the theoretical story: that IGOs increase cooperation. This chapter develops and tests an alternative theory consistent with the distributive ideological framework. The previous chapter showed that the distribution of IGO membership reflects geopolitical ideological conflict between states. That same ideological conflict also lies at the root of some, but not all, militarized disputes. For example, during the Cold War, the Soviet Union and the United States frequently engaged in militarized disputes over Marxist insurgencies or governments. Since the end of the Cold War the United States and other Western powers have fought wars against states that have violated norms embedded in the Western liberal international system, most notably Yugoslavia (Serbia), Iraq, and Afghanistan. Not all militarized disputes fit this ideological narrative. There is no particular reason that territorial disputes between neighbors are always about global ideology, although some are. If, as this book contends, the geopolitical implications of IGO membership are more ideological than functional, then we should expect that IGO membership matters primarily for disputes over geopolitical rather than particularistic stakes, such as territory.

Chapter 4 argues that effective non-universal IGOs advance cooperation among their members *and* intensify gaps with excluded parties. IGOs harmonize member policies, provide exclusive benefits for their members, insulate them from coercive retaliation by other IGO members, and sometimes develop mechanisms to act collectively and coercively against those that are outside the IGO. Moreover, IGOs do not just solve specific problems. As the previous chapter demonstrated, states self-select into the world's IGOs as they are more comfortable with their ideology. If IGOs are effective, then membership exacerbates the consequences of these diverging ideologies.

This book's theory has several observable implications regarding the link between IGO memberships and militarized conflict. I highlight two. First, shared IGO membership should affect only the likelihood of geopolitical ideological militarized conflict. Major powers are much more likely to have both the ability and the incentive to be involved in militarized disputes over global issues. I find robust evidence that shared IGO memberships are correlated with reduced onset of militarized conflict when at least one state is a major power but not between contiguous states or pairs of states involved in territorial disputes.

Second, the propensity of conflict should be correlated not with the number of shared IGO memberships but with ideological divergence in the pattern of IGO memberships, measured by a state's ideal point estimated from the matrix of IGO memberships (as in the previous chapter). Ideological sorting into or out of institutionalized coalitions rather than the number of shared ties drives variation in conflict and cooperation. The regression analyses find that distances between IGO ideal points are strongly and robustly correlated with increased conflict but not shared IGO memberships.

These findings are especially important because the abilities of IGOs to affect major power behavior on militarized conflict have traditionally been questioned the most.[5] The distributive argument, is not, however that IGOs constrain major powers. Or rather, they may only constrain them vis-à-vis states that share the same institutionalized commitments. The theory and empirical evidence is consistent with the view that IGOs matter but not that more IGOs necessarily make the world a more peaceful place. IGOs are not just means to reduce or prevent militarized conflict; they may also exacerbate policy differences and affect the availability of coercive options and are sometimes the means through which violent conflict is organized. Thus, IGOs affect the distribution of militarized conflict.

The chapter begins with an evaluation of existing theories, which highlight the functional or socialization effects of IGOs. These theories make two types of arguments. First, IGOs help prevent bargaining failures during crises. Second, IGOs stimulate cooperation that may prevent situations where force is threatened. I discuss each in turn.

Information, Commitment, and Bargaining Failure

Informational arguments marry the rationalist institutionalist emphasis on the informational role of institutions with the bargaining theory of war's claim that wars might result from failures to communicate private information. This is an uneasy marriage.

Bargaining theory starts from the observation that war is costly and that it usually ends with an agreement.[6] Rational leaders should prefer to reach that agreement without costly fighting. Leaders get a better deal if their opponents believe that they are willing to make few concessions short of war. This gives rational leaders incentives to understate what they are willing to give up to avoid violent contests. If leaders have incentives to lie, then they also have difficulties communicating their true resolves. Thus, bargaining may fail. As James Fearon put it, "The cause of war cannot be simply lack of information, but whatever it is that prevents its disclosure."[7]

By contrast, institutional theories typically argue that the International Monetary Fund (IMF), the Intergovernmental Panel on Climate Change, the World Bank, and other IGOs develop expertise that (some) states do not have independently.[8] Centralized institutions solve coordination problems and stimulate collective information gathering and the development of expertise.[9] Yet centralized institutionalized solutions are typically less effective than decentralized costly signaling when problems of private information are more prominent.[10]

Boehmer, Gartzke, and Nordstrom recognize this issue but argue that IGOs with extensive institutional structures nonetheless help in "credibly communicating strategic variables that otherwise remain the private domain of states."[11] They claim that more homogenous institutions should be superior at this task because they better preserve secrecy.

How might this work? States that desire secrecy typically prefer to act outside of formal IGOs. For example, the greater transparency of formal IGOs has led to a move toward clubs in some areas of governance.[12] Yet neutral IGOs may have some independent intelligence gathering capabilities. Examples are the International Atomic Energy Agency (IAEA) and the Organization for the Prohibition of Chemical Weapons (OPCW), which employ inspectors who verify whether parties abide by an agreement to destroy or stop developing a military capability. Yet access to these organizational assets is not limited to states that share many IGO memberships. For example, Syria simply ratified the Chemical Weapons Convention and joined the OPCW *after* an agreement was reached to abandon its chemical weapons.[13] Similarly, the IAEA helps make a negotiated settlement with Iran over nuclear nonproliferation more credible by potentially revealing information about cheating. This solution is available to all states. Indeed, the IAEA's role in preventing conflict is most pertinent in precisely those countries that are poorly integrated into the world's IGOs, such as Iran. More interventionist institutional solutions potentially substitute for a lack of trust although information revelation can also exacerbate conflict.[14]

Second, IGOs could impose sanctions, embargoes, and other costly measures that help distinguish resolved and less resolved parties by raising the cost of competition.[15] The theory is that states that endure sanctions may distinguish themselves from less resolved others. This mechanism recognizes that costly signaling more effectively discloses private information than centralization. It is not clear why joint membership in many IGOs should increase the likelihood of such costly competition. To the contrary, the empirical evidence suggests that states that are well integrated into IGOs often implement sanctions against states on the fringes.[16] The role of institutions in this process is not that joint membership reduces conflict by revealing private information but that institutions may make collective actions on sanctions against others easier to achieve.[17] This fits the distributive rationale better than the informational one.

Third, IGOs can be mediators. Again, it is not clear why the number of joint IGO memberships should make effective mediation more likely. Simply being a part of the UN system provides ample access to mediation services. Moreover, IGOs may have disadvantages communicating private information. A mediator who primarily cares about peace has incentives to encourage restraint regardless of the private information she is passed on.[18] Finally, there is very little evidence that revealing private information through mediation plays a major role in resolving conflict. In a review,

Andrew Kydd points out that "remarkably little empirical work has been devoted to the specific hypothesis that information provision reduces conflict, which is a key analytical foundation for the literature."[19] Kydd highlights one study that investigates the use of information by the UN in Cambodia, Cyprus, the Golan Heights, and Namibia.[20] This study finds that the informational role of the UN mattered primarily in information-poor environments. This is not about credibly revealing private information but about better dissemination of publicly available information (a coordination problem). IGOs do provide other advantages as negotiators, such as the promise of peacekeeping to enforce agreements. Peacekeeping is available to all states, regardless of IGO memberships, and it works by making agreements more credible rather than by revealing private information about the resolve of belligerents.[21]

Fourth, the position of states in the IGO network may influence information flows. For example, Dorussen and Ward argue that if two states have many strong ties to a third actor, then that third actor is more likely to have private information about either side and may thus be a more effective mediator.[22] Moreover, a dyad that is more centrally embedded in the network of IGOs should have greater overall information transmission and therefore a reduced probability of conflict. Dorussen and Ward offer no specifics about how IGOs facilitate the revelation of private information. Nevertheless, they find negative correlations between the strength of indirect ties via IGOs and conflict, although the correlation is not significant when two countries have an embassy.

Brandon Kinne offers a more precise causal mechanism. Entry into IGOs functions as a screening device to separate trustworthy and less trustworthy states.[23] If state A has many joint IGO memberships with states that state B also has joint memberships with, then this signals that state A may be a trustworthy partner for state B. This is predicated on the idea that joining IGOs is a sufficiently costly activity that helps separate trustworthy partners for cooperation from less trustworthy ones.[24] Kinne offers the example of post–Cold War Georgia, which joined IGOs that were heavily tilted toward Western states and avoided those dominated by Russia.

This theory recognizes that costly private action is a more effective way to reveal private information than centralization. Yet the mechanism fits the distributive theory better. Georgia's decision to join Western IGOs rather than Russian-dominated IGOs signals a shift to policies and allegiances favored by the West. This creates conflict with Russia while bringing Georgia closer to countries in the West. The conflict over Ukraine's trade agreement with the EU follows a similar interpretation.

To summarize, IGOs plausibly help states resolve commitment problems when they bargain in the shadow of conflict. Yet this does not depend on differential membership patterns. The most important commitment devices such as peacekeeping, weapons inspections, and judicialized dispute resolution are available regardless of a state's or dyad's integration into the world's institutions.

A Distributive Ideological Theory

A second strand of literature argues that formal IGOs increase cooperation by centralizing information, coordinating policies, offering independent monitoring, settling disputes, lowering transaction costs, resolving commitment problems that arise from domestic politics, increasing the shadow of the future, and socializing states into shared norms.[25] If IGOs reduce cheating and effectively resolve low-level disputes, then this may remove some of the reasons states issue violent threats. IGOs may increase interdependence and lengthen the shadow of the future, thus raising the stakes for issuing violent threats in pursuit of short term goals.[26] IGOs may increase the ability to act collectively against uncooperative behavior by a member. Joint IGO memberships may result in preference convergence,[27] which in turn can mitigate the outbreak of militarized conflict.[28] Others argue that institutionalized social interactions create security communities in which states develop common identities or shared perceptions of their security interests.[29] This may be so even in communities designed primarily for commercial purposes.[30] Again others claim that institutionalized cooperation of this type is much more likely to succeed among democracies and that thus only joint membership in IGOs dominated by democracies has a pacifying effect.[31]

These are all plausible arguments for why increased institutionalized cooperation can reduce militarized conflicts among members. Yet these claims highlight only one side of the theoretical story. First, the distribution of IGO memberships reflects geopolitical conflict between states. Exclusionary IGOs are typically not created to enhance the social welfare of all. They are the result of the efforts of some to constrain the efforts of others.[32] This leads to ideological sorting. Moreover, at least some (but not all) militarized disputes are about the same types of geopolitical ideological divides.

Second, well-functioning IGOs that harmonize policies and/or increase cooperation among their members may simultaneously widen the gap with those on the outside. I first explain both points and then discuss their observable implications.

IDEOLOGY AND THE PORTFOLIO OF IGO MEMBERSHIPS

Chapter 6 showed that there is considerable ideological structure underlying patterns of IGO memberships. IGO membership reflects ideological sorting. IGOs are more likely to invite countries for membership that have similar ideologies and that do not provide a security risk to existing members.[33] International militarized disputes are at least some of the time about these geopolitical ideological conflicts. During the Cold War, there were many militarized conflicts motivated by fears that a country's government was (about to be) taken over by communists (or capitalists). The Vietnam War, the Korean War, and the war in Afghanistan are obvious examples.

Since the end of the Cold War, the acquisition of weapons of mass destruction by revisionist states, support for terrorism, human rights violations, and violations of the territorial integrity norm have all (in various combinations) been the stated cause of militarized disputes and have dominated global institutional politics. IGOs played a direct role in many of these disputes. Examples are the conflicts in Iraq, Kosovo, and Libya. Another set of examples is Russia's militarized disputes with Georgia and the Ukraine, which were at least partly over these countries' feared switches of institutional allegiances.

This raises the possibility that observed correlations between IGO memberships and institutionalized conflicts are due to sorting into IGOs. Differences in the portfolio of IGO memberships may reflect but not cause geopolitical contestation. This is consistent with the distributive theory. But as suggested in chapter 3, it is also plausible that institutional memberships sharpen geopolitical divisions.

THE DUAL EFFECTS OF WELL-FUNCTIONING EXCLUSIONARY IGOS

If rational functionalists are correct that IGOs help some states create a social surplus through cooperation, then this may create competitive disadvantages for other states and thus redefine the competitive landscape. Indeed, IGOs may well be created for that purpose. Let's recall former U.S.

president Barack Obama's announcement of the Trans-Pacific Partnership (TPP) in these terms: "We can't let countries like China write the rules of the global economy. We should write those rules, opening new markets to American products while setting high standards for protecting workers and preserving our environment."[34] The TPP's purpose was to get better market access for U.S. exporters but at terms that favor U.S. ideology and interests over those of a rival state: China. This is why the United States intended to partner with like-minded states (e.g., Canada) and states that depend greatly on access to its market (e.g., Vietnam). Tying Vietnam's policies, practices, regulations, and economic activities more closely to those of the United States and like-minded states could have been a source of conflict with China in the same way that Ukrainian and Georgian agreements with the EU and the United States were a source of conflict with Russia.

Export losses due to exclusion from PTAs correlate with increased probability of militarized disputes within dyads.[35] Peterson suggests that the economic loss itself increases threat and thereby conflict. I suggest that ideology plays a role too. If the PTA were organized along principles acceptable to the excluded country, then joining the PTA (or a separate one with similar attributes) would be relatively straightforward. In this important sense, this argument differs from the idea that relative gains impede cooperation.[36]

Economists have long argued against club-like arrangements because they create select groups with special privileges and thereby undermine the aspiration for global free trade.[37] Even the WTO deliberately omits states like Iran, Iraq, Afghanistan, Syria, the Sudan, and North Korea. The WTO's enforcement mechanisms lower the relative price of taking protectionist measures against nonmembers versus members.[38] For example, the United States uses "Special 301" reports to initiate multilateral disputes against fellow WTO members, but it can take direct unilateral sanctions against nonmembers.[39] Thus, nonmembers face the prospect of having their market access withdrawn instantaneously.

Effective trade institutions solve political holdup problems among their members.[40] They make it more difficult to use market access as a tool of coercive diplomacy. The WTO has a security exception, which was applied in the case of sanctions against Russia over its invasion of Ukraine. Yet membership creates a barrier for imposition over lesser issues. In October 2015, the United States had trade sanctions in place against nineteen countries. All but Russia were non-WTO members.[41] The Iranian government has sought access to WTO membership since 1996 and has announced its intention to continue this quest once sanctions over nuclear proliferation are lifted.[42] Until now, the United States has refused such access, presumably at least in part because it would limit the use of some coercive tools.

John Ikenberry has argued that the United States has used institutions to credibly signal restraint to other participants in the liberal international order.[43] Yet the other side of this story warrants emphasizing as well. Forming exclusionary liberal institutions creates conflict with governments less enamored of liberal principles. This suggests another side to the argument that IGOs form a third leg of the Kantian tripod and help preserve the liberal peace.[44] Michael Doyle argued in the second article of his seminal series on the liberal peace that liberal states frequently go to war against illiberal states for liberal reasons.[45] IGOs have been instrumental in organizing collective coercive actions against illiberal states and marginalizing illiberal states. For example, multilateral sanctions backed by an IGO succeed more often because IGOs help enforce that those who initiate the sanctions actually follow through.[46] Joint IGO membership is correlated with a lower rate of sanction imposition even though countries that share many IGOs interact more and have more conflicts, including sanction threats.[47]

Even weak IGOs could raise competitive fears. Membership in IGOs that purely coordinate is still associated with converging domestic economic policies.[48] The flip side is that this policy harmonization increases the gap with nonmembers. Members of a development bank have access to lending that other states do not, which might worsen the conditions under which they can borrow in a competitive lending market. Yet new institutions can also diverge on ideology. The Asian Infrastructure Investment Bank (AIIB) was motivated in part by dissatisfaction with the ideology espoused by the World Bank, especially its emphasis on human rights, environmental issues, and governance issues. Moreover, there are competitive fears: the World Bank is dominated by the United States whereas the AIIB will be controlled by China. It would be silly to argue that individually such IGOs increase the chances of militarized conflict. But patterns of membership across a range of IGOs may create contested patterns of inclusion and exclusion.

I have emphasized non-security institutions because the implications for conflict are least straightforward. Obviously, alliance members enjoy protection that outsiders do not. The security dilemma dictates that this makes other states less secure.[49] John Mearsheimer, who generally believes that institutions have no effects,[50] argues that the possibility of

NATO expansion was one of the main instigators for Russia's actions against Ukraine in 2014.[51] Alliances help countries defend themselves, but they are also vehicles for collective militarized action,[52] as illustrated by recent NATO interventions in Kosovo, Afghanistan, and Libya. The Economic Community of West African States (ECOWAS) and other regional organizations have similarly played an important role in collective military actions (and sanctions).

OBSERVABLE IMPLICATIONS

I highlight two ways in which the distributive approach can be distinguished from functionalist explanations. First, most militarized conflicts reflect either disputes between contiguous states, usually over territory, or disputes in dyads that involve at least one major power.[53] Scholars label these two classes of dyads "politically relevant" and sometimes limit their analyses to them.[54] The distributive theory implies that shared IGO memberships correlate with a relative absence of militarized disputes in dyads that contain at least one major power but not in contiguous dyads or dyads that are involved in a territorial dispute.

This distributive argument implies that disparities in IGO membership should be correlated with militarized disputes over the rules, norms, and ideologies that govern the international system but not with disputes that don't. With some exceptions, such as Cuba's intervention in Angola, minor powers rarely get involved in military disputes over global issues outside their home region unless it is part of a multilateral effort. By contrast, major powers both have the interest and the ability to partake in militarized disputes over global policy or ideological issues.

Other militarized conflicts have little to do with global political issues. For most of their histories, Ecuador and Peru have had similar positions on global issues and have fought multiple border wars. Theories based on the bargaining models of war are typically explicitly motivated by the idea that IGOs help states resolve negotiations of border disputes peacefully. To be clear, my argument is not that institutions cannot help states reach peaceful bargains over territory. Bilateral treaties, such as border treaties, can help resolve border conflicts.[55] IGOs, like the International Court of Justice, can also facilitate such solutions.[56] But there is no good theoretical reason to expect that the number of shared IGOs matters for these types of disputes.

Second, the distributive theory posits that we should not just look at the relative frequency of shared memberships but take account of overall (dis)similarities in the portfolio of IGO memberships. In the distributive perspective differential patterns of IGO memberships reflect conflicting institutionalized interests over outcomes. Scholars in international relations have long used Kendall's tau or Euclidean distance (S) to calculate similarities in alliance portfolios or UN votes.[57] Yet a more recent literature applies empirical spatial models to UN votes[58] or treaty choices[59] to estimate ideal points in a low-dimensional policy space. Dissimilarity is the distance between the ideal points of two countries.

In a number of studies, similarity measures based on network theory correlate more strongly with conflict than counts of direct IGO ties.[60] As the previous chapter argued, these network measures may well summarize similarity in patterns of IGO memberships better than a simple count of shared memberships (they use more information). But that doesn't necessarily imply a social network interpretation. Unlike the spatial model, the network approaches are typically not based on an explicit data generation model. Network analyses often measure structural equivalence,[61] often by taking the Euclidean distance between membership patters, which is equivalent to using S-scores (see also the previous chapter).[62] Others employ algorithms to divide states into different clusters, cliques, or communities of states that have similar patterns of IGO memberships. Yet another approach is to measure IGO network centrality.[63] Centrality is a measure of social prestige or of being a hub central to information provision. But there is also a distributive underpinning. A state that is less central may be one that is marginalized and more susceptible to coercive action than are states that are well integrated into IGOs.

Data and Method

I follow conventions in the literature by regressing the shared number of IGO memberships on the occurrence of a militarized interstate dispute as coded by the Correlates of War (COW) dataset. The analysis relies on both militarized interstate dispute (MID) and IGO data from 1880 until 2010.[64] I present separate findings for the post-1945 period. I focus on MIDs in which force was used (hostility levels 4 and 5).

All results hold both with all IGO memberships and with only interventionist IGOs as defined by Boehmer, Gartzke, and Nordstrom. In addition, the model includes the number of IGOs in the system in a given year. The overall number of IGOs both could be correlated with shared IGOs and could covary with propensity for conflict in a given year. Major power status and contiguity data both come from the COW project.[65]

Consistent with the literature, I estimate a logit model with dyad-year as the unit of analysis. Observations drop after the initiation of a dispute for the duration of the dispute. The model includes a third-degree polynomial for the time since the last dispute.[66] This operates as a hazard function.

The models also include possible confounding variables.[67] First is the presence of a formal alliance between two states.[68] States that are joint members of many IGOs or have similar geopolitical ideologies may also be more likely to form alliances (or vice versa). Second is the minimum level of democracy in a dyad, measured by Polity scores. Jointly democratic states are more likely to have many shared IGO memberships and less likely to engage in militarized conflict. Third, the model includes the absolute value of the capability ratio between two states (measured with CINC scores). It could be that states with large discrepancies in capabilities have fewer joint IGO memberships. Fourth, the appendix presents models that include the average export dependence between the two states to examine whether economic interdependence confounds the relationship between IGO membership and MID initiation.[69] Introducing this variable leads to a drop in observations but does not affect the main results. All independent variables are lagged by one year.

The models for the post–World War II period also include the UN ideal point distance between states. States with differing ideological positions should be more likely to engage in militarized disputes with each other. Others have already shown the correlation between UN voting and militarized disputes.[70] The introduction here is important primarily because the previous chapter showed that states sort ideologically into IGOs. As such, shared IGO membership could simply be a proxy for ideological similarity. Yet this chapter posits that the pattern of IGO memberships has an additional effect, especially in dyads that involve a major power.

An important choice is how to deal with the interdependence in the observations. The default in the literature is to simply include standard errors clustered by dyad. This seems insufficient for the present purpose, although the main results are consistent with this approach (see the appendix). There are many fixed characteristics among pairs of states that are correlated both with their propensity to join many IGOs and with their likelihood of conflict. Fixed dyad effects control for these unobserved time-invariant dyad characteristics.[71] Yet the fixed effects specification excludes all dyads that never engaged in any MID, and it is problematic for variables that change little or not at all over time, such as contiguity and major power status.[72] I therefore present results with both fixed and random effects specifications. In interpreting the findings, it is important to acknowledge that the fixed effects sample includes only those dyads that have ever engaged in an MID.

Results

MAJOR POWER STATUS AND CONTIGUITY

The first hypothesis is that shared IGO memberships reduce conflict onset only in dyads that include at least one major power. By contrast, shared IGO memberships should have little impact in contiguous dyads or among states undergoing border disputes. The model includes an interaction between shared IGO memberships and whether two states share a border or are separated by less than 150 miles over sea. Table 7.1 presents the findings.

The coefficient on shared IGO membership is inconsistent across specifications. It changes signs between the random and fixed effects models. This suggests that the random effects model insufficiently controls for stable factors that lead states to be in the same IGOs relatively often.[73] The interaction between the presence of a major power in a dyad and the number of shared IGO memberships is consistently negative and significant. This holds regardless of the time period, whether or not fixed effects are included, and whether or not control variables are introduced. This suggests that among major power dyads, conflict disproportionally takes place among dyads that have relatively few shared IGO memberships. By contrast, the coefficient on shared IGO memberships in contiguous states is inconsistent. In fixed effects models, the coefficient on shared IGO memberships is positive and significant in contiguous dyads. There is thus no evidence that increasing shared IGO memberships in dyads that have engaged in a conflict (the sample in a fixed effects analysis) reduces the probability of conflict. By contrast, within pairs of states that include a major power increased IGO membership is correlated with reduced conflict onset.

Figure 7.1 interprets the interaction effects graphically (based on a random effects model). Militarized disputes disproportionally occur between contiguous states, regardless of IGO memberships, and within dyads that involve a major power and that share relatively few IGO memberships. The bottom panel shows the same finding with interventionist IGO memberships. A noncontiguous dyad that includes a major power and that has about ten shared interventionist IGO memberships is no more likely to experience conflict onset than a noncontiguous dyad with-

Table 7.1. Logit analysis of conflict onset

Variable	Full period		1946–2010	
	Random effects	Fixed effects	Random effects	Fixed effects
Major power status	2.76***	1.24***	2.90***	−0.81
	(0.12)	(0.20)	(0.25)	(1.04)
Shared IGOs	0.03***	−0.02***	0.05***	−0.05***
	(0.00)	(0.01)	(0.01)	(0.01)
Major power × Shared IGOs	−0.03***	−0.01***	−0.05***	−0.03***
	(0.00)	(0.00)	(0.01)	(0.01)
Contiguity	2.90***		4.31***	
	(0.14)		(0.24)	
Contiguity × Shared IGOs	0.00	0.02***	−0.03***	0.03***
	(0.00)	(0.00)	(0.01)	(0.01)
Ideal point distance			0.52***	0.30***
			(0.05)	(0.08)
Democracy	−0.06***	−0.04***	−0.06***	−0.02
	(0.01)	(0.01)	(0.01)	(0.01)
Alliance	−0.04	−0.07	0.13	−0.29
	(0.09)	(0.11)	(0.14)	(0.19)
Capability ratio	−0.00**	−0.00	−0.00	−0.00
	(0.00)	(0.00)	(0.00)	(0.00)
Shared region	0.73***		0.99***	
	(0.12)		(0.16)	
Number of IGOs in system	−0.00***	0.00	−0.00***	0.00***
	(0.00)	(0.00)	(0.00)	(0.00)
Observations	731,807	54,826	582,217	17,951
Number of dyads	19,238	806	18,893	445

Standard errors in parentheses. Peace years polynomial and constant omitted.
$*p < .1. **p < .05. ***p < .01.$

out a major power. This finding is particularly significant because the effect of IGO memberships on major power behavior has traditionally been questioned.

Consistent with the literature, ideal point distance increases the probability of conflict while joint democracy lowers it.[74] The other covariates exhibit no systematic and significant correlations with conflict onset. All results are robust to excluding these covariates.

Table 7.2 is identical to table 7.1 except that contiguity is replaced by the presence of a territorial dispute between states as coded by the COW project.[75] The results are similar: increased numbers of shared IGO memberships increase the probability of conflict onset among pairs of states that include a major power but not among pairs of states involved in a territorial dispute. The fixed effects analysis implies that the correlation of a mili-

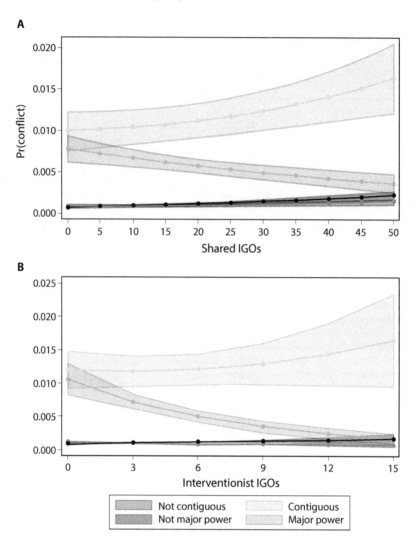

FIGURE 7.1. Interaction effects between contiguity, major power status, and IGO membership on militarized dispute onset.

tarized conflict does not decrease when two states join more IGOs together. By contrast, the likelihood of conflict onset with a major power does decrease as two states join more IGOs together.

REPLICATIONS

To illustrate the robustness of the interaction between major power status and IGO memberships, I replicated three seminal studies. Figure 7.2 summarizes the key findings. The appendix has more details.

Table 7.2. Territorial disputes, IGO membership, and conflict onset

Variable	Full period		1946–2010	
	Random effects	Fixed effects	Random effects	Fixed effects
Major power status	2.74***	1.37***	2.69***	−0.67
	(0.12)	(0.20)	(0.24)	(1.03)
Shared IGOs	0.03***	−0.00	0.03***	−0.02**
	(0.00)	(0.01)	(0.01)	(0.01)
Major power × Shared IGOs	−0.03***	−0.02***	−0.04***	−0.03***
	(0.00)	(0.00)	(0.01)	(0.01)
Territorial dispute	1.30***	0.81***	1.26***	0.07
	(0.14)	(0.15)	(0.29)	(0.33)
Territorial dispute × Shared IGOs	0.00	0.00	0.00	0.00
	(0.00)	(0.00)	(0.00)	(0.00)
Ideal point distance			0.52***	0.28***
			(0.05)	(0.07)
Contiguity	2.56***		3.16***	
	(0.12)		(0.16)	
Democracy	−0.06***	−0.04***	−0.06***	−0.02
	(0.01)	(0.01)	(0.01)	(0.01)
Alliance	0.02	0.03	0.13	−0.29
	(0.09)	(0.11)	(0.14)	(0.19)
Capability ratio	−0.00**	−0.00	−0.00*	−0.00
	(0.00)	(0.00)	(0.00)	(0.00)
Shared region	0.64***		0.98***	
	(0.12)		(0.16)	
Number of IGOs in system	−0.0***	0.00	−0.00**	0.00***
	(0.00)	(0.00)	(0.00)	(0.00)
Observations	731,807	54,826	582,217	17,951
Number of dyads	19,238	806	18,893	445

Standard errors in parentheses.
*$p < .1$. **$p < .05$. ***$p < .01$.

First, Jon Pevehouse and Bruce Russett find that IGOs with more democratic membership reduce conflict, but overall number of shared IGO memberships does not.[76] The dependent variable is the occurrence of a fatal MID in the 1885–2000 period. Democratic IGOs are those where the average member has a Polity score of 7 or higher. Panel A shows that shared IGO memberships do correlate with lower conflict onset in this analysis but only for dyads that include a major power. Dyads including at least one major power but with very few shared IGO memberships are especially conflict prone. However, once states have joined about thirty IGOs, dyads including a major power are about as peaceful as dyads without major

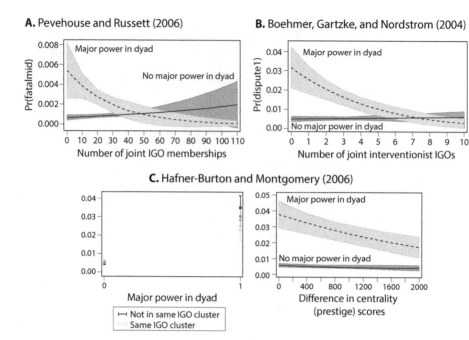

A. Pevehouse and Russett (2006)

B. Boehmer, Gartzke, and Nordstrom (2004)

C. Hafner-Burton and Montgomery (2006)

FIGURE 7.2. Replications of link between IGOs and MIDs.

powers. Moreover, the democratic IGO finding is not robust to a logarithmic transformation (its distribution is extremely skewed), whereas the interactive effect is.

Boehmer, Gartzke, and Nordstrom argue that only some IGOs are likely to reduce militarized conflict.[77] First, only interventionist IGOs with institutionalist mechanisms for mediation, arbitration, and other means to coerce state decisions are able to help states credibly reveal private information in crises. Second, IGOs are more effective as they are more homogenous in their membership as these are better at maintaining the secrecy required for effective private information transmission. IGO heterogeneity is measured using dyadic similarity in UN voting records. A regression analysis on MIDs from 1950 to 1991 supports these hypotheses. In a replication, I find that shared interventionist IGO memberships reduce conflicts only in dyads that contain at least one major power (see panel B). Moreover, IGO homogeneity membership no longer correlates with conflict in the regressions that include the interaction.

Emilie Hafner-Burton and Alex Montgomery examine how the way states are integrated into the network of IGOs affects their propensity to engage in conflict.[78] First, the network of IGOs may consist of different clusters. They find that membership in the same cluster is correlated with reductions in conflict. Second, high disparities in network prestige may affect conflict propensity, although the theory is unclear about the direction of this effect. They find that shared IGO memberships have a positive correlation with conflict when including these network variables. Yet after introducing major power interactions, shared IGO memberships, shared cluster membership, and "prestige" (eigenvalue centrality) differences are negatively correlated with dispute initiation only in dyads that include at least one major power (see panels c and d).

In short, the evidence in this section indicates that dyads including a major power are less likely to experience conflict when two states share many IGO memberships. This does not hold for contiguous states or states in a border dispute.

IGO PORTFOLIOS

Table 7.3 includes the W-NOMINATE estimates of ideal point differences in IGO memberships. This reduces the number of observations in the full period, as only in 1900 were there sufficient IGOs to estimate these ideal points. Moreover, the World War II period is missing due to the separation into two periods.

The results provide strong support for the hypothesis that the propensity to engage in conflict correlates positively and significantly with differences in the IGO ideal points of states. This finding holds across both periods, in random and fixed effects specifications, when covariates are included or excluded, and across alternative definitions of militarized conflict. Figure 7.3 illustrates the substantive size of the correlation (based on the full period). Two states with identical ideal points are about 67 percent less likely to experience a conflict than two states one standard deviation (0.26) above zero.

Figure 7.4 reports regressions where both ideal point estimates and IGO ideal point estimates are interacted with major power status and contiguity. The IGO ideal point distance strongly increases the probability of a militarized conflict in a dyad that includes a major power but not in a contiguous dyad that does not include a major power. In the post–World War II environment the same holds true for UN ideal point distance.

These findings suggest that some militarized conflicts are about ideological contestation whereas others are not. As the examples earlier in this

Table 7.3. Logit regressions with fixed and random dyad effects on the likelihood of militarized conflict

Variable	1900–2010		1946–2010	
	Random effects	Fixed effects	Random effects	Fixed effects
Major power	2.83***	1.27***	2.73***	−1.04
	(0.16)	(0.27)	(0.27)	(1.01)
Shared IGOs	0.04***	−0.02**	0.05***	−0.04***
	(0.01)	(0.01)	(0.01)	(0.01)
Major power × Shared IGOs	−0.04***	−0.03***	−0.05***	−0.02*
	(0.00)	(0.01)	(0.01)	(0.01)
Contiguity	3.83***		4.58***	
	(0.18)		(0.26)	
Contiguity × Shared IGOs	−0.02***	0.01	−0.03***	0.02**
	(0.00)	(0.01)	(0.01)	(0.01)
IGO ideal point distance	0.98***	1.06***	0.61**	1.49***
	(0.16)	(0.25)	(0.25)	(0.52)
UN ideal point distance			0.47***	0.30***
			(0.05)	(0.08)
Democracy	−0.06***	−0.04***	−0.06***	−0.02**
	(0.01)	(0.01)	(0.01)	(0.01)
Alliance	−0.07	−0.15	0.12	−0.34*
	(0.10)	(0.12)	(0.14)	(0.20)
Capability ratio	−0.00	0.00**	−0.00	0.00*
	(0.00)	(0.00)	(0.00)	(0.00)
Shared region	0.65***		0.82***	
	(0.14)		(0.17)	
IGOs in the system	−0.00***	0.00***	−0.00	0.01***
	(0.00)	(0.00)	(0.00)	(0.00)
Observations	574,734	35,938	475,477	17,315
Number of dyads	13,753	624	13,729	420

Standard errors in parentheses.
*$p < .1$. **$p < .05$. ***$p < .01$.

book illustrated, two neighboring states may well have a conflict over territory. Whether these neighboring states share a global ideology or many IGO memberships may matter little for the likelihood that this conflict turns violent. But major powers also pursue geopolitical interests. Sharing IGO memberships and a global ideology with a major power strongly correlates with the absence of militarized disputes.

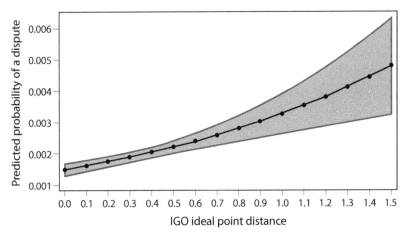

FIGURE 7.3. IGO ideal point distance and MID onset.

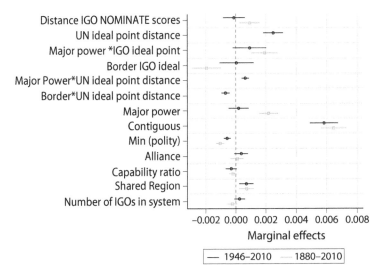

FIGURE 7.4. Marginal effects on MID onset. Peace years polynomial
not displayed. Variables rescaled to improve comparability.

Conclusion

This chapter applied the theoretical framework to a particular empirical
regularity: the correlation between shared IGO memberships and militarized disputes. Existing theoretical explanations for this correlation highlight the functional benefits of IGOs in preventing bargaining failures and

increasing cooperation. IGOs may well help states overcome bargaining failures. But there is little reason that variation in IGO membership reflects variation in access to this function. Simply being a UN member should suffice.

Variation in IGO membership portfolios reflects ideological differences between states. These ideological differences are sometimes also at the root of militarized disputes, although there are also militarized disputes that are nonideological. Moreover, if IGOs stimulate cooperation among their members, then in a competitive environment they might also exacerbate ideological conflict with outsiders. These insights offer a new way to understand the correlation between shared IGO memberships and militarized conflict.

The empirical section displays two key findings. First, variation in shared IGO memberships correlates with variation in conflicts in dyads that include a major power but not among contiguous dyads or dyads involved in territorial disputes. This is consistent with the idea that the IGO membership portfolio reflects ideological sorting and that militarized conflict is sometimes about the same ideological issues that divide states in their IGO membership patterns.

Second, distance between two states IGO portfolios, measured by ideal points in an empirical spatial model, correlates with increased likelihood of conflict. This is so regardless of whether a dyad includes a major power. The ideal point difference reflects institutionalized differences of interests between states. It is not purely an ideological difference but that different policies are entrenched in institutional commitments. Again, this suggests that IGO memberships can harmonize but also differentiate states. More direct evidence for this is that the proportion of non-shared IGO memberships is correlated with an increased probability of conflict.

Some words of caution are in order. Most importantly, the correlation between IGO memberships and conflict may not reflect any causal relationship at all. Empirical studies like this cannot control for all the (unobservable) factors that may relate to both joint IGO membership and militarized conflict. The best we can do is to evaluate the logic of underlying theories, specify a range of contrasting observable implications, and draw careful model-based inferences.

At the very least, these findings suggests that the distributive perspective should be on the table when thinking through the potential pacifying effects of IGOs. The theoretical and empirical stakes in this debate are high. One implication of the distributive perspective is that more IGOs do not necessarily equate to more peace, even if we believe that IGOs matter for war and peace. A new IGO like the TPP could theoretically harmonize policies, increase interdependence, and create peaceful forms of dispute resolutions among its members while at the same time exacerbating conflict with those on the outside. This is also true in the aggregate: IGOs have both pacifying and contentious aspects. To return to Terry Moe's observation, we should examine both sides of institutions.

CHAPTER EIGHT

Ideology and the Investment Regime

THIS CHAPTER examines how ideological contestation has shaped the institutions that protect foreign investment from expropriation. The investment regime consists of more than three thousand mostly bilateral treaties that contain provisions that protect private investors against expropriation and contractual breaches from foreign governments.[1] Many of these treaties give private investors access to binding arbitration at the International Centre for Settlement of Investment Disputes (ICSID) or another (international) venue. Arbitration panels can issue substantial awards against governments, which are enforceable in the domestic courts of the world's main financial centers.[2] Investment arbitration has become one of the more controversial components of the liberal international order. Its apparent beneficiaries are typically large multinational corporations that win financial compensation from developing country governments.[3]

From the rational functional perspective, the investment regime helps states and private investors overcome a time inconsistency problem that hinders mutually beneficial investment. Governments have incentives to promise favorable treatment in order to attract investors. Governments may have incentives to not follow through on these promises after the initial investment has been made. Private investors may refrain from investing if they fear that the host government would expropriate the investment or enact policies that negatively affect the value of an investment. Investment agreements allow capital-importing states to send a credible signal that they will not expropriate foreign investors.[4] This potentially allows for more efficient allocation of capital across borders than would otherwise be possible.[5]

This functionalist theory may also explain institutional design. Barbara Koremenos's Continent of International Law database codes investment agreements as solving problems of uncertainty, commitment, and enforcement but not distribution.[6] Binding arbitration with direct private access and enforceable decisions best solves these strategic problems. Host states with the greatest need to make credible commitments, for instance because their domestic court system is lacking, are most likely to commit to bilateral investment treaties (BITs).[7]

Recent scholarly assessments suggest that this narrative is at least partially misleading.[8] The evidence that investment agreements increase investment is inconsistent at best. Governments in capital-exporting countries were primarily interested in political and legal objectives rather than increasing investments when they designed model investment agreements. There is very little evidence that private firms lobbied governments in capital-exporting countries for investment protection through treaties and arbitration. Especially in the United States, investors appeared satisfied with the status quo, which involved protection through sometimes heavy-handed diplomatic involvement. Instead, this literature points to the agency of international bureaucrats,[9] the bargaining power of capital-exporting states,[10] and the bounded rationality of governments in developing countries[11] as key factors in explaining the creation and diffusion of investment agreements.

This chapter explains how a focus on competition in a low-dimensional ideological space helps us make sense of the emergence of the investment regime and adjustments to it. From the U.S. perspective, the investment regime is partially about protecting the specific assets of American investors. Yet this could be achieved through other means. The institutional regime is also about advancing principles favored by the United States over alternative principles advocated by the Soviet Union and other states. There was intense ideological conflict over what the rules for the treatment of investments should be during the Cold War. The Soviet Union advocated that states should pursue nationalization on their path toward collective ownership of the means of production. Especially Latin American countries advocated for rules that placed foreign investors on equal legal footing with domestic investors and that permitted extensive government regulation of multinational companies. The United States and other Western capital exporters pursued a set of rules that discouraged nationalization and demanded prompt and adequate compensation for foreign investors. The movement for more legalized protection and arbitration took off when customary rules that favored the West came under fire. The investment regime came about from attempts by powerful capital-exporting states to generalize constraints on less powerful states. Even though the regime is not multilateral in the traditional sense, it does advance a set of general principles.

This chapter first details ideological conflict during the Cold War. It then uses the framework from chapter 4 to analyze the role of ideology in determining what countries did and did not sign BITs with the United States. Finally, the chapter shows that governments that changed their ideological orientations since originally negotiating BITs are the most likely to renegotiate or end treaties. The rational functional rationales of investment agreements must be understood against the backdrop of fierce ideological competition in a low-dimensional space.

Ideological Conflict and the Emergence of the Investment Regime

Expropriation of investments from foreign corporations has long been a source of tensions between governments. Both the United States and European powers have used political and military tools effectively to protect assets or to extract compensation from governments, especially in Latin America.[12] This practice continued well into the twentieth century. For example, Iran's nationalization of assets owned by British and U.S. companies resulted in a major foreign policy crisis and eventually a CIA-supported coup in 1953.[13] Wikileaks cables reveal that U.S. diplomats continue to routinely intervene on behalf of corporations in investment disputes with governments.[14]

The United States has long advanced legal and institutional mechanisms alongside more coercive tools of statecraft. Using coercion on behalf of major corporations was sometimes costly and unpopular and drew the United States into conflicts when they would have preferred to remain on the sidelines.[15] Moreover, the United States sought to create convergence on a set of principles that all states it regularly interacted with could agree on. As chapter 4's framework suggests, the United States would be better off if more states that it interacts with adopt policies regarding the treatment of foreign investors that are closer to its ideal point. Coordination would help shape expectations about where conflict and cooperation are most likely to emerge even if it does not prevent all conflict on individual cases.

Most importantly, the United States sought to advance minimum standards for the treatment of foreign investors, the Hull rule, named after U.S. secretary of state Cordell Hull.[16] The Hull rule requires "prompt, adequate and effective" compensation for expropriations of foreign investments. The Hull rule was a by-product of a 1938 dispute between the U.S. secretary of state and his Mexican counterpart over confiscations of agrarian and oil assets owned by U.S. citizens and firms.[17] Hull did not invent the idea that governments should compensate investors for expropriation. He referred to earlier precedent set by the Permanent Court of International Justice, for instance.[18] Yet Hull's formulation came to be seen as authoritative among most capital-exporting countries.

The Hull rule mattered because many courts and governments in the United States and Europe accepted it as binding customary international law (CIL).[19] CIL is the "general and consistent practice of states followed by them from a sense of legal obligation."[20] CIL gets its force not from countries ratifying a treaty but from practice. States need to accept the rule as legally binding and behave as if this is so. For example, the United States has not ratified the UN Convention on the Law of the Sea, but it has accepted the twelve-nautical-mile territorial waters rule as part of CIL. Yet CIL norms are also vulnerable to change as states change practices or denounce a rule. For example, the CIL norm of absolute sovereign immunity eroded, and more states started to allow lawsuits against sovereigns over commercial disputes.[21]

The Hull rule is now embedded in virtually all modern investment agreements. Yet the rule long faced strong ideological opposition, and it was not always obvious that it would prevail. Communist governments, led by the Soviet Union, insisted that governments have an inherent right to nationalize and collectivize means of production. Indeed, communist doctrine holds that the means of production *should* be collectively held, which implies that expropriation is not just allowable but desirable.

States that had only recently become independent from Western colonial domination also objected to granting foreign corporations special rights. These states viewed Western corporations and their assets as legacies of colonial exploitation. Latin American countries have long adhered to the Calvo doctrine, which states that foreigners should not have rights that are not also accorded to nationals.[22] The adaptation of the Calvo doctrine into domestic constitutions made compensation and jurisdiction matters of national law in many Latin American states, which had opposed U.S. efforts to embed investment provisions in the proposed International Trade Organization after World War II even if they aligned with the United States in other ways.[23] The development strategies of many newly independent states focused on import substitution, which meant that they sought to replace foreign imports with domestic production. Governments sought to regulate and tax multinational corporations and their investments in order to further this objective. This culminated in a large number of expropriations in the 1960s and 1970s, especially in natural resources.

Many governments that nationalized foreign investments were not ideologically committed to communism. Instead, nationalization was a way to assert sovereignty and control over valuable assets (statism). Yet U.S. presidents feared that forceful intervention on behalf of U.S. companies would drive these governments toward the Soviet Union and communism.[24] This made some presidents reluctant to intervene. U.S. companies successfully lobbied Congress to pass the 1962 Hickenlooper Amendment, which required the government to withhold all foreign aid to governments that had expropriated U.S. property, despite explicit objections from the Kennedy administration.

While U.S. administrations sometimes resisted implementing the Hickenlooper Amendment, there was still pressure to punish foreign governments for expropriating U.S.-held property. For example, when Sukarno first established new conditions on foreign petroleum companies and then nationalized a series of industries, Lyndon Johnson felt pressured to act but also warned that "if we cut off all assistance, Sukarno will probably turn to the Russians."[25] Sukarno did indeed turn to the Russians but was overthrown in a 1965 coup, supported by the U.S. government.

The issue of expropriation became a major battleground for Cold War politics. Figure 8.1 summarizes the ideological conflict. On the one side, the United States and its Western allies promoted principles that required "prompt, adequate, and effective" compensation, and on the other side the Soviet Union and its allies saw expropriation as an essential step in the spread of communism.

These ideological positions were intrinsically intertwined with traditional power politics. If a country turned toward communism, it also became increasingly dependent on the Soviet Union. Rules that restrict expropriation and guarantee compensation clearly benefitted capital-rich capitalist countries. Many developing countries were somewhere in the

FIGURE 8.1. Ideological conflict over foreign investor protection.

middle, desiring greater control over especially natural resources but not always wanting to move toward communism and the Soviet sphere of influence. Since most foreign investors came from Western countries, their position favoring greater protection was also self-serving. As explained throughout this book, the analytic purchase of ideology comes not from a separation between interests and ideas but from the way ideology structures conflict and cooperation over institutions.

During the 1960s, newly independent developing countries started to become a more influential independent voice in international institutions. They exploited their emerging numerical majority in the UN General Assembly (UNGA) to draft Resolution 1803 (1962), which reaffirms that states have "permanent sovereignty over their natural wealth and resources."[26] The resolution carves out limited circumstances that allow states to nationalize property but also notes that "the owner shall be paid appropriate compensation, in accordance with the rules in force in the State taking such measures in the exercise of its sovereignty and in accordance with international law." The resolution raises the possibility of international adjudication, but only after exhaustion of domestic remedies, meaning that foreign investors would first have to go through the domestic court system before filing international arbitral claims. This is an important principle that is not part of most contemporary investment agreements.

The Soviet Union proposed an amendment that would strike the phrase "and in accordance with international law" from the resolution. This move directly targeted the Hull rule, which was the most important rule of international law governing this issue. Even votes on nonbinding resolutions can be informative as to whether a customary rule is still operative. The Soviet amendment was defeated by a vote of thirty-four to forty-eight, with twenty-one abstentions. Figure 8.2 demonstrates that the vote was highly ideological. The figure plots each country's vote against its ideal point in

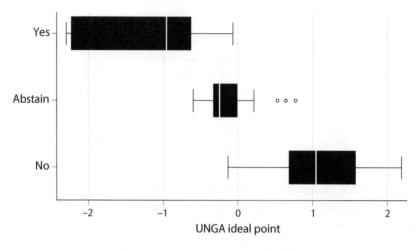

FIGURE 8.2. UN ideal point and votes on the Soviet Union amendment to Resolution 1803 that would have stripped references to international law.

the preceding session, which did not include any votes on investment issues. Countries ideologically closer to the United States tended to vote against the amendment, whereas those in the middle abstained. Governments of developing countries more favorably disposed toward the Soviet ideological position voted in favor of the amendment.

This initial victory by the United States and its allies did not last. In the early 1970s, developing countries used their growing numeric control of the UNGA to advance the New International Economic Order (NIEO).[27] The NIEO sought to overhaul the global economic system, including a North-South transfer of primary goods, energy, technology, and knowledge as well as debt forgiveness and preferential trading arrangements for poorer countries. This culminated in the Charter of Economic Rights and Duties of States, which was brought to the UNGA floor in 1974.

The United States and other Western states had strong incentives to at least pay lip service to the NIEO architects. Concerns that former colonies would switch to the Soviet side were persistent. Henry Kissinger traveled to New York to make an explicit effort to signal U.S. endorsement of the goals of the NIEO movement. Yet the status of foreign investment and expropriation proved to be a stumbling block that prevented the United States from voting in favor of the resolution. Article 2 of the Charter of Economic Rights essentially adopted the Calvo doctrine. It stated, "No State shall be compelled to grant preferential treatment to foreign investment." The charter omitted references to international law as a set of guid-

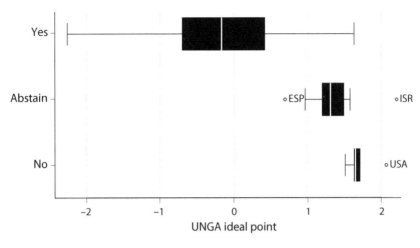

FIGURE 8.3. UN ideal point and vote for the Charter for Economic Rights.

ing principles for solving investment disputes.[28] If the United States were to endorse this position even in a nonbinding vote, it would accept that the Hull doctrine was no longer the governing CIL principle. U.S. ambassador John Scali put it this way:

> The United States delegation regrets that the compromise solution which resolution 1803 (XVII) embodies was not reproduced in this Declaration. If it had been, on this count the United States would gladly have lent its support. Resolution 1803 (XVII) provides, among other things, that, where foreign property is nationalized, appropriate compensation shall be paid in accordance with national and international law; it also provides that foreign-investment agreements by and between States shall be observed in good faith. By way of contrast, the present Declaration does not couple the assertion of the right to nationalize with the duty to pay compensation in accordance with international law. For this reason, we do not find this formulation complete or acceptable. The governing international law cannot be, and is not, prejudiced by the passage of this resolution.[29]

While the charter passed with an overwhelming majority, figure 8.3 shows that the final vote took place along ideological lines. Countries ideologically close to the United States mostly abstained or voted no. Nonetheless, international support for the Hull rule had clearly waned. It was against this backdrop that the move toward a treaty-based regime started in earnest.

The Move to Investment Treaties

At the same time that developing countries asserted their abhorrence of the Hull rule, they also started signing BITs cementing that same rule (and more) into binding treaty law.[30] Germany, which had lost all of its foreign investments in the aftermath of World War II, was the first to sign such an agreement with Pakistan in 1959.[31] German investors could not rely on their government to protect interests, given Germany's constrained foreign policy posture in the first decades after World War II.[32] At this time, there was little interest among British or U.S. companies for more legalized forms of investment protection.[33] The United States began contemplating BITs in 1977, shortly after the UNGA had adopted the Charter of Economic Rights and Duties, although the United States waited until 1983 to draft a model investment agreement.[34] The United States continued to use other tools of statecraft to protect individual investors.[35]

The objective of investment treaty programs was to shape a legal regime that fit the Western liberal ideology. The purpose was not just to protect investments but also to sway other countries away from socialism or other ideological frameworks that privileged a strong role for the state in the domestic economy r. The treaties went well beyond previously existing CIL. Most notably, in the 1980s BITs started to include provisions for international arbitration without exhaustion of domestic remedies.

There is already a good bit of evidence that the U.S. BIT program was driven more by political and legal considerations than by a concern for increasing investments. Former negotiators emphasize that concerns about the erosion of international legal standards were a major driving force for the State Department lawyers.[36] U.S. model BITs were shaped by an ideology that separated politics and markets and that stipulated an important but limited role for the law to enforce contracts.[37] The United States was mostly unwilling to depart from this model BIT, preferring no agreement to one that would water down principles. Taylor St. John documents how shared ideological ground between George H. W. Bush and Argentinean president Carlos Menem made Argentina an ideal partner for a first more extensive BIT.[38] Argentina abandoned the Calvo doctrine as part of this agreement, which was a meaningful policy concession that Argentina has probably come to regret. A similar logic applies to Poland and other Central and Eastern European states.[39] A former negotiator wrote that the treaties were useful "because they symbolize a commitment to economic liberalism."[40]

Quantitative studies have shown that variation in both China's BITs[41] and U.S. BITs[42] are driven more by international political considerations than investment opportunities. Todd Allee and Clint Peinhardt find that the preferences and bargaining power of capital-exporting governments better explain design variation than the capital-importing government's needs to make credible commitments.[43]

The spatial modeling framework from chapter 4 embeds political and ideological concerns with concerns about interdependence. Equation 8.1 gives the utility for country i for adopting a policy p as a function of how far that policy is from the country's ideal point θ_i and the distance between its policy and those of other states (D_{ij}) weighted by the dependence on other states ($w_{i,j}$).

$$U_i(p) = -|\theta_i - p| - \sum_{j \neq i}^{N}((w_{i,j})^* D_{ij}) \qquad \text{(eq. 8.1)}$$

A government's utility increases the closer its policy is to its domestically preferred policy θ_i and the closer it is to the policies of states on whom it depends. The second part of this equation captures the potential benefits of coordination. Large deviations from what a country would prefer to do for domestic reasons are more likely the more a country depends on other states with very different policies. A BIT in this context can be seen as an attempt to decrease D_{ij}, more specifically an attempt to move policies from capital-importing (host) countries closer to the ideal points of the United States and other capital-exporting countries. In addition, BITs have the functionalist goals of providing enforcement when agreements would not be self-enforcing (see chapter 4).

From the host country perspective, a BIT is less attractive the more it requires a shift away from its ideal point. However, this can be offset the more dependent the host country is on the home country. In the bilateral setting, implementing a BIT imposes a policy cost $|\theta_i - p|$. If we assume that the BIT moves policy close to the U.S. ideal point, this cost increases in the ideal point distance to the United States. Yet the cost of not having a BIT is increasing in both dependence on the United States and the ideal point gap: $w_{i,USA}^* D_{iUSA}$. That is, maintaining policies that are far removed from the U.S. ideal point is more costly as interdependence with the United States increases.

The framework posits an interactive effect between ideology and interdependence. Countries that are heavily dependent on the United States may have a greater willingness to depart from their preferred policies whereas countries that are ideologically closer may be willing to sign BITs regardless of interdependence. Moreover, BITs should matter less for ideologically similar countries. These countries can coordinate more easily without institutions. Investor expectations about likely expropriation without compensation are shaped not just by a government's willingness to sign an investment agreement but also by a government's overall set of policy commitments that are reflected in its ideology.

From the U.S. perspective, the biggest utility gains come from commitments from countries whose policies are far removed from its ideal point. Argentina shifted away from the Calvo doctrine. Poland was shifting away from socialism. Getting those countries to shift matters both because they are sizeable countries that make sizeable policy shifts and because these shifts should make it more likely that other countries will also shift (see the second part of equation 8.1). The United States can use its economic might to shift these countries' policies.

EVIDENCE FROM U.S. BIT PROGRAMS

Figure 8.4 shows evidence for such an effect in the context of the U.S. BIT program. The model replicates a study by Adam Chilton.[44] Chilton found no evidence that countries with greater economic interdependence on the United States were more likely to sign BITs faster. Instead, he found that countries that were formerly communist and those that received large amounts of military aid were most likely to sign BITs quickly. This suggests a political interpretation of the U.S. BIT program.

Figure 8.4 replicates Chilton's baseline model but adds the UN ideal point distance with the United States and its interaction with the natural log of the annual U.S. FDI outflows, the key indicator Chilton uses to measure interdependence.[45] In addition, figure 8.4 also includes an analysis with the proportion of host country exports that go to the United States.[46] This measure better captures the dependence of the host country on the United States. In both cases, we expect economic interdependence to moderate the effect of ideological differences.

The model also includes the natural log of the annual U.S. exports to the potential partner country in each year.[47] The appendix also presents models that control for democracy, measured using Polity, and a twelve-point Investment Protection index from the Political Risk Services Group, which both appear to attract FDI according to the literature.[48] The results are qualitatively identical. The model is estimated as a logit model with a third-degree time polynomial.[49] The full tables are in the appendix.

The analysis confirms that countries with similar ideal points to the United States were much quicker in signing BITs. The policy adjustments

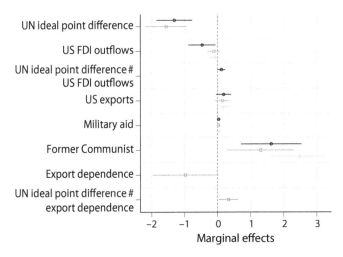

FIGURE 8.4. Logit analysis of signing BITs with the
United States among non-OECD countries.

for these countries were smaller and the treaties easier to negotiate. However, this relationship holds only at low levels of FDI outflows or export
dependence. Figure 8.5 analyzes the marginal effect of UN ideal point on
BIT signing at different levels of FDI outflows.[50] At low levels of FDI outflows, greater UN ideal point distance is associated with a much lower
probability of BIT signing. Yet at moderate or high levels of FDI outflow,
the relationship is no longer significantly different from zero.[51]

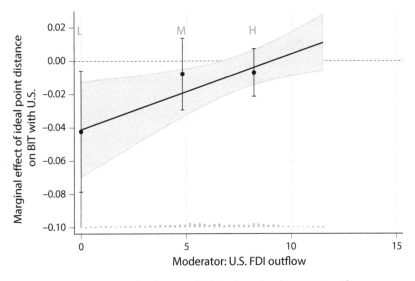

FIGURE 8.5. Interaction between UN ideal point and U.S. FDI outflows.

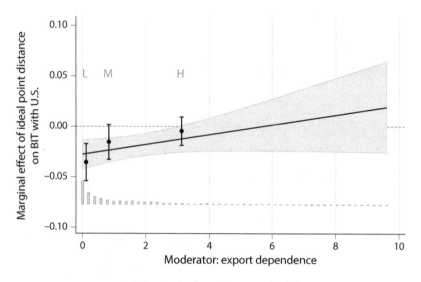

FIGURE 8.6. Interaction between export dependence on
the United States and ideal point distance.

Figure 8.6 demonstrates the same effects for export dependence. Countries with large ideal point differences with the United States are less likely to sign BITs, but this is no longer so at higher levels of export dependence. Economic dependence induces countries to make larger policy concessions, as predicted by chapter 4's framework.

MOVING BEYOND THE DYAD

The theoretical framework offers a natural way to move beyond the dyad. States do not make decisions about whether to engage in a bilateral investment treaty in isolation of what other states have done. The BIT literature already recognizes this point. For example, Andrew Guzman argues that developing countries initially signed BITs because even though they would have collectively been better off resisting, capital-importing countries individually had an interest in making their investment environment seem more attractive relative to their competitors.[52]

This argument nicely illustrates the two sides of international institutions. Even if a treaty is Pareto optimal for the parties involved, it changes the calculus for others, which may make them worse off. Some countries did not initially prefer BITs until other countries had signed on. Moreover, as the number of BITs ballooned, the competitive advantage of signing a BIT disappeared. So we may see countries shifting their policies without seeing very large social welfare benefits. That is, the main effect of BITs could be that it led countries to change policies in a direction desired by capital-exporting countries. Opposition to the BIT regime has mostly come from countries that have been negatively affected by arbitral rulings and where the domestic government ideology has become hostile to the liberal international order, such as in Venezuela, Ecuador, and Bolivia. These countries have started to opt out of the regime.[53]

The second part of equation 8.1 captures this basic logic. The more states shift their policies, the greater the cost for others to remain on the sidelines. The framework thus predicts that the early adopters would be states with similar ideologies to Western states and states with large interdependencies. Yet over time the pressure on others to join grows. Importantly, the second term of equation 8.1 also recognizes that states have fewer incentives to shift as long as a sufficient share of their export market remains ideologically close *and* uncommitted to BITs. The implication is that the presence or absence of economically strong states that espouse alternative ideologies shapes the incentives of all states to join institutions that aim to shift states toward the liberal side of the spectrum. When the Soviet Union was a prominent potential trading partner, states with divergent ideal points had less strong incentives to sign BITs. Moreover, the growth of China as a potential alternative source of trade and investment reduces the incentives of states with divergent ideological preferences to make concessions.

Elkins, Guzman, and Simmons have advanced a related argument.[54] Their primary argument is that host states have incentives to sign BITs when their export market competitors have already done so. This is congruent with the second part of equation 8.1. They conceptualize interdependence ($w_{i,j}$) as sharing the same export market, noting that this is a good proxy for investment opportunities. In their analysis, D_{ij} is the presence or absence of a treaty between a pair of states. They operationalize this through a spatial weight, which is the average number of BITs in force among other host countries weighed by $w_{i,j}$.

Figure 8.7 incorporates this idea in the case of the U.S. BIT program using Chilton's data. The model includes a measure of what proportion of a state's export partners (weighed by export dependence) already have a BIT with the United States. The findings show strong evidence that the more export partners have already signed on (and thus the larger the gap for a state that has not yet signed on), the more likely it is that a state will sign a BIT with the United States in any given year. This also holds when controlling for whether the state already has a BIT in place with another country, which presumably lowers the cost of entering a new agreement with the

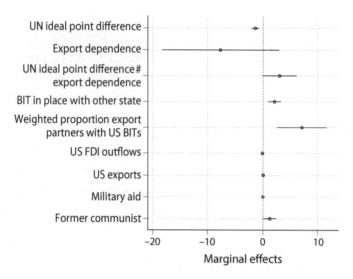

FIGURE 8.7. Logit regression on signing BIT with the United States.

United States. However, a larger ideal point difference with the United States continues to be associated with a lower probability of BIT signing.

The evidence indicates that the attractiveness of a treaty is decreasing in the ideal point distance from the United States but increasing as more states with which the country has strong interdependencies have already signed similar treaties. This theory thus endogenizes that the treaty becomes more attractive as more other states have signed.

This argument also offers a potential explanation for the modest effects of BITs on FDI inflows. Pairs of countries with large interdependencies and similar ideologies can resolve the underlying strategic problem without resorting to strong treaties. BITs may matter more for countries with different ideological commitments, but these countries may also be more likely to violate such agreements given that these governments have different ideas about how private foreign property rights should be protected. For example, Haillie Lee has found that investor claims lead to reductions in investments only in those countries that rarely vote with the United States in the UN.[55] This suggests that investors draw fewer conclusions from single investment disputes when their overall assessment of the country suggests that it is on board with the liberal order.

Renegotiation

The spatial model can also help us understand why dissatisfied states sometimes renegotiate treaties. Yoram Haftel and Alex Thompson argue

that states renegotiate when they learn new information about the consequences of treaty commitments through their experiences in legalized dispute settlement.[56] Yet the spatial model also suggests that renegotiation
should be more attractive when states have diverged in terms of their ideological preferences. That is, the probability of treaty renegotiation should
increase if the two states have grown farther apart ideologically since first
negotiating the treaty. Anecdotally, some governments that have experienced many disputes and have also changed ideologically from the time
they signed BITs, such as Bolivia, Ecuador, and Venezuela, have renegotiated (or exited) more BITs than other governments that have also experienced many disputes but have changed less ideologically, such as Argentina.[57] Indeed, several left-wing governments in Latin America have
rediscovered the Calvo doctrine as part of a more general move toward a
greater role for the state in the economy.[58]

Figure 8.8 tests this proposition more systematically by replicating
model 1 from Haftel and Thompson.[59] The dependent variable is an indicator of whether an existing BIT was renegotiated or terminated in a given
year (from 1962 to 2010). The core independent variable of the original
study is a count of all new investment claims filed against both governments in a given year.[60] The only change from the original model is that it
adds the change in the distance between UN ideal points since the negotiation of the original treaty (lagged by one year). The theory expects that if
the ideal point distance increases, so will the likelihood of renegotiation or
termination.

The model also includes a series of control variables: whether a country
is a new EU member, whether at least one country in the dyad is undergoing a democratic transition, changes in the GDP per capita gap since the
treaty went into force, changes in the host country's FDI flows as a percentage of GDP since the treaty went into force, whether at least one party has
a common law system, and whether they share colonial ties. Moreover, the
model includes a count of how many other BITs the two parties together
had renegotiated up until that point. The main model is a Cox hazard
model, but the findings also hold in probit and (rare event) logit specifications with time polynomials to model the changing risk over the duration
of an agreement. The full results and robustness checks are in the appendix. The main finding holds in all specifications run by Haftel and
Thompson.

Figure 8.8 shows that the main result from Haftel and Thompson
holds: the more legalized disputes respondent governments have been
involved in, the greater the likelihood of renegotiation. Yet there is also

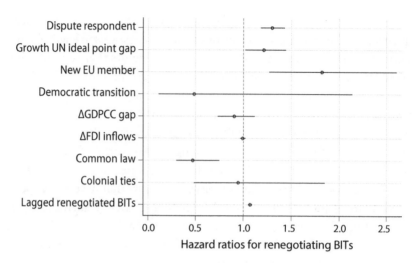

FIGURE 8.8. Ideological change and BIT renegotiation. Source: Based on model 1, Haftel and Thompson, "When Do States Renegotiate Investment Agreements?"

evidence that increasing ideological divergence matters. A one-standard-deviation increase in the ideal point distance in any year is associated with an increase in the probability of negotiation by an estimated 23 percent. That is a sizeable effect.

This finding illustrates how the theoretical framework developed in this book can be used to analyze change in the international system, including resistance to the liberal international system. Most sizeable changes in the global ideology of states follow domestic political leadership changes that alter the support basis for ruling coalitions.[61] There are predictable foreign policy consequences if governments come to power that have very different ideas about the appropriate role of the state vis-à-vis businesses and individuals.

Conclusion

The regime to protect foreign investments emerged from fierce competition in a low-dimensional ideological space over how foreign investments should be protected. The United States and other Western capital-exporting states fought hard not just to protect individual investors but also to generalize the principle that any expropriation should be followed by prompt and adequate compensation. This idea clashed with communist and socialist ideologies but also with postcolonial dependency theory, which influenced ideas about self-determination and freedom from Western influence. Bilateral investment agreements with dispute settlement came about only after it had become clear that the Hull rule could not survive as a CIL principle. Governments that were ideologically closer to the United States were more likely to sign up to BITs. Moreover, growing ideological discrepancies between governments are correlated with an increased likelihood of renegotiation or ending of agreements.

This analysis does not undermine the idea that investment agreements with binding arbitration help states make credible commitments. Yet we should also analyze why states are asked to make credible commitments to a certain set of principles to begin with. Moreover, this perspective offers insight into the challenges to the investment regime.

CHAPTER NINE

Populism and Backlashes against International Courts

How do ideological changes affect backlashes against liberal international institutions? Chapter 6 found that states ideologically sort into international institutions. The preceding chapter found that states whose UN ideal points grew further apart since they originally signed an investment agreement are more likely to renegotiate or terminate that agreement. This is consistent with existing evidence that ideological distance with IGO members correlates with exit from IGOs.[1] Thus, changes in government ideal points along the main dimension of ideological contestation correlate with both entry into and exit from international institutions.

However, not all ideological change corresponds neatly to the main global dimension. For example, the rise of populism is widely perceived to threaten international institutions.[2] This chapter applies the book's conceptual framework to this development with an empirical application to international courts. Chapter 5 argued that ideological contestation can undermine trust in expertise authority. Cas Mudde's widely accepted definition of populism is that it is a "thin-centered ideology that considers society to be ultimately separated into two homogeneous and antagonistic groups, 'the pure people' versus 'the corrupt elite' and which argues that politics should be an expression of the volonté générale (general will) of the people."[3] Populists can be more left or right leaning on socioeconomic issues. Some populist leaders, like Brazil's president Jair Bolsonaro, closely associate themselves with U.S. leadership, whereas others, such as Venezuela's Hugo Chávez and Nicolás Maduro, mobilize against U.S. leadership. Thus, populism runs orthogonal to the main global ideological dividing lines. Yet populists share a resistance to especially the countermajoritarian

aspects of liberalism. Mudde calls populism an "illiberal democratic response to undemocratic liberalism."[4]

This chapter advances two main arguments. First, populism forms an
ideological basis for backlashes against international courts and potentially other expert-based liberal international institutions. Chapter 5 discussed how interpretive expert authority relies on trust and how trust is
subject to deliberate attempts at destruction, especially when the veracity
of the expert messages cannot be verified. International courts with liberal mandates are often set up to protect the groups who are the targets
of populist ire. Investment tribunals, regional economic courts, and even
human rights courts protect property rights, which often favor ruling
elites or foreign investors. Human rights courts evaluate large numbers of
claims from prisoners, immigrants, and other minority groups who may
be the target of populist identity politics. When international institutions
deliver interpretations that protect elites or minorities against whom
there is a preexisting populist mobilization, then populists can charge that
the institution is biased. Moreover, populism offers an ideology for why
these countermajoritarian institutions should not have authority in the
first place. Strong populist movements or populist presidents make it
more likely that governments opt for challenging the authority of institutions over alternative strategies such as (reluctant) acceptance, noncompliance, or avoidance.

This argument implies that backlashes against international courts are
not just about sovereignty. Populist attacks on international courts often
closely track efforts to curb domestic courts. Moreover, the argument implies that leaders may instigate backlashes against international institutions to attract popular support. By contrast, much of the literature assumes that the public constrains leaders from violating international law
and that international courts serve as substitutes for poorly functioning
domestic courts. Within countries there is ideological diversity about the
desirability of liberal international institutions. Some political parties,
media, and civil society groups see international courts not as tools to protect them from the illiberal tendencies of elites but as tools for liberal elites
to cement their preferred policies against the "will of the people."

The secondary argument is that populism is too thin an ideology to
form effective coalitions for effectively reforming international courts.
Since populists vary in their positions along the primary dimension of
ideological contestation, populist concerns about the liberal institutional
order vary greatly and do not form a solid basis for forming new institutions. Selective exit is a more common outcome than effective reform. This

argument bears similarity to the claims about statism. In the present day, ideological opposition to liberalism is thin in the sense that it does not offer a cohesive alternative vision of how international and domestic societies should be organized. Instead, we are witnessing a move toward transactional foreign policies.

The chapter proceeds with an explanation of what the backlash against international courts is. It identifies twenty-eight backlashes that targeted the formal authority of international courts. I then evaluate two explanations derived from existing theories: a functionalist cost-benefit argument and an account that links legalization to democratization and the backlash to democratic backsliding. I then explain the theoretical links between populism and the backlash against international courts. The next section establishes the descriptive claim that a large percentage of backlashes are indeed started by leaders widely identified as populist in the literature. The chapter offers narrative evidence that backlash episodes were often about property rights or minorities who were the subject of preexisting domestic populist mobilization, that leaders used populist rhetoric to undermine a court's authority, and that populist backlashes against international courts often coincide with backlashes against domestic courts over similar issues.

What Are Backlashes against International Courts?

Both the numbers of international courts[5] and their judgments increased markedly throughout the 1990s and the early 2000s.[6] Yet more recently there have been backlashes against investment arbitration,[7] NAFTA dispute settlement,[8] the Court of Justice of the European Union (CJEU),[9] international human rights courts,[10] the European Court of Human Rights (ECtHR),[11] the Inter-American Court of Human Rights (IACtHR),[12] African regional courts,[13] and the International Criminal Court (ICC).[14] There is a good deal of consistency in how scholars use the term "backlash." A backlash refers to government actions that aim to curb or reverse the authority of an international court. Although a court decision may trigger a backlash, a backlash ultimately targets the court rather than just the ruling. Backlash differs from noncompliance or partial compliance,[15] even if systematic noncompliance could undermine the court's authority.

Despite consistency in the overall definition of a backlash, there has not been a systematic effort to operationalize the concept. I offer an operationalization here. A first type of backlash targets a court's general authority.

For example, Zimbabwe succeeded in eliminating the Southern African Development Community (SADC) tribunal.[16] The United States may be in the process of accomplishing the same thing using the same tactic by vetoing new appointments to the World Trade Organization's (WTO) Appellate Body.[17] This category also includes reform attempts that had the clear objective to curb a court's authority, even if these did not succeed. I consider only instances where governments introduce concrete reform proposals. For example, the United Kingdom used its Council of Europe chairmanship to propose reforms whose clear objective was to limit the ECtHR's authority.[18]

A second type of backlash applies only to a court's authority over an individual country. Governments do not always have the option to eliminate a court altogether, but they can typically extract themselves from a court's jurisdiction. For example, Venezuela pulled out of the IACtHR, Rwanda withdrew its declaration granting its citizens access to the African Court on Human and Peoples' Rights, and Burundi has left the ICC. Bolivia, Ecuador, Indonesia, Poland, South Africa, and Venezuela have sought to withdraw themselves from investment arbitration where possible.[19] I also include instances where governments have made explicit and credible threats to exit even if they haven't (yet) followed through. For example, South Africa's High Court blocked South Africa president Jacob Zuma's attempt to withdraw from the ICC. Similarly, British prime minister Theresa May stated repeatedly that the United Kingdom should leave the ECtHR, and the Conservative Party endorsed this policy in its party manifesto.[20]

This operationalization focuses on efforts to curb a court's formal institutional authority. There are other ways that governments may threaten a court's authority. This includes broad critiques that seek to delegitimize a court but that fall short of threatening exit. Including such critiques may introduce bias if critical speeches by populists draw more attention. For example, a speech by Hungarian prime minister Viktor Orbán on the ECtHR may draw more publicity because there is a preexisting concern about the Hungarian government's commitment to human rights. Moreover, it is difficult to draw the line regarding which criticisms do and do not threaten a court's authority. The operationalization also excludes temporary suspensions due to declared emergencies, such as the Turkish suspension of the European Convention on Human Rights in 2016 under populist president Tayyip Erdogan. Finally, it includes only backlashes by members of a court, thus excluding the recent backlash by the Trump administration against the ICC. The theory may well apply to such instances, but I limit the focus of the empirical examination to formal institutional authority.

Table 9.1 identifies twenty-eight episodes of backlash against eleven different international judicial institutions. The table is based on an extensive search of the secondary literature. The online appendix includes more detail and references. The table lists countries from all continents (other than Australia) and includes the world's most powerful states as well as some of the smaller states. This list aims to be exhaustive given the limits defined here. Yet both the literature and events are evolving rapidly, so it is possible that the list excludes some episodes that would qualify.

Table 9.1. Backlashes against international courts between 1990 and 2018

Tribunal	State	Leader	Issue	Strategy	Outcome
ACtHPR	Rwanda	Kagame	Free speech	Exit	Abrogation of declaration giving individuals access
ATJ	Ecuador	Correa	Trade rules	Threaten to exit	Backlash shifted into legal means instead
ATJ	Venezuela	Chávez	Peru and Colombia's free trade agreements with the U.S.	Exit	Exit
CACJ	Costa Rica	Solís	Cuban immigration	Exit	Exit then returned
CACJ	Guatemala	(several)	Civil war crimes	Refuse to appoint judges	Marginal role in the court
EACJ	Kenya	Kibaki	Choice of judges	Reform	Partial reform
ECHR	Russia	Putin	Authority over national courts	Threaten exit	Domestic reform
ECHR	United Kingdom	Cameron/May	Prisoner rights, extradition	Threaten exit, reform	Partial reform
ECOWAS	Gambia	Jammeh	Human rights violations against journalists	Reform	Reform failed
IACtHR	Bolivia	Morales	Domestic interference	Reform/replacement	Failed
IACtHR	Dominican Republic		Granting of citizenship	Threaten to denounce	Unclear
IACtHR	Ecuador	Correa	Freedom of speech	Reform	Failed
IACtHR	Peru	Fujimori	Terrorism	Exit	Exit then returned

Table 9.1. (continued)

Tribunal	State	Leader	Issue	Strategy	Outcome
IACtHR	Trinidad and Tobago	Banday	Death penalty	Exit	Exit
IACtHR	Venezuela	Chávez	Prisoner rights/allegations of imperialism	Exit	Exit
ICC	Burundi	Nkurunziza	Allegations of bias against Africans, political violence	Exit	Exit
ICC	Gambia	Jammeh	Allegations of bias against Africans	Exit	Exit, then returned following ouster of Jammeh
ICC	Kenya	Kenyatta	Electoral violence	Exit, reform	Unclear
ICC	Philippines	Duterte	Human rights violations in antidrug policies	Threaten to exit	Exit
ICC	South Africa	Zuma	Allegations of bias against Africans	Threaten to exit	Unclear
ISDS	India	Modi	Require arbitration in domestic institutions	Exit	Partial exit
ISDS	Indonesia	Widodo	Unfairness of arbitration rulings	Exit	Partial exit
ISDS	Poland	Duda	Unfairness of arbitration rulings	Threaten to exit	Government appears to have reversed course
ISDS	Bolivia	Morales	Unfairness of arbitration rulings	Exit	Partial exit
ISDS	Ecuador	Correa	Unfairness of arbitration rulings	Exit	Partial exit
ISDS	Venezuela	Chávez	Unfairness of arbitration rulings	Exit	Partial exit
SADC	Zimbabwe	Mugabe	Land reform	Blocking appointment new judges	Effectively ended tribunal
WTO	United States	Trump		Blocking appointment of new judges	Unclear

Explanations for Backlash

While there is a growing literature on backlashes against international courts, this literature has not yet developed a general theory of why back-lashes occur. Some of the literature focuses on explaining the success or failure of backlash attempts,[21] outlining the implications for international courts[22] and legal academia,[23] and mapping backlashes.[24] Other scholars develop explanations for backlashes in specific contexts.[25] There are good reasons to do so. Opposition to investment dispute settlement and human rights courts likely has diverse causes. There is no reason to presume that the IACtHR and ECtHR are under scrutiny for the precise same reasons. That said, we might draw some interesting theoretical lessons from examining backlash as a general phenomenon in the same way that legalization and delegation to international courts have been studied in general ways.[26] I draw on the legalization literature to propose two plausible political science theories of backlash: rising implementation costs and a reversal in democratization.

IMPLEMENTATION COSTS

The first, and most obvious, theory links backlash to the rising number of binding international court judgments. Governments should be more likely to trigger backlashes when the cumulative implementation costs increase such that they exceed the benefits of staying inside the regime.[27] It would seem perfectly rational for Bolivia, Ecuador, and Venezuela to limit their exposure to investor-state dispute settlement (ISDS) following large financial awards against them. Chapter 8 already discussed evidence that states are more likely to renegotiate BITs when there have been more ISDS awards against them.[28]

A court "going too far" in the eyes of the target government sometimes triggers backlashes. For example, Russia had minimally implemented ECtHR rulings for decades—paying monetary compensation but not changing policies to prevent future violations.[29] This changed following a judgment that awarded $2.5 billion to Yukos shareholders.[30] The Putin government responded with a new law that grants Russian courts the right to decide whether Russia needs to implement ECtHR judgments.[31] Not surprisingly, the Russian courts found that there was no reason for Russia to comply with the *Yukos* ruling.[32] Yet even in the Russian case, the EC-tHR's most controversial ruling for the public was related to identity—the

2012 *Markin* ruling, which stated that military servicemen cannot be re-fused parental leave when such leave is available to servicewomen.[33]

The cost of implementing judgments surely plays a role in backlash. Yet this theory does not explain why some countries do not engage in backlash when faced with high-cost judgments, why some backlashes are triggered over judgments that are not that costly to implement, and why some of the highest stakes judgments have not triggered backlashes. For example, many states (e.g., Mexico) with large International Centre for Settlement of Investment Disputes (ICSID) awards stay in the system. Some countries, like China and Germany, have responded to adverse rulings by strengthening investor protections rather than resisting the system.[34] Italy has had more than twice as many ECtHR judgments against it as the United Kingdom without threatening exit. In the United Kingdom, relatively easy to implement judgments on prisoner voting rights and extradition spurred a backlash, where earlier judgments on Northern Ireland and homosexuals in the military did not.[35]

One answer is that implementation costs are not just material but also political.[36] This is surely accurate. However, any theory that makes such a claim must specify why some judgments at some times in some countries are politically costly. Without such a theory, the argument becomes circular. We observe high political costs only when politicians vent their rage about a judgment or a court. The proposed link between domestic populist mobilization and international court backlashes is partially an argument about when judgments are more likely to become so controversial that they might trigger backlashes.

DEMOCRATIZATION

Theorists have long linked the growing importance of international courts and law in investment, trade, and human rights to democratization.[37] These theories typically posit that international courts help address a time inconsistency problem. Governments sometimes have incentives to promise that they will improve human rights, respect property rights, prosecute war criminals, and adhere to the provisions of trade agreements. Yet they may also have incentives to violate those promises later. Democratizing states have strong incentives to make credible commitments to international human rights and to "lock-in" democracy.[38] Many democratizing states in the 1990s were also transitioning to market economies. These states often did not have strong property rights protections and needed foreign investment. This provided incentives to sign BITs and commit to ISDS.[39]

If democracy and democratization are responsible for commitments to international courts, then more recent democratic reversals may be responsible for backlash. Populism is often associated with a backlash against liberal democracy. To some extent, the arguments overlap. Yet the credible commitment logic assumes that deviating from international court judgments should be politically unpopular. The presumption is that civil society and public opinion mobilize on behalf of international law rather than against it.[40] International courts are supposed to protect a democratic public from the kleptocratic tendencies of elites. If leaders could gain electorally from defying international courts, then a commitment to them does not make reform promises more credible.

Moreover, democratization theories assume that international courts are a substitute for poorly functioning domestic courts. Countries with well-functioning domestic legal systems have fewer problems committing to protect investor and human rights. Thus, countries with middling domestic legal institutions have the most to gain from committing to international courts.[41] By contrast, the populism argument posits that backlashes against domestic and international courts often go hand in hand.

If governments lose interest in liberalization, then they also have incentives to withdraw from human rights courts and investment treaties. This is an ideological rather than an institutional explanation. If illiberal leaders come to power, then their interest in commitments to international liberal institutions should decrease even if a country still is an electoral democracy. This suggests a (potentially) democratic but illiberal logic of backlash to international courts.

Populism and the International Judiciary

The argument proceeds in two steps. First, populists often identify themselves as involved in a struggle with groups that international courts with liberal mandates are set up to protect. International courts will sometimes come down with rulings that populists can use to mobilize support. Opposing these court rulings can be a source of popularity for leaders who rely on populist mobilization. Second, populism offers an ideology to challenge the authority of a court rather than just the ruling. From a populist perspective, international courts fail to reflect the vox populi both because these institutions are international *and* because they are countermajoritarian.

POPULISM AND BACKLASHES [157]

These two claims operate together. International courts become salient only after rulings fuel preexisting populist mobilization. Without an ideology to challenge the legitimacy of the institution, leaders could challenge a ruling narrowly or refuse to comply. Before substantiating both parts of this argument in more detail, I first discuss the definition of populism.

WHAT IS POPULISM?

There is an emerging convergence in the literature on Cas Mudde's definition of populism as a thin-centered "ideology that considers society to be ultimately separated into two homogeneous and antagonistic groups, 'the pure people' versus 'the corrupt elite' and which argues that politics should be an expression of the volonté générale (general will) of the people."[42] This thin-centered ideology creates some commonalities among populist leaders. But these leaders are also diverse in their thicker ideologies. Chapter 2 argued that ideologies have implications for (1) what is ethically good, and (therefore) what is bad, (2) how society's resources should be distributed, and (3) where power appropriately resides.[43] Populism as a thin ideology is clearest about the third part: the people should rule. Or, as Margaret Canovan puts it, "Populists claim legitimacy on the grounds that they speak for the people."[44]

Populists define themselves in opposition to a corrupt elite on both distribution and virtue, but they differ in just how they do so. For example, Latin American populist presidents of the last two decades have included those who have advocated for more market-oriented (neoliberal) policies, such as Peru's Alberto Fujimori and Argentina's Carlos Menem.[45] These populists attack special interests, such as organized labor or corporatist interests, that prevent deserving people from succeeding. They tend to succeed in inflationary crises when more left-wing policies seem less attractive.[46] But Latin American populists have also included leftist politicians like Venezuela's Hugo Chávez, Bolivia's Evo Morales, and Ecuador's Rafael Correa, who have mobilized around their opposition to neoliberalism and neoimperialism.[47]

Despite their differences on socioeconomic policy, these leaders are united by claims that they were fighting corrupt elites on behalf of the people. Populists also frequently accuse elites of pushing dominant values of tolerance that repress a silent majority. Just who does and does not belong to "the virtuous people" depends on the domestic mobilization narrative.[48] Some populists adopt a full-on nativist ideology. Populists have also used race, ethnicity, gender, sexuality, and other categories as criteria of exclusion. Identity plays a role in most populist movements, although Latin American populism has typically focused more on the material (distributional) side, whereas European populism leans toward a heavier focus on identity.[49]

WHY (INTERNATIONAL) COURT RULINGS SOMETIMES UPSET POPULISTS

International courts are part of the liberal international institutional order. The texts that international courts interpret typically advance core liberal objectives such as increasing civil liberties, advancing the functioning of domestic markets, and promoting the flow of goods, capital, and people across borders. In interpreting their legal texts, international courts often come down with judgments that clash with populist mobilization around property and minority rights. Populists do not necessarily dismiss the ideas of property or minority rights. Instead, populists object to court judgments that interfere with domestic populist narratives about whose rights deserve to be protected. As Jan-Werner Müller warns, populists are not necessarily against institutions, just those that "in their view, fail to produce the morally (as opposed to empirically) correct political outcomes."[50]

Property rights are a core liberal principle and a major preoccupation of international judicial institutions. Most obviously, the purpose of investment treaties is to protect foreign investors from expropriation and other government actions that devalue the investment but violate existing treaties or contracts, even if such actions are popular with majorities.[51] Property rights cases (protocol 1, article 1) are the second most common kind of ECtHR case and regularly feature in the IACtHR. The Andean tribunal primarily resolves intellectual property rights cases.[52] Regional economic courts also have large caseloads concerning the protection of property rights.

Distributive conflict over ownership of natural resources, land, and other wealth is central to populist mobilization in many countries. Property rights is a liberal principle but can also be conservative: it protects those who already own property. Populists have argued that expropriation can be legitimate if the initial acquisition of property by corrupt elites was unjust. For example, many populist movements in Africa have mobilized around inequity in land rights, often in response to heritages from colonial times.[53] In Latin America, left-wing populists have mobilized in opposition to historical inequities in ownership of media, natural resources, companies, and land as well as multinational corporations.[54]

The idea that elites should create international courts to protect them from majoritarianism is not new. Friedrich von Hayek wrote in the final chapter of the *Road to Serfdom* that "an international authority which effectively limits the powers of the state over the individual will be one of the best safeguards of peace. The International Rule of Law must become a safeguard as much against the tyranny of the state against the individual as against the tyranny of the new super-state over the national communities."[55] In the 1950s, French and British leaders on the right, most notably Winston Churchill, actively campaigned for a strong ECtHR and the inclusion of a protocol on property rights out of fear that future left-wing majorities would expropriate the wealthy.[56] As historian Marco Duranti puts it, the ECtHR became "a mechanism for realizing what Socialists described as a discredited conservative agenda too unpopular to be enacted through democratic means."[57] This presents an alternate view of the ECtHR as an attempt not to lock in democracy[58] but to lock in ideological principles.

Liberalism demands that individuals have a core set of civil liberties that states have an obligation not to infringe upon (negative rights) or even an active duty to guarantee (positive rights).[59] The rise of judicial review and the inclusion of human rights in constitutions and international law have contributed to a trend where courts, including international courts, are increasingly asked to offer judgments on what Ran Hirschl calls issues of mega-politics: "core political controversies that define the boundaries of the collective or cut through the heart of entire nations."[60] Examples are judicial interference over the outcome of elections or alleged misbehavior by leaders, judicial scrutiny of core executive prerogatives in fiscal policy, foreign affairs, and national security, and, especially, cases that are about the definition of the polity, such as cases that impinge on citizenship, the status of religion, or other aspects of identity. Hirschl argues that judicial involvement on such politically charged issues "make the democratic credentials of judicial review most questionable."[61]

International courts take part in this trend. The ICC makes judgments about whether sitting presidents have committed criminal offenses. Regional human rights courts have issued judgments about citizenship, religion, immigration, and other issues that directly concern the identity of polities. The CJEU and African regional economic courts have also issued controversial rulings on civil liberties protecting women, LGBT individuals, ethnic minorities, and other vulnerable groups.[62] Investment tribunals do not just evaluate straight expropriation but increasingly evaluate regulations and policies of democratically elected governments, including on identity-related issues such as the habitat of indigenous peoples.[63]

My argument is that not all judgments on minority rights activate populist opposition but only those judgments that fit with preexisting domestic ideological mobilization around these mega-politics questions. Indeed, controversy often arises over the very same issues with domestic courts. For example, in the United Kingdom populist movements center on excluding certain groups of immigrants and criminals from the virtuous people. I will show later that populists were already mobilizing in opposition to British courts that ruled in favor of prisoner or immigrant rights before they shifted their attention to the ECtHR. By contrast, rulings on LGBT rights did not generate a backlash as there was no populist mobilization targeting LGBT people.

International courts are not always maximally liberal in their interpretations. Indeed, international courts have developed interpretive strategies that allow them to proceed with restraint. For example, investor/state arbitral tribunals have adapted the ECtHR's margin of appreciation doctrine to allow democratic states leeway in how they respect property and minority rights.[64] Investors lose many cases where they claim that regulatory actions by democratically elected governments have harmed the value of their investments.[65] Yet international courts are often in a position where they have to decide whether a domestically unpopular minority deserves protection from international law. Many of these cases impinge on some aspect of a polity's identity. In this sense the "judicialization of politics"[66] almost inevitably spurs a politicization of the judiciary.[67]

POPULISM AND RESISTANCE TO THE
AUTHORITY OF INTERNATIONAL COURTS

It is not sufficient that international courts sometimes issue controversial rulings. Governments have responded to adverse rulings through noncompliance, partial compliance, and reluctant compliance.[68] We also need to understand why governments sometimes escalate unhappiness about a ruling (or series of rulings) to backlash.

One explanation, as alluded to before, is that some rulings are simply so costly that exit or other forms of backlash become more attractive. This is certainly part of the story. Yet populism offers an ideology that opposes the very idea that an international court should have authority over issues of distribution, identity, or other matters that fall within the normal provenance of democratic politics.[69] Populist leaders may benefit electorally from attacking the institutional system rather than just the rulings.

As stated before, a commonality among populists is that politics should be an expression of the vox populi. This allows populists to challenge the decisions of countermajoritarian institutions not just as wrong but also as illegitimate. Both left- and right-wing populist leaders have eroded judicial independence in Latin America.[70] The Polish and Hungarian governments have reconfigured their highest courts and limited judicial independence.[71] By contrast, it is not always clear that populism undermines other aspects of liberal democracy. For example, there is a lively debate among populism scholars on whether elections with populist parties increase voter turnout.[72]

The international character of courts matters in two ways. First, it offers an additional ground for populist leaders to attack the authority of an institution based on sovereignty or identity. It is much easier to challenge an institution as unrepresentative of the will of the people if the judges are foreign and take decisions in foreign locales.

Second, in many instances governments do not have the same means to influence international courts. Domestic courts can be stacked with like-minded judges. It is not as easy to stack international courts. In some instances, a government can effectively kill a court if they have the right to veto new appointments. More typically, reforming an international court requires a multilateral coalition. Given diverse thicker sources of ideological mobilization, it can be difficult to amass successful coalitions for populist leaders. Indeed, the empirical illustrations show that populist-inspired reform attempts have at best had modest influence. This illustrates the limits of populism in a multilateral context. It also makes exit a more likely strategy. However, populists do not always follow up on exit threats. Populists may have domestic incentives to issue exit threats, but there could be international benefits to stay within a regime. This again points to the need to consider backlash as a strategy rather than an outcome.

Empirical Evidence

The proposed theoretical link between populism and backlashes against international courts has a range of observable implications. Governments that rely strongly on populist mobilization should be more likely to initiate backlashes. The trigger should be judgments that directly map into domestic populist mobilization narratives over identity or the distribution of property. Populist backlashes should highlight that an international court is undeserving of its authority, which properly belongs to the people. Backlashes against international courts should go hand in hand with efforts to curtail domestic courts. Individual-level opposition to international courts should be correlated with individual-level opposition to domestic courts.[73] Domestic public opinion should not be a constraint but an incentive for attacks on the court by populist leaders. Attacks on the authority of international courts should be especially popular among the supporters of populist leaders or parties.

It is impossible to test all these implications in a single book chapter. They cover different levels of analysis, variation in occurrences of (as well as motivations for) backlashes, and a wide variety of international courts and countries across the globe. I instead evaluate the empirical plausibility of the theory and discuss research designs that may be used to examine individual observable implications more rigorously. First, I examine what proportion of backlashes are indeed initiated by leaders widely considered to be populist. I then offer narrative evidence that at least some of these backlashes follow the logic of the theory.

How Many Backlashes Are Initiated by Populist Leaders?

Table 9.2 lists the backlash episodes from table 9.1 by whether the leader relies heavily on populist mobilization. Despite an emerging consensus on a definition, there is no consensus on how to measure whether a leader is populist. There is, however, a literature on Latin America and Europe with a fair degree of consensus on whether leaders or the parties they represent are populist. The remaining leaders were evaluated based on the secondary literature. There are three leaders for whom the sources gave mixed assessments (indicated by an asterisk): Kenyatta, Putin, and Cameron/May. To be conservative, I characterized all of them on the "not populist" side. The online appendix offers more detail on sources.

Eighteen of the twenty-eight backlash episodes originated from populist leaders. This is purely a descriptive statement rather than a causal or even correlational statement. To start with the obvious, the table selects on the dependent variable. It includes only instances of backlash. Even if we had a dataset of all leaders that coded whether they could be considered populist (or not), then there would still be substantial inferential challenges. For example, the base propensity for engaging in backlash depends on exposure to international courts, which is difficult to establish given that the dependent variable consists of many courts. It would, for instance,

Table 9.2. Populism and backlashes against international courts

Tribunal	Populist	Not populist
ACtHPR		Rwanda (Kagame)
ATJ	Ecuador (Correa), Venezuela (Chávez)	
CACJ		Costa Rica (Solís), Guatemala
EACJ		Kenya (Kibaki)
ECOWAS	Gambia (Jammeh)	
ECtHR		UK (Cameron/May*), Russia (Putin*)
IACHR	Bolivia (Morales), Ecuador (Correa), Peru (Fujimori), Venezuela (Chávez)	Dominican Republic, Trinidad and Tobago (Banday)
ICC	Gambia (Jammeh), Philippines (Duterte), South Africa (Zuma)	Kenya (Kenyatta*), Burundi (Nkurunziza)
ISDS	India (Modi), Indonesia (Widodo), Poland (Duda), Bolivia (Morales), Ecuador (Correa), Venezuela (Chávez)	
SADC	Zimbabwe (Mugabe)	
WTO DSU	United States (Trump)	

be possible to examine whether populist leaders are more likely to renegotiate BITs or leave ICSID following unfavorable rulings.

That a leader is characterized as populist does not mean that the backlash fits the proposed theory. Moreover, there are some leaders who are not populist but have relied on populist mobilization strategies, such as the U.K. backlash against the ECtHR. The remainder of the chapter offers short narratives of individual backlash episodes to examine the plausibility of the theory.

Property Rights

Populists often mobilize around claims that those who control land, natural resources, or other property are morally undeserving of this ownership. They propose either redistribution to deserving others or nationalization such that the people rather than the corrupt elite benefit from natural resource wealth. International court judgments that constrain domestically popular redistribution initiatives have instigated several backlashes.

Land rights have been the most important engine for populist movements in Africa.[74] The populist charge centers on inequitable and undeserving disproportionate landownership by ethnic or racial minorities, often dating back to colonial times. In most sub-Saharan countries property rights are poorly protected in domestic law. This creates incentives for majorities to expropriate minorities.[75] International courts have not had much success in substituting for poor domestic property rights protections.

The most dramatic example is the SADC tribunal, which was eliminated altogether after ruling in favor of a white farmer, Mike Campbell, in a dispute over land seizures.[76] Mugabe described the 2008 ruling as "nonsense, absolute nonsense. . . . We have courts here in this country that can determine the rights of people."[77] Zimbabwe's domestic courts, including its supreme court, were initially receptive to legal complaints from farmers who had been expropriated without compensation.[78] However, in the early 2000s Mugabe's government replaced the (mostly white) judges that had frustrated land seizures with more sympathetic judges, partially in response to protests at courthouses and elsewhere.[79] This was part of a campaign to decolonize the judiciary and return power to the people.[80] The Zimbabwean government could have simply refused to implement the judgment given that domestic courts would surely have not enforced it. Instead, Mugabe's government immediately launched a campaign to delegitimize the tribunal, challenging its legal mandate and refusing to supply a Zimbabwean judge, ensuring that the tribunal did not have sufficient judges to hear new cases. Eventually, his tactics succeeded and the tribunal was abandoned altogether.[81]

The theoretical expectation is not that all land rights rulings by international courts should trigger backlashes but that only those that intersect with preexisting domestic mobilization should. Elites opposed IACtHR rulings in favor of indigenous land rights.[82] But there was no preexisting populist mobilization against indigenous peoples and no backlash against the IACtHR even if governments did not always comply in full and did not shy away from criticizing the court.

A second form of populist mobilization around property rights targets "neoliberalism" or at least the version of it pushed by foreign actors. The clearest examples are the left-wing populist movements in especially Latin America, which have mobilized around their opposition to neoliberalism and its advocates, especially the World Bank, the International Monetary Fund (IMF), and the United States. Elite and foreign control of natural resources and domestic policies are at the center of the local populist mobilization.[83]

The backlash against investment arbitration serves as the most straightforward illustration. It is no coincidence that Latin America's left-wing populist governments, Bolivia, Ecuador, and Venezuela, are the ones that have ended their commitments to ICSID.[84] Bolivia and Ecuador even altered their constitutions to prohibit international investment arbitration. The opposition to ICSID was in part driven by costly adverse judgments.[85] But as chapter 8 already alluded to, it was also ideological.[86] In each country, there was preexisting mobilization against neoliberalism and neoimperialism.[87] These governments had been arguing for some time that foreign direct investment promotes imperialism and hinders the distribution of benefits from natural resources to the people. Venezuela left the Andean Community in 2006, objecting to bilateral free trade agreements that fellow member states Peru and Ecuador negotiated with the United States.[88] Chávez claimed that "it makes no sense for Venezuela to remain in the CAN, a body which serves only the elites and transnational companies and not our people, the Indians and the poor."[89]

Each government preceded its attack against the international tribunals by curtailing domestic courts. A 2011 referendum gave Ecuador's Correa the authority to reform the judicial system and pack the courts with his followers.[90] Venezuela's Chávez reduced the institutional requirements for appointing like-minded judges on courts.[91] In Bolivia, the Morales government introduced direct elections for national judges by the people, which increased confidence in the judiciary among government supporters but decreased overall confidence in the judiciary.[92]

Yet Latin-American left-wing populists are not the only ones who have lashed out at investment arbitration using populist rhetoric. The right-wing government in Poland announced its intention to get rid of BITs, also following (and during) domestic institutional reforms that were widely perceived to reduce judicial independence.[93] India's government led by prime minister Modi passed a constitutional amendment to alter the judicial appointment system, but India's Supreme Court struck it down citing it as a threat to judicial independence.[94] Indonesia's Widodo government is the outlier in that it has mobilized more strongly around sovereignty issues and foreign intervention with its domestic court system, especially over severe penalties for drug offenders.

That reductions in domestic judicial independence and commitment to international investment arbitration appear to coincide is puzzling given conventional theories, which see a commitment to international investment arbitration as a substitute for poor domestic property rights protections (see chapter 8). In this view, then, countries that limit judicial independence domestically should incur the highest cost in terms of reduced foreign investments if they also seek to exit the investment arbitration regime.

Yet the examples presented here suggest that both left-wing and right-wing populist governments have nonetheless been willing to proceed on both tracks, even if exiting ICSID and canceling BITs do not automatically exempt a country from ISDS.[95]

Minority Rights and Identity

A second liberal countermajoritarian task for international courts concerns the protection of unpopular minorities. I highlight four regularities. First, backlashes often occur over judgments that fit preexisting populist mobilization around the identity of the polity. Second, backlashes often coincide with domestic court curbing. Third, populist leaders often believe that their instigation of a backlash increases their popularity. Fourth, populist efforts to reform international courts often fail to garner enough support because local mobilization efforts have diverse thicker ideological roots.

Even though the Conservative governments in the United Kingdom are not populist per se, the British backlash against the ECtHR illustrates all four points and clearly relied on populist rhetoric. In 1998, the United Kingdom passed the Human Rights Act, which incorporated the European Convention on Human Rights (ECHR) into domestic law. This was a relatively uncontroversial act at the time.[96] Its main effect was that British courts could now evaluate human rights claims by British citizens. Inevitably, most human rights cases were filed by prisoners, who sometimes won. These judgments became increasingly controversial. For example, in 2003 the *Daily Mail* ran a populist editorial saying that "Britain's unaccountable and unelected judges are openly, and with increasing arrogance and perversity, usurping the role of Parliament, setting the wishes of the people at nought and pursuing a liberal, politically correct agenda of their own."[97]

Michael Howard, then the leader of the Conservative Party, tapped into this sentiment: "I believe that these are essentially matters for Parliament—for elected representatives, accountable directly to the people—to decide. . . . The Act has led to taxpayers' money being used for a burglar to sue the man whose house he broke into and a convicted serial killer being given hard-core porn in prison because of his 'right to information and freedom of expression.'"[98] Until then, the ECtHR had barely emerged into these public debates. Yet the ECtHR's judgment in *Hirst v. UK* (2005) launched a perfect storm.[99] The court ruled that a British law that banned all prisoners from voting constituted a violation of the ECHR. The plaintiff had murdered his landlady with an axe and was photographed allegedly celebrating his court victory while smoking a joint and drinking champagne.[100]

The ECtHR judgment was not difficult to implement. The U.K. government needed to provide a rational basis for why some prisoners should not be able to vote, such as those who had committed a felony. But when the government proposed such a bill in 2011, it was defeated by an overwhelming majority (234–22).[101] Few parliamentarians wanted to be on the record as supporting prisoner voting rights amid growing populist sentiment. Prime Minister David Cameron, supposedly arguing for the cabinet's proposal, stated during the debate that "it makes me physically ill to even contemplate having to give the vote to anyone in prison."[102]

The negative attention also affected public opinion: whereas 71 percent of the British public supported the ECtHR in 1996, in 2011 only 19 percent believed that the ECtHR had been a "good thing" and only 24 percent agreed that the United Kingdom should remain a member of the court.[103] Some Tory MPs tried to capitalize on this by organizing a parliamentary vote to leave the ECtHR. Richard Bacon, the MP introducing the initiative, stated the populist rationale for stripping away the ECtHR's authority rather than just fighting the judgment: "Although I do object to the idea of prisoner voting, my much more fundamental objection is to the idea that a court sitting overseas composed of judges from, among other countries, Latvia, Liechtenstein and Azerbaijan, however fine they may be as people, should have more say over what laws should apply in the UK than our constituents do through their elected representatives."[104]

The motion received support from only seventy-one MPs and was not backed by the government. Negative sentiment against the ECtHR increased following its 2012 judgment that prohibited the United Kingdom from extraditing Islamic preacher and suspected terrorist Abu Qatada to Jordan for fears that he might be tortured there. The judgment upset then–home secretary Theresa May so much that she argued that "it isn't the EU we should leave but the ECHR and the jurisdiction of its court."[105] Cameron responded, "He has no right to be here, we believe he is a threat to our country. We have moved heaven and earth to try to comply with every single dot and comma of every single convention to get him out of our country. It is extremely frustrating and I share the British people's frustration with the situation we find ourselves in."[106] As a *Guardian* editorial put it, "This strategy allows the Conservative party to bang a populist drum on crime and immigration while blaming foreign European judges— all in one hit."[107]

Cameron used the United Kingdom's chairmanship of the Council of Europe to propose reforms that were "a blueprint for clipping the Strasbourg Court's wings and weakening supranational review of member states' human rights practices."[108] Yet the country was unable to create a coalition that would support the most far-reaching reforms. The final Brighton Declaration was much milder than the initial draft.[109] Moreover, neither the May nor the Johnson governments have not (yet) followed through on the promise to exit the court.

Another illustration is Ecuadorian president Correa's attempt to curb the Inter-American Commission on Human Rights after the commission interfered with domestic legal actions against journalists who wrote about the business dealings of one of Correa's relatives and opened up other investigations into Ecuador's treatment of journalists.[110] Correa framed his reform attempts as part of a struggle against the traditional families that controlled Ecuador's media and the imperial influence of the United States. As Correa put it,

> The thing is that the [Inter-American Commission on Human Rights] creates conflicts. Based in Washington, it thinks that it knows the reality of our peoples and on many occasions it has allied itself with the powers that be, which are part of the problem and not the solution, in the name of the sublime concept of freedom of expression. It is one thing for that to belong to businesses dedicated to the communications media and another for freedom of expression to be turned into a capacity for blackmail and manipulation. I believe that it is a bureaucracy that got used to acting at its own risk; it is heavily influenced by the vision of hegemonic countries who see freedom of expression as free enterprise.[111]

Correa did not want to get rid of the institution altogether but wanted to eliminate "the last vestiges of neoliberalism and neocolonialism" and "look for something that is new, better, and truly ours."[112] Yet the proposal to limit external funding for the commission's free speech investigations and move the commission out of Washington, D.C., failed to gather much support beyond the other three leftist populist leaders that were party to the convention (Venezuela, Bolivia, and Nicaragua).

Venezuela, under Hugo Chávez, exited the IACtHR in 2012 over a ruling that an antigovernment terrorist, who had since moved to the United States, had been treated inhumanely in Venezuela. Noncompliance would have been a viable option. Chávez had stacked the domestic constitutional court with sympathetic judges. The domestic court concluded that the Inter-American Commission on Human Rights was not superior to the

Venezuelan Constitution and that they could hold IACtHR judgments un-enforceable.[113] Yet the Chávez government, which had long accused the court of being a mouthpiece of the United States, withdrew.

The case of the Dominican Republic follows a different logic. The Do-minican Constitutional Tribunal in 2013 ordered the executive to review and retroactively rescind the citizenship of Dominicans of Haitian de-scent.[114] This was a popular measure against a minority group that had long suffered discrimination. The IACtHR found that Dominican ruling breached inter-American prohibitions on discrimination, forcible expul-sions, and a duty to prevent statelessness. The tribunal responded not just by criticizing or ignoring the IACtHR judgment but by ruling that the Dominican Republic's acceptance of the IACtHR's jurisdiction was uncon-stitutional.[115] The Dominican government at the time and the court do not fit the populism label, even if the backlash originated in the kind of identity politics popular with populists.

African backlashes against the ICC have a diverse set of motivations. Especially in the cases of Burundi and Kenya, they were clearly motivated by (the threat of) actual prosecutions against government leaders. This fits traditional sovereignty arguments well. Yet there was also a broader mo-bilization against the presumed anti-African bias of the court, which fits preexisting populist mobilization on identity in some countries.

For example, in the Gambia Jammeh won the 1996 presidential elec-tion after having been one of the leaders of a 1994 coup that overthrew the previous government. Jammeh's populist appeals centered on pan-Africanism.[116] The new constitution vested the power in the president to appoint judges. Jammeh appointed a large number of foreign judges who had loyalty only toward him[117] and curbed judicial independence.[118] Jam-meh launched a failed campaign against the Economic Community of West African States (ECOWAS) Court, in which he was unable to garner support to restrict the court's jurisdiction on human rights issues.[119] In 2016, amid a heated election, Jammeh labeled the ICC the "International Caucasian Court" and initiated Gambian withdrawal from the court.[120] Jammeh believed that such a public campaign, highlighting the court's anti-African bias, would boost his support given his traditional mobiliza-tion strategies. Instead, Jammeh lost the election and, after an ECOWAS-authorized Senegalese intervention, handed over power to Barrow, who reentered Gambia into the ICC.

Similarly, in South Africa, President Jacob Zuma's basis for domestic populist mobilization long relied on anti-Western and pan-African rheto-ric.[121] Zuma has also been embroiled in a series of struggles with a strong and independent Constitutional Court,[122] including over the arrest of the indicted Sudanese president Omar al-Bashir during his visit to South Africa.[123] As mentioned before, the court declared the government's declaration to leave the Rome Treaty a violation of the constitution.

This again illustrates that populist backlashes do not always succeed. Strong institutions can constrain populists. The efforts to form a multilateral coalition in the African Union to leave the ICC en masse failed. Populist leaders do consider the benefits that institutions bring and may not always follow through on threats that are sometimes offered for domestic political reasons.

Conclusions and Implications

The theory and evidence in this chapter suggest that at least some backlashes against international courts were initiated by governments based on preexisting populist mobilization narratives that also played a role in curtailing domestic courts. But there are other reasons for backlashes, including the increase in binding and meaningful judgments and democratic reversals. Moreover, populist backlashes are not always successful. Populism as a thin ideology provides a thin basis for multilateral reform coalitions, making (partial) exit a more likely outcome than reform. Leaders who rely on populist mobilization may have incentives to reap short-term rewards from threatening to exit courts even if they do not immediately follow through. Moreover, some countries have returned to the jurisdiction of international courts after populists were defeated, as illustrated by the examples of Gambia after Jammeh and Peru after Fujimori. These considerations are important if we are to understand the potential impact of populism on international courts and international institutions more generally.

One theoretical implication is that domestic politics theories of international institutions ought to go beyond theorizing about variations in domestic institutions. Ideology is crucially important if we wish to understand why governments (threaten to) opt out of international institutions. I have focused on one type of opposition to liberal ideology—populism—and one kind of international institution—courts. But the argument may well apply more generally given that most international institutions are countermajoritarian from a domestic perspective.

The evidence offered here is at best a plausibility probe. More rigorous inquiries would require new data collection and research designs. They would also have to focus on narrower observable implications than the range discussed in this chapter. For example, it should be possible to examine whether reductions in domestic judicial independence indeed often precede withdrawals from the jurisdiction of international courts or whether populist leaders are more likely to exit BITs or ICSID following negative arbitration outcomes. Another potentially useful approach would be to examine whether judgments on land reform, prisoners, or immigrants indeed create more of an outcry where preexisting populist mobilization on these issues exist. Moreover, the study of public opinion and international courts is in its infancy. We do not know whether voters for populist parties or individuals with populist attitudes are indeed more favorably disposed toward leaving the jurisdiction of international courts. Survey experiments might examine whether populist frames about international courts are indeed successful in persuading individuals. Finally, we do not know to what extent these backlashes are truly independent events or are linked in some way that may create tipping point effects.

Another important open question is what international courts can do about this challenge. Some suggest that courts could avoid backlash by not "overlegalizing" sensitive issues.[124] Courts have developed strategies for this purpose. For example, the ECtHR's margin of appreciation doctrine allows the court to grant governments some leeway in implementing the European Convention on Human Rights. For example, the 2009 *Lautsi* judgment reasoned that an Italian law that mandates a crucifix in each public school classroom violates freedom of religion. The decision caused immediate uproar. President Silvio Berlusconi, not known for his piousness, called it "one of those decisions that make us doubt Europe's common sense."[125] The populist right-wing Northern League, again not exactly a religious party, used local government control to distribute crucifixes in the main squares of villages and to enact bylaws that compelled shopkeepers to display the crucifix.[126] Italian populists argued that the crucifix had become a symbol of Italian identity (rather than religion), with an undertone of excluding Islam from that identity.[127] The ruling also faced the unprecedented opposition of thirteen state parties that joined in amicus briefs.

In 2011, the ECtHR's Grand Chamber reversed the unanimous chamber judgments fifteen to two, arguing that "the decision whether or not to perpetuate a tradition falls in principle within the margin of appreciation of the respondent State."[128] In other words, the ECtHR wrote that it should grant a great deal of deference to states in deciding cases of identity. There is more general evidence that the ECtHR has become more restrained in response to criticisms.[129] Moreover, investment tribunals have adopted the margin of appreciation doctrine and have become more predisposed toward states after withdrawals from ICSID or investment agreements.[130] How judicial bodies respond to increased scrutiny is a promising area for future research.

International courts may not always have enough information to assess the political sensitivity of their judgments.[131] The *Lautsi* case is an example. The initial chamber judgment didn't elaborate much on its societal implications, and there was little attention and no third-party government submissions. That changed for the Grand Chamber judgment. The theory advanced here suggests that the court may have to understand preexisting domestic populist mobilization if it wants to assess whether a judgment may trigger a backlash. Yet judges may not always be in the best position to engage in these types of political judgments or to evaluate whether populist threats are credible. This could lead to backlashes that the judges had preferred to avoid or to overreactions where courts become more cautious across the board in an attempt to prevent backlashes. If so, the implications of populist backlashes reach well beyond the immediate effects of the occasional withdrawals and institutional reforms.

CHAPTER TEN

Conclusion

IMPLICATIONS FOR THE LIBERAL INTERNATIONAL ORDER

Ideology and Multilateralism

The potential demise of the Western liberal institutional order preoccupies scholars of international institutions.[1] The concerns are twofold. First, nonliberal and/or non-Western states are becoming more powerful and are attempting to change existing institutions and create institutions that better fit their interests and worldviews. Second, populist and antiglobalization movements challenge the commitment of democratically elected Western governments to the liberal international order, most notably the United States.

Both of these are ideological challenges. The challengers to the current system have fundamentally different visions of how global society and domestic societies should be organized and how power should be allocated. Multilateral institutions seek to spread generalized principles of conduct. Defenders of the liberal international institutional order worry about the partial collapse of the Trans-Pacific Partnership (TPP), the creation of the Asian Infrastructure Investment Bank (AIIB), the hamstrung World Trade Organization (WTO), the U.S. exit from the World Health Organization (WHO), and the increased Chinese influence in global institutions because they believe that international institutions led by China will produce more illiberal outcomes than those led by the United States or other powerful liberal democracies. Moreover, they worry that the United States and other powerful states may abandon multilateralism and adopt more transactional approaches to settle international disputes.

Yet theories of international institutions have largely omitted ideology. This book has offered a framework that helps analysts think through familiar theoretical issues regarding international cooperation while highlighting the centrality of distributive ideological conflict. The goal was not just to argue that ideology is important but also to make it a tangible concept for applied social science research. Unidimensional models and measures are enormous simplifications but are useful analytic and empirical tools. The dynamic positions of states along a single ideological dimension correlate with a large number of consequential outcomes in multiple issue areas. There is strong and persistent ideological sorting into institutions. This suggests that there is considerable structure underlying state preferences. States often find the same other states on the opposite side of the fence.

The positions of states in this ideological space partially reflect domestic politics, economics, and institutions. Governments typically pursue domestic policies that go in a similar ideological direction as their foreign policy positions. Governments that pursue market-based reforms and privatizations are also more likely to lift capital controls and favor trade rules that bar other states from subsidizing industries. Governments that pursue nationalizations and price controls are likely to be more protectionist and resist international interventionism. Democracies on average have different foreign policy ideologies than nondemocracies. Market economies on average pursue different foreign policy ideologies than nonmarket economies. Left-wing governments systematically pursue different foreign policy goals from right-wing governments. Yet ideology cannot be reduced to any single characteristic. Foreign policy ideology does not always follow from domestic ideology. It may well be the reverse. Governments may be enticed by trade or security incentives to implement domestic policy reforms that take the country in a new direction. More likely, there is a mutually reinforcing relationship. Joining an international institution may incentivize some domestic reforms, which then have international implications, and so on. The key is that policy positions are bundled: understanding how a government positions itself on some issues allows others to form reasonable expectations about preferences on different issues, including issues that are yet to arise. This makes ideology an important basis for multilateral institutionalized cooperation. Multilateralism seeks to spread adherence to general principles.[2] Multilateral politics is at least partially a contest over the desirability of these principles themselves. Multilateral politics can often be understood as an attempt to move the policy status quo in a particular direction in a low-dimensional ideological space.

Throughout the book, I have been careful to argue that not all distributive politics is ideological. There is lots of transactional politics over particularistic interests. Producers entice governments to protect their products from international competition, which may entice liberal-minded governments to offer state subsidies or protectionist tariffs. Governments sometimes compete with ideological allies and cooperate with ideological adversaries. The United States and Saudi Arabia are strategic partners not because they share an ideological vision of how the world should be organized but because they care about the stability of oil production and the defense of their territories. The EU and the United States have many trade disputes over particularistic stakes. The absence of shared ideology makes multilateralism less likely as a form of international cooperation. The relationship between the United States and Saudi Arabia is transactional. The EU and the United States have long resolved their trade disputes through the General Agreement on Tariffs and Trade and the WTO.

Ideological visions often coincide with particularistic interests. The United States defended the general idea that global rules should protect foreign investors from expropriation and sought to build coalitions of like-minded states. At the same time, the United States continues to use coercive tools of statecraft to protect specific investors. Special interest politics and ideological politics often coexist. Nevertheless, they have vastly different implications. Most notably, spreading principles can have system-wide effects in a way that protecting special interests does not. A successful effort by the United States to spread general principles that protect foreign investments has much larger spillover effects than efforts to just protect the interests of U.S. firms.

Moreover, even if the incentives to join institutions are particularistic, the geopolitical implications can often be understood only in ideological terms. The Ukraine vignette that opened this book illustrates this point. Ukrainian producers may well have lobbied the Ukrainian government to join a trade agreement with the EU. Yet that agreement was understood as a move toward the West and away from Russia, with implications for a wide range of foreign policies and allegiances as well as domestic policies and institutions.

Ideologies can be understood in part as a rational response to the costliness of political information. In the context of long-term institutionalized cooperation with multiple partners, ideologies help governments understand the likely consequences of institutional commitments. Ideologies are interdependent propositions about what is ethically good, how resources should be distributed, and where power appropriately resides. The interdependent nature of these propositions implies that moving along the ideological continuum on one issue incentivizes a government to make similar adjustments on other issues.

Multilateral institutions arise from attempts by states to shift the policies of other states toward their ideal points. The more countries shift their policies, the more attractive it can become for others, especially dependent states, to do the same. This means that institutions can affect even states that are not part of the initial coalition that formed the institution. Chapter 6 presented evidence that states indeed sort ideologically into intergovernmental organizations (IGOs). Chapter 7 showed that ideologically cohesive IGOs can ameliorate conflicts with insiders but can exacerbate conflict with outsiders. Joint IGO memberships affect militarized disputes only if the distributional stakes have global ideological implications as opposed to when disputes are purely over particularistic stakes, such as territory.

Chapter 8 showed that ideological conflict shaped the institutionalization of foreign investor protections in consequential ways. If and how foreign investments were worthy of special protections was an ideologically contested question. When the version preferred by the United States and other capital-exporting states threatened to lose out, these states started to use their economic might to shift the policies of others toward their ideal points. States that later shifted their ideal points away from the United States are more likely to renegotiate or exit investment agreements.

Chapter 5 analyzed expert-based institutions in the context of ideological conflict. The analysis showed that ideological conflict creates opportunities for transnational and supranational actors, as long as these experts are able to solve their own coordination dilemmas. Yet ideological conflict also creates challenges. Chapter 9 showed how the rise of populism results in backlashes against international courts.

The theoretical framework offers a way to think about institutionalization rather than a theory of any specific institution. The various empirical chapters are meant as illustrations of the kinds of questions the framework could shed light on rather than as a set of definitive tests that discriminate the distributive ideological perspective from other theoretical frameworks. Indeed, as chapter 3 pointed out, the insights from the distributive ideological perspective are at least partially complementary to other theoretical approaches.

This book's core objective is to highlight the importance of ideology for understanding global institutionalized conflict and cooperation. Much more needs to be done. This book has focused on international distributive conflict while acknowledging that many of the reasons why states pursue ideological directions come from domestic politics. While scholars have analyzed left-right divisions, much more can be done on new ideological dimensions of contestation, including the rise of populism, nationalism, and identity politics. Even internationally, ideological divisions are surely much more complex than portrayed in this book. Not all politics is one-dimensional. And the first dimension on Middle East issues may look different from the first dimension on human rights or nuclear issues. There is ample room for refinement. The modeling framework is also undeveloped. Much of the discussion was informal and tentative. The idea was to offer a way to think through the strategic dilemmas that have spurred the functionalist literature in the context of ideological conflict.

The goal for the remainder of this conclusion is not to declare a winner in a contest of theories. Instead, this conclusion offers thoughts on how the distributive ideological framework helps us think through questions regarding the future of the Western liberal order and how to define a research agenda for theoretically informed and empirically rigorous research on this important question.

Ideological Challenges to the Liberal Institutional Order

The end of the Cold War meant not just the downfall of one superpower in a bipolar conflict but also the virtual collapse of the main ideological opponent of liberalism: communism. As Fukuyama predicted, there has been no new ideology that both challenges liberalism and provides a cohesive alternative with global appeal.[3] Yet this book has highlighted that there are thinner ideological visions that challenge liberalism and the liberal order. These include challenges from rising illiberal powers as well as domestic political movements in liberal states. In some ways these ideological changes amplify each other, whereas in other ways they contravene each other. I highlight four ways in which these ideological challenges may affect the liberal institutional order.

First, both ideological challenges share in large part a view that international institutions should minimize interference in the domestic affairs of states, albeit for different reasons. Among non-Western states the emphasis on nonintervention originates partially in colonial heritage and resistance toward neocolonialism. The concern is that Western-dominated liberal international institutions provide justifications and tools to intervene in poorer, non-Western states. For example, the international financial institutions impose conditions that reflect liberal ideology, investment ar-bitrations privilege multinational corporations and complicate domestic environmental and economic regulatory policies, and the International Criminal Court selectively intervenes in African conflicts.

Populist and nationalist antiglobalization movements in Western states often challenge the undemocratic and cosmopolitan nature of interna-tional institutions.[4] However, they should primarily be understood as chal-lenges to the liberal nature of these institutions. The principles embedded in the WTO encourage job displacement from more developed to less de-veloped states, international human rights law protects immigrants and convicted criminals, and regulatory harmonization imposes foreign ideas in how a society is run.

Liberal international institutions have become much more intrusive and broad based since the end of the Cold War.[5] The radical nature of the transformation in the 1990s is still often underestimated. At the same time that multilateral institutions drastically deepened, these institutions also became much more inclusive in terms of membership. Deepening means both that institutions expanded the range of policy issues on which they pushed a mostly liberal agenda and that the commitments to these institu-tions became more legalized. The WTO expanded its membership, devel-oped its legalized dispute settlement understanding, and extended its sub-stantive commitments to include intellectual property rights, government procurement, and so on. The EU expanded its membership, added a com-mon currency and a central bank, and boosted human rights and other novel policy commitments. Peacekeeping became a set of multidimen-sional activities that included state building and postconflict justice. There are similar examples in just about all issue areas.

This era of institutional innovation has come at the very least to a tem-porary standstill. There is no group of powerful ideologically similar states that can write the rules for the world in 2020. Global institutions are more inclusive, and states with ideal points far removed from those of the United States now have the ability to block attempts to move the status quo to-ward the United States and its allies. In addition, there is much less ap-petite within the United States and many of its allies to broaden and deepen multilateralism.

Both ideological challenges point toward stagnation at best. And as chapter 9 illustrated, they may also point to backlash in some areas. Human rights are an obvious target. Illiberal states have always rejected more intrusive human rights institutions, and much of the populist and nationalist backlash in democracies also targets human rights institutions, especially in Europe. We should remember that inserting human rights into preferential trade agreements, the World Bank, and binding international courts really proliferated only in the 1990s. The Universal Declaration of Human Rights was nonbinding. The UN's global human rights treaties have few teeth. It is not clear that any of these institutions have had an effect on manifestly illiberal states. Instead, most of the literature suggests that human rights agreements affect only democratizing states that want to make their commitments to reform more credible.[6] An institutional order that partially retreats from intrusive human rights commitments may still be more liberal than the order that existed in the 1970s or 1980s.

A second source of ideological contestation concerns the appropriate role for the state in domestic political economies. This is in many ways a continuation of the old East-West conflict. Ideological challengers, most notably China, often contend that economic institutions like the WTO and the International Monetary Fund (IMF) should advance principles that allow especially developing country governments to be more interventionist in their domestic economies. Understanding the ideological context of these struggles may guide empirical research. The ideal points estimated from UN votes should be good predictors of who supports and opposes specific reforms, especially if interacted with interdependence (as in chapter 8). That is, as countries become more dependent on China, more countries with middle-of-the-road ideal points could switch their allegiance over institutional policies.

The COVID-19 crisis may encourage an ideological shift toward a greater role for the state in the economy. The crisis has exposed the vulnerabilities of global capitalism and global supply chains. Governments have had to resort to protectionist measures and border closures in order to manage the crisis. Democratically elected governments have faced severe criticism for allowing national pharmaceutical and other critical industries to disappear due to mergers and outsourcing. Changing this would require government subsidies and/or discriminatory regulations that violate the fundamental principles underlying existing trade law.

Traditionally contestation over multilateral institutions in liberal democracies has taken place along similar lines as the socioeconomic left-right conflict, which is often at least partially about the role of the state and the market in the domestic economy. However, globalization has transformed the ideological space in many democracies.[7] The traditional parties have moved closer together on the classic left-right socioeconomic cleavage. An orthogonal dimension that emphasizes values and identity conflict has become more prominent.[8] In many countries, ideological competition now primarily occurs on what was previously a secondary dimension of ideological contestation.

The transformation of domestic ideological spaces matters for international institutions not just because some, more nativist, parties tend to oppose globalization and international institutions, as discussed above. It also matters because the new cleavage does not lend itself for multilateral coalition formation. The meaning of left-right ideological conflict has strong similarities across countries and directly feeds into global ideological conflict. This means that left-right changes in governments have somewhat predictable consequences for government policies toward multilateral economic institutions.[9] By contrast, value and identity conflict is only partially transnational and may be orthogonal to left-right contestation.[10] It is much less predictable how value and identity-based challenges to international economic institutions will proceed. For example, U.K. prime minister Boris Johnson was firmly committed to the WTO while campaigning fiercely on Brexit.

The difficulty that emerges is that even if there may be very good functional reasons to form new and effective multilateral institutions, or reform existing ones, it may be difficult to organize the coalitions that could create them. The outcome may well be one where states selectively exit institutions while others muddle through with the existing rules.

A third ideological challenge is to the privileged role of the West in international institutions. Challenges to institutional power in IGOs are not just about China (or another specific country) wanting a greater say but about getting non-Western countries a greater say. This creates a basis for coalition formation in a low-dimensional space that might be missed by distributive analyses that focus more narrowly on what each state gets for itself. It yields an empirical prediction that governments closer to China ideologically are more likely to support reforms that give China greater authority, whereas governments further removed from China do not. Moreover, this principle creates resistance in liberal democracies. This has always been the case, but to the extent that nationalism and identity politics have strengthened, this may also intensify opposition to multilateralism that grants a greater say to non-Western countries. Indeed, some right-wing authoritarian parties have made Western identity and civilizational discourses salient features of their political programs.

This gives non-Western states incentives to create new IGOs that replicate functional tasks of existing IGOs but that are organized around alternative principles. This book has discussed regional development banks, the AIIB, and various plurilateral trade agreements as primary examples. Most non-Western challenges to the liberal institutional order are centered on nonintervention and a desire to reallocate authority. The AIIB is an effort to organize a development bank that puts China in charge and that promises not to interfere with the domestic affairs of states. Non-Western challenges to the Responsibility to Protect (R2P) norm center both on the problems of interfering in domestic affairs and on concerns that R2P might institutionalize a form of neocolonialism. For example, Brazil, China, and others are developing principles about "responsibility while protecting."[11]

A focus on ideology may help us understand what is and what is not being challenged. The principles highlighted here offer a more limited challenge than communism ever did. There is no evidence that non-Western states are creating a "World without the West."[12] They are more interested in toning back some of the most interventionist aspects of the institutional system and in gaining influence within existing institutions. States are not lining up to replace the WTO, the World Bank, or the IMF. They are not creating an alternative world order based on principles that are antithetical to the existing world order, even if they sometimes create competing institutions that challenge some aspect of that order.

That said, we are likely to see continued ideological sorting into IGOs that duplicate functions. This may lead to ideological polarization, where countries' membership portfolios start to diverge along ideological lines. This ideological polarization could have consequences for security relationships if the analysis in chapter 7 is correct.

A fourth, and perhaps more fundamental, ideological challenge concerns multilateralism as a form of international cooperation. I have characterized both populism and non-Western opposition as driven by "thin ideologies." They do not offer comprehensive visions of how a good society should be organized. They are united in their opposition to liberalism but not united by a strong vision of how domestic and international political, economic, and social relations should be organized.

There are two sides to this observation. First, organizing around thin ideological principles limits the scope of challenges. It is difficult to form sustained coalitions with extensive agendas based on thin shared principles. For example, the BRICS countries have, despite a lot of attention, cooperated only in shallow ways. Moreover, the challenges are constrained by preexisting institutions. Historical institutionalists are surely correct that precedent and sequencing matter. This doesn't mean that change cannot occur. For example, Phillip Lipscy has convincingly argued that it is much easier to reform institutions in policy areas where states have better outside options.[13] Development lending is an example. Interdependence is pretty minor in this policy area. States can lend unilaterally, multilaterally, or with small coalitions of like-minded states. The ease of creating alternatives makes outside options more credible and reform more likely. In other policy areas interdependencies are stronger and it is harder to organize collectively to alter the institutional status quo.

Similarly, populist and nationalist antiglobalization movements are likely to lead to important individual withdrawals from international institutions but not wholesale efforts at reshaping them. There is an insufficiently thick ideological basis for doing so. Brexit is a good example. The United Kingdom is hardly the only country in which populists have rallied against the EU. In European party systems Euroscepticism is no longer just for fringe parties.[14] Yet there is not enough common ground between these populist movements to build a coalition to reform the EU. The only viable options are exit, defiance, and obstruction. By contrast, there is very little exit from international institutions based on the non-Western challenge.

The flip side is that thin ideologies threaten the very idea of multilateralism. Multilateralism as an attempt to coordinate behavior on the basis of generalized principles requires a thick ideology. States have to understand on what set of interdependent principles they are organizing. In the absence of such an understanding, multilateral politics reduces to transactionalism in which states use multilateral institutions only if these institutions advance their immediate interests. It is not necessarily clear that more transactional trade politics will result in more conflict. It may simply lead to different types of conflicts that are more about specific assets than about the principles that govern the world. A world that moves away from multilateralism would be a world preoccupied with short-term coalitions and conflicts rather than long-term alliances and institutions.

Introduction

1. Ruggie, "Multilateralism," 571.

2. Cox, "Ideologies and the New International Economic Order"; Cox, "Gramsci, Hegemony and International Relations."

3. E.g., Ikenberry, "Liberal Internationalism 3.0."

4. Statement by the president on the Trans-Pacific Partnership, www.whitehouse.gov/the-press-office/2015/10/05/statement-president-trans-pacific-partnership.

5. For an overview, see Voeten, "Making Sense of the Design of International Institutions." Chapter 3 returns in depth to contrasts with the existing literature.

6. Keohane and Nye, *Power and Interdependence*, 10.

7. Kentikelenis and Babb, "Making of Neoliberal Globalization."

8. Risse-Kappen, *Cooperation among Democracies*.

9. Knight, *Institutions and Social Conflict*; Moe, "Political Institutions"; Voeten, "Making Sense of the Design of International Institutions."

10. Moe, "Political Institutions."

11. Dreher, Sturm, and Vreeland, "Global Horse Trading"; Thacker, "High Politics of IMF Lending."

12. Chapter 3 contains more literature review and references. I keep references to the literature at a minimum in the introduction.

13. Chapter 2 details the use of ideology in the literature.

14. Downs, *Economic Theory of Democracy*. There is more detail in chapter 2.

15. Dixit and Londregan, "Ideology, Tactics, and Efficiency in Redistributive Politics."

16. Goldstein, "Political Economy of Trade."

17. Krasner, "Tokyo Round."

18. E.g., Finnemore and Sikkink, "International Norm Dynamics and Political Change"; March and Olsen, "Institutional Dynamics of International Political Orders."

19. The term is from Rosenboim, *Emergence of Globalism*, 33, who uses it in her discussion of Raymond Aron's thought on how the post–World War II order would be shaped by competing ideology.

20. Doyle, "Kant, Liberal Legacies, and Foreign Affairs."

21. Doyle, "Kant, Liberal Legacies, and Foreign Affairs, Part 2."

22. Chapter 7 elaborates and provides evidence for ideological coalitions for militarized disputes.

23. Fukuyama, "End of History?"

24. Ruggie, "International Regimes, Transactions, and Change."

25. Helleiner, "Economic Liberalism and Its Critics."

26. Zürn, "Global Governance and Legitimacy Problems."

27. Downs, *Economic Theory of Democracy*.

28. For good overviews, see Martin, "Interests, Power, and Multilateralism"; Stein, "Coordination and Collaboration."

29. Dewan and Shepsle, "Recent Economic Perspectives on Political Economy, Part II," 561.

30. Again, there are notable exceptions, mostly in the security area, including Morrow, "Spatial Model of International Conflict"; Voeten, "Outside Options and the Logic of Security Council Action"; Reed et al., "War, Power, and Bargaining."

31. Voeten, "Outside Options and the Logic of Security Council Action."

32. Keohane and Nye, *Power and Interdependence*.

33. E.g., Grossman and Helpman, "Protection for Sale."

34. For such an explanation of the WTO, see Carnegie, *Power Plays*.

35. Goldstein, "Political Economy of Trade."

36. Sell and May, "Moments in Law."

37. Davis and Wilf, "Joining the Club."

38. "Clinton's Words on China."

39. Weissmann, "Waking the Sleeping Dragon."

40. Bown, "Unappreciated Hazards of the US-China Phase One Deal."

41. Note that the Trump administration negotiated separately with Canada and Mexico over NAFTA and concluded separate agreements.

42. Gallagher, "Understanding Developing Country Resistance to the Doha Round."

43. Gruber, *Ruling the World*.

44. Walt, "Collapse of the Liberal World Order"; Kagan, "Twilight of the Liberal World Order"; Barma, Ratner, and Weber, "World without the West."

Chapter 2

1. Mearsheimer, "False Promise of International Institutions."

2. This is part of most definitions in the institutions literature writ large (e.g., Knight, *Institutions and Social Conflict*.

3. Voeten, "Political Origins of the UN Security Council's Ability to Legitimize the Use of Force"; Thompson, "Coercion through IOs."

4. This differs slightly from otherwise like-minded institutional theorists such as Jack Knight and Avner Greif who define institutions as equilibria. My quibble is that institutions are not equilibria but efforts to construct equilibria or to coordinate behavior on an equilibrium. Greif and Kingston, "Institutions"; Knight, *Institutions and Social Conflict*.

5. Stone, "Informal Governance in International Organizations."

6. Finnemore, "Norms, Culture, and World Politics."

7. Goldstein and Keohane, *Ideas and Foreign Policy*.

8. Wendt, *Social Theory of International Politics*; Keohane, *After Hegemony*; Mearsheimer, *Tragedy of Great Power Politics*; Waltz, *Theory of International Politics*.

9. Jahn, "Liberal Internationalism."

10. E.g., Moravcsik, "Taking Preferences Seriously."

11. Kahler, "Rationality in International Relations."

12. E.g., Hall, "Moral Authority as a Power Resource."

13. Gilpin, *Political Economy of International Relations*.

14. Kramer, "Ideology and the Cold War."

15. Mearsheimer, "False Promise of International Institutions"; Mearsheimer, "Bound to Fail."

16. Owen, "When Do Ideologies Produce Alliances?"; Owen, *Liberal Peace, Liberal War*; Haas, "Ideology and Alliances"; Haas, "Ideological Polarity and Balancing in Great Power Politics."

17. Glaser et al., "Correspondence."

18. E.g., Jahn, "Liberal Internationalism"; Rathbun, "Politics and Paradigm Preferences"; Weber, *International Relations Theory*.

19. E.g., Cox, "Ideologies and the New International Economic Order"; Cox, "Gramsci, Hegemony and International Relations"; Birchfield, "Contesting the Hegemony of Market Ideology."

20. Le Melle, "Race in International Relations."

21. Hemmer and Katzenstein, "Why Is There No NATO in Asia?" Note that this is an argument about identity, but it could easily be rephrased as about ideology.

22. Jost, Federico, and Napier, "Political Ideology."

23. Converse, "Ideology and Discontent," 206; Jost, Federico, and Napier, "Political Ideology."

24. Based on Hinich and Munger, *Ideology and the Theory of Political Choice*, 11. For overviews of alternative definitions, see Gerring, "Ideology"; Jost, Federico, and Napier, "Political Ideology."

25. Downs, *Economic Theory of Democracy*, 96.

26. Marinov and Goemans, "Coups and Democracy."

27. Cox, "Ideologies and the New International Economic Order"; Gill and Law, "Global Hegemony and the Structural Power of Capital."

28. Fukuyama, "End of History?"

29. E.g., Barma, Ratner, and Weber, "World without the West."

30. Lipscy, *Renegotiating the World Order*.

31. Leffler, *For the Soul of Mankind*; Leffler, "Cold War"; Gaddis, "Cold War, the Long Peace, and the Future."

32. Doyle, "Kant, Liberal Legacies, and Foreign Affairs."

33. Lacher, "Embedded Liberalism, Disembedded Markets."

34. Tourinho, "Co-constitution of Order."

35. Doyle, "Stalemate in the North-South Debate." Much more on this in chapter 8.

36. For a good discussion, see Kahler, "Who Is Liberal Now?"

37. Fukuyama, "End of History?"

38. Fukuyama, "End of History?," 14–15.

39. Freeden, "Is Nationalism a Distinct Ideology?" Note that populism is also often defined as a thin ideology, albeit distinct from nationalism. Mudde, "Populist Zeitgeist."

40. Kasa, Gullberg, and Heggelund, "Group of 77 in the International Climate Negotiations."

41. Xi Jinping, "Working Together to Forge a New Partnership."

42. Narlikar and Tussie, "G20 at the Cancun Ministerial."

43. Stuenkel, "BRICS and the Future of R2P."

44. Huber, "Values and Partisanship in Left-Right Orientations."

45. Rudra and Tobin, "When Does Globalization Help the Poor?"

46. E.g., Garrett, "Capital Mobility, Trade, and the Domestic Politics of Economic Policy"; Milner and Judkins, "Partisanship, Trade Policy, and Globalization."

47. E.g., Fordham, "Economic Interests, Party, and Ideology in Early Cold War Era U.S. Foreign Policy"; Rathbun, *Partisan Interventions*.

48. Kriesi et al., "Globalization and the Transformation of the National Political Space."

49. Mudde, "Populist Zeitgeist."

50. Voeten, "Populism and Backlashes Against International Courts."

51. Hooghe, Lenz, and Marks, "Contested World Order."

52. There is a huge literature on this. See Keck and Sikkink, *Activists beyond Borders*; Risse and Sikkink, *Persistent Power of Human Rights*; Simmons, *Mobilizing for Human Rights*.

53. Hafner-Burton, "Trading Human Rights."

54. E.g., French, "China in Africa."

55. Gaddis, "Cold War, the Long Peace, and the Future," 236.

56. Dougan and Munger, "Rationality of Ideology."

57. Downs and Jones, "Reputation, Compliance, and International Law."

58. Ruggie, "Multilateralism."

59. E.g., Simmons, Dobbin, and Garrett, "Introduction."

60. Tobin and Busch, "A BIT Is Better Than a Lot."

61. Gowa and Mansfield, "Power Politics and International Trade"; Gowa, *Allies, Adversaries, and International Trade*.

62. Gray, "International Organization as a Seal of Approval"; Gray, *Company States Keep*.

63. E.g., Hafner-Burton and Montgomery, "Power Positions"; Greenhill, *Transmitting Rights*; Greenhill and Lupu, "Clubs of Clubs"; Kinne, "IGO Membership, Network Convergence, and Credible Signaling in Militarized Disputes"; Ingram, Robinson, and Busch, "Intergovernmental Network of World Trade."

64. Arrow, *Social Choice and Individual Values*; McKelvey, "Intransitivities in Multidimensional Voting Models and Some Implications for Agenda Control"; Hinich, "Equilibrium in Spatial Voting"; Shepsle, "Institutional Arrangements and Equilibrium in Multidimensional Voting Models."

65. Morgan, "Issue Linkages in International Crisis Bargaining."

66. Voeten, "Clashes in the Assembly"; Bailey, Strezhnev, and Voeten, "Estimating Dynamic State Preferences from United Nations Voting Data"; Bailey and Voeten, "Two Dimensional Analysis of Seventy Years of United Nations Voting."

67. Kim and Russett, "New Politics of Voting Alignments in the United Nations General Assembly"; Doyle, "Stalemate in the North-South Debate"; Bailey and Voeten, "Two Dimensional Analysis of Seventy Years of United Nations Voting."

68. Poole and Rosenthal, "Spatial Model for Legislative Roll Call Analysis"; Poole and Rosenthal, *Congress*.

69. Poole and Rosenthal, *Congress*.

70. Poole and Rosenthal, "D-Nominate after 10 Years."

71. Keohane, "Institutionalization in the United Nations General Assembly."

72. Carter and Stone, "Democracy and Multilateralism"; Dreher, Nunnenkamp, and Thiele, "Does US Aid Buy UN General Assembly Votes?"; Wang, "U.S. Foreign Aid and UN Voting."

73. Gartzke, "Kant We All Just Get Along?"; Oneal and Russett, "Kantian Peace"; Reed et al., "War, Power, and Bargaining."

74. Sweeney, "Severity of Interstate Disputes."

75. Wolford, *Politics of Military Coalitions*.

76. Dreher and Gassebner, "Does Political Proximity to the U.S. Cause Terror?"

77. Alesina and Dollar, "Who Gives Foreign Aid to Whom and Why?"

78. Thacker, "High Politics of IMF Lending."

79. Girod and Tobin, "Take the Money and Run."

80. Koremenos, "Contracting around International Uncertainty."

81. Ward and Dorussen, "Standing alongside Your Friends."

82. Neumayer, "Distance, Power and Ideology."

83. Liao and McDowell, "No Reservations."

84. This is a simple index of voting agreement where abstentions are halfway between yes votes and no votes. This is identical to Lijphart, "Analysis of Bloc Voting in the General Assembly" and Signorino and Ritter, "Tau-b or Not Tau-b."

85. Voeten, "Data and Analyses of Voting in the UN General Assembly."

86. Poole and Rosenthal, "D-Nominate after 10 Years"; Poole and Rosenthal, "Spatial Model for Legislative Roll Call Analysis."

87. In this case, there are two cut-points given that abstentions are a common vote choice distinct from absences. More details are in Bailey, Strezhnev, and Voeten, "Estimating Dynamic State Preferences from United Nations Voting Data."

88. Doyle, "Stalemate in the North-South Debate."

89. Bailey, Strezhnev, and Voeten, "Estimating Dynamic State Preferences from United Nations Voting Data." We used plagiarism software to identify identical resolutions and manually checked resolutions that were more than 90 percent identical to detect subtle but important changes in language.

90. Gladstone, "Trump Administration Defends Cuba Embargo at U.N., Reversing Obama."

91. Bailey and Voeten, "Two Dimensional Analysis of Seventy Years of United Nations Voting."

92. Poole and Rosenthal, *Congress*.

93. Bailey and Voeten, "Two Dimensional Analysis of Seventy Years of United Nations Voting."

94. This is the absolute ideal point distance times –1.

95. E.g., Mansfield and Pevehouse, "Democratization and International Organizations."

96. Marshall, Jaggers, and Gurr, "Polity IV Project."

97. E.g., Gartzke, "Capitalist Peace."

98. Chinn and Ito, "What Matters for Financial Development?"; Gartzke, "Capitalist Peace."

99. E.g., Garrett, "Capital Mobility, Trade, and the Domestic Politics of Economic Policy"; Milner and Judkins, "Partisanship, Trade Policy, and Globalization."

100. See also Bailey, Strezhnev, and Voeten, "Estimating Dynamic State Preferences from United Nations Voting Data."

101. Hanania, "Are Liberal Governments More Cooperative?"

102. Bailey, Strezhnev, and Voeten, "Estimating Dynamic State Preferences from United Nations Voting Data."

103. As measured by Chinn and Ito, "What Matters for Financial Development?"

104. Based on measures developed in Beck et al., "New Tools in Comparative Political Economy."

105. E.g., Voeten, "Clashes in the Assembly"; Mattes, Leeds, and Carroll, "Leadership Turnover and Foreign Policy Change"; Dreher and Jensen, "Country or Leader?"

106. Ikenberry, "Liberal Internationalism 3.0."

107. Doyle, "Kant, Liberal Legacies, and Foreign Affairs"; Ruggie, "International Regimes, Transactions, and Change."

Chapter 3

1. Ikenberry, *After Victory*.

2. Haas, *Beyond the Nation-State*, 6.

3. Saint-Simon, *Declaration of Principles*. See also Craig, *Routledge Encyclopedia of Philosophy*; Mazower, *Governing the World*.

4. Haas, *Beyond the Nation-State*.

5. Carr, "League of Peace and Freedom."

6. Pedersen, "Back to the League of Nations"; Kim, "'Surreptitious Introduction.'"

7. Mazower, *Governing the World*, 192–93.

8. Mitrany, *Working Peace System*.

9. "Petits pas, grands effets" can be translated as "small steps, big effects."

10. Although there is by no means consensus on this. See, for instance, Moravcsik, *Choice for Europe*; Milward, *Reconstruction of Western Europe, 1945–51*.

11. Mazower, *Governing the World*.

12. Haas, *Beyond the Nation-State*.

13. Haas, *Beyond the Nation-State*.

14. Although for a critique see Moravcsik, "Preferences and Power in the European Community"; Milward, *European Rescue of the Nation State*.

15. Haas, *Obsolescence of Regional Integration Theory*.

16. Haas, "Turbulent Fields and the Theory of Regional Integration."

17. Hix, "Parliamentary Behavior with Two Principals"; Marks and Steenbergen, *European Integration and Political Conflict*; Marks, Wilson, and Ray, "National Political Parties and European Integration"; Tsebelis and Garrett, "Legislative Politics in the European Union."

18. Hooghe, Marks, and Wilson, "Does Left/Right Structure Party Positions on European Integration?"; Hooghe and Marks, "Postfunctionalist Theory of European Integration."

19. Tillman, "Authoritarianism and Citizen Attitudes towards European Integration."

20. Moravcsik, *Choice for Europe*.

21. Stone, *Controlling Institutions*; Dreher, Sturm, and Vreeland, "Global Horse Trading."

22. Kentikelenis and Babb, "Making of Neoliberal Globalization."

23. E.g., Alter, "Who Are the 'Masters of the Treaty'?"; Alter and Meunier-Aitsahalia, "Judicial Politics in the European Community European Integration and the Pathbreaking Cassis de Dijon Decision"; Burley and Mattli, "Europe Before the Court"; Sweet and Brunell, "Constructing a Supranational Constitution." For a critique, see Carrubba, Gabel, and Hankla, "Judicial Behavior under Political Constraints."

24. Newman, "Building Transnational Civil Liberties."

25. Posner, "Making Rules for Global Finance."

26. Kaczmarek and Newman, "Long Arm of the Law."

27. Haas, "Do Regimes Matter?"

28. Slaughter, *New World Order*.

29. Fioretos, "Historical Institutionalism in International Relations."

30. Burley and Mattli, "Europe Before the Court"; Alter, "Agents or Trustees?"; Stone Sweet and Brunell, "Trustee Courts and the Judicialization of International Regimes."

31. Carrubba, Gabel, and Hankla, "Judicial Behavior under Political Constraints"; Larsson and Naurin, "Judicial Independence and Political Uncertainty"; Voeten, "Politics of International Judicial Appointments."

32. Hooghe and Marks, "Postfunctionalist Theory of European Integration"; Hooghe, Lenz, and Marks, *Theory of International Organization*.

33. Hooghe and Marks, "Cleavage Theory Meets Europe's Crises"; Rauh and Zürn, "Authority, Politicization, and Alternative Justifications"; Tallberg and Zürn, "Legitimacy and Legitimation of International Organizations."

34. Among the seminal works are Keohane, *After Hegemony* and the various articles/chapters in Krasner, *International Regimes*; Oye, *Cooperation under Anarchy*.

35. For an overview, see Bolton and Dewatripont, *Contract Theory*.

36. Two excellent influential articles are Stein, "Coordination and Collaboration"; Martin, "Interests, Power, and Multilateralism."

37. Koremenos, Lipson, and Snidal, "Rational Design of International Institutions."

38. Koremenos, "Continent of International Law."

39. Koremenos, *Continent of International Law*, 84.

40. Fearon, "Bargaining, Enforcement, and International Cooperation"; Morrow, "Modeling the Forms of International Cooperation"; Drezner, "Bargaining, Enforcement, and Multilateral Sanctions."

41. Moravcsik, "Taking Preferences Seriously."

42. In Koremenos's coding scheme, BITs are not coded as addressing distributive problems.

43. Gertz, Jandhyala, and Poulsen, "Legalization, Diplomacy, and Development."

44. Voeten, "Politics of International Judicial Appointments"; Carrubba, Gabel, and Hankla, "Judicial Behavior under Political Constraints"; Elsig and Pollack, "Agents, Trustees, and International Courts."

45. Voeten, "Outside Options and the Logic of Security Council Action."

46. E.g., Pollack, "Delegation, Agency, and Agenda Setting in the European Community"; Hawkins et al., *Delegation and Agency in International Organizations.*

47. Hooghe, *Measuring International Authority*; Hooghe, Lenz, and Marks, "Contested World Order"; Zürn, "Politicization of World Politics and Its Effects."

48. Bendor and Meirowitz, "Spatial Models of Delegation."

49. Ikenberry, "Constitutional Politics in International Relations"; Ikenberry, *After Victory.*

50. Schweller, "Problem of International Order Revisited."

51. Pierson, "Increasing Returns, Path Dependence, and the Study of Politics."

52. Mearsheimer, "False Promise of International Institutions"; Mearsheimer, *Tragedy of Great Power Politics.* For a recent restatement, see Rosato, "Inscrutable Intentions of Great Powers."

53. These counterpoints are very well and more expansively explained in Glaser et al., "Correspondence."

54. Schelling, *Strategy of Conflict.*

55. Mearsheimer, "Back to the Future."

56. Glaser et al., "Correspondence."

57. Downs, Rocke, and Barsoom, "Managing the Evolution of Multilateralism."

58. Downs, Rocke, and Barsoom, "Is the Good News about Compliance Good News about Cooperation?"

59. E.g., McKelvey, "Intransitivities in Multidimensional Voting Models and Some Implications for Agenda Control"; Shepsle and Weingast, "Structure-Induced Equilibrium and Legislative Choice."

60. Tourinho, "Co-constitution of Order."

61. Shepsle and Weingast, "Structure-Induced Equilibrium and Legislative Choice."

62. Pierson, "Increasing Returns, Path Dependence, and the Study of Politics"; Farrell and Newman, "Domestic Institutions beyond the Nation-State"; Fioretos, "Historical Institutionalism in International Relations."

63. E.g., Finnemore, "Norms, Culture, and World Politics"; Barnett and Finnemore, *Rules for the World*; Johnston, *Social States*; Reus-Smit, "Constitutional Structure of International Society and the Nature of Fundamental Institutions"; McNamara, *Currency of Ideas*; Checkel, "International Institutions and Socialization in Europe"; Meyer et al., "World Society and the Nation-State"; Ruggie, "International Regimes, Transactions, and Change"; Kratochwil, *Rules, Norms, and Decisions*; Hurrell, *On Global Order.*

64. Ruggie, "Multilateralism."

65. Ruggie, "International Regimes, Transactions, and Change"; Lacher, "Embedded Liberalism, Disembedded Markets."

66. Leffler, *Preponderance of Power.*

67. Fearon and Wendt, "Rationalism and Constructivism in International Relations Theory."

68. I briefly discussed the nonpositivist literature in the preceding section. This book is in less direct conversation with that literature.

69. Wendt, "Constructing International Politics," 73.

70. Wendt, "Collective Identity Formation and the International State," 386.

Chapter 4

1. For good overviews, see Martin, "Interests, Power, and Multilateralism"; Stein, "Coordination and Collaboration."

2. Keohane and Nye, *Power and Interdependence*, 8.

3. Farrell and Newman, "New Politics of Interdependence Cross-National Layering in Trans-Atlantic Regulatory Disputes."

4. Keohane and Nye, *Power and Interdependence*.

5. There may be issue areas where coordination works only if states adopt the exact same policies. In those cases, let $D_{ij} = 0$ iff $p_i = p_j$ and 1 otherwise. Or we may have a combination of the two. For example, the high privacy standard country would surely be happier if the low standard country improved some of the way but full trade may still depend on complete harmonization. This can be modeled by taking some weighted average between the two.

6. Switching cost can of course be extensive in some policy areas and can easily be added to the utility function.

7. See for an example of this study of bilateral investment treaties, which will be discussed in more detail in chapter 8. Elkins, Guzman, and Simmons, "Competing for Capital."

8. Rodrik, *Globalization Paradox*.

9. The tie-breaking assumption is that states continue with their status quo policy.

10. Martin, "Interests, Power, and Multilateralism."

11. Arrow, *Social Choice and Individual Values*.

12. Romer and Rosenthal, "Political Resource Allocation, Controlled Agendas, and the Status Quo"; Gilligan and Krehbiel, "Collective Decisionmaking and Standing Committees"; Shepsle, "Institutional Arrangements and Equilibrium in Multidimensional Voting Models"; Krehbiel, *Pivotal Politics*.

13. Hardin, *Indeterminacy and Society*.

14. Shepsle and Weingast, "Why so Much Stability?," 86.

15. Shepsle, "Institutional Arrangements and Equilibrium in Multidimensional Voting Models"; Shepsle and Weingast, "Structure-Induced Equilibrium and Legislative Choice."

16. E.g., Cox and McCubbins, *Legislative Leviathan*; Romer and Rosenthal, "Political Resource Allocation, Controlled Agendas, and the Status Quo"; Krehbiel, *Pivotal Politics*.

17. Farrell and Saloner, "Coordination through Committees and Markets."

18. Johns, "Courts as Coordinators Endogenous Enforcement and Jurisdiction in International Adjudication."

19. McAdams and Nadler, "Coordinating in the Shadow of the Law"; Huth, Croco, and Appel, "Bringing Law to the Table."

20. Farrell and Saloner, "Coordination through Committees and Markets."

21. Farrell and Newman, "New Politics of Interdependence Cross-National Layering in Trans-Atlantic Regulatory Disputes."

22. Gillingham, *Coal, Steel, and the Rebirth of Europe, 1945–1955*.

23. Gillingham, *Coal, Steel, and the Rebirth of Europe, 1945–1955*, xi.

24. Milward, *Reconstruction of Western Europe, 1945–51*.

25. Milward, *Reconstruction of Western Europe, 1945–51.*

26. Riker, *Art of Political Manipulation.*

27. E.g., Moravcsik, *Choice for Europe.*

28. E.g., Sweet and Sandholtz, "European Integration and Supranational Governance."

29. Krasner, "State Power and the Structure of International Trade"; Gruber, *Ruling the World.*

30. Voeten, "Outside Options and the Logic of Security Council Action."

31. Lipscy, "Explaining Institutional Change."

32. Axelrod and Keohane, "Achieving Cooperation under Anarchy"; Oye, *Cooperation under Anarchy*; Martin, "Interests, Power, and Multilateralism"; Fearon, "Bargaining, Enforcement, and International Cooperation."

33. Zürn, "Global Governance and Legitimacy Problems"; Zürn, Binder, and Ecker-Ehrhardt, "International Authority and Its Politicization."

34. Kahler and MacIntyre, *Integrating Regions*; Ravenhill, "'New East Asian Regionalism.'"

35. Kono, "Making Anarchy Work"; Haftel, "Commerce and Institutions."

36. Maggi and Morelli, "Self-Enforcing Voting in International Organizations."

37. Maggi and Morelli, "Self-Enforcing Voting in International Organizations."

38. Ikenberry, "Institutions, Strategic Restraint, and the Persistence of American Postwar Order."

39. Carnegie, "States Held Hostage"; Carnegie, *Power Plays.*

40. E.g., Oye, *Cooperation under Anarchy.*

41. Downs, Rocke, and Barsoom, "Managing the Evolution of Multilateralism."

42. E.g., Ahiakpor, "Success and Failure of Dependency Theory"; Cardoso, "Consumption of Dependency Theory in the United States."

43. Lipscy, "Explaining Institutional Change."

44. Pierson, "Increasing Returns, Path Dependence, and the Study of Politics."

45. Lipscy, *Renegotiating the World Order.*

46. Poast and Urpelainen, "How International Organizations Support Democratization."

47. Krehbiel, *Pivotal Politics.*

Chapter 5

1. E.g., Epstein and O'Halloran, "Administrative Procedures, Information, and Agency Discretion"; Gilligan and Krehbiel, "Collective Decisionmaking and Standing Committees." For excellent overviews of formal models, see Gailmard and Patty, "Formal Models of Bureaucracy"; Bendor and Meirowitz, "Spatial Models of Delegation."

2. E.g., Martin, "Interests, Power, and Multilateralism"; Hawkins et al., *Delegation and Agency in International Organizations*; Johnson and Urpelainen, "International Bureaucrats and the Formation of Intergovernmental Organizations"; Koremenos, *Continent of International Law.*

3. Johnson and Urpelainen, "International Bureaucrats and the Formation of Intergovernmental Organizations."

4. Most rationalist analyses cited in the chapter's introduction explicitly or implicitly use this model.

5. Bendor and Meirowitz, "Spatial Models of Delegation."

6. Crawford and Sobel, "Strategic Information Transmission"; Gailmard and Patty, "Formal Models of Bureaucracy."

7. Gilligan and Krehbiel, "Collective Decisionmaking and Standing Committees"; Gilligan and Krehbiel, "Asymmetric Information and Legislative Rules with a Heterogeneous Committee."

8. Gailmard and Patty, "Formal Models of Bureaucracy."

9. Thompson, "Coercion through IOs," 2006.

10. Donno, "Who Is Punished?"; Hyde, "Catch Us if You Can"; Kelley, "Assessing the Complex Evolution of Norms."

11. Nielson and Tierney, "Delegation to International Organizations."

12. Johnson and Urpelainen, "International Bureaucrats and the Formation of Intergovernmental Organizations."

13. Hawkins et al., *Delegation and Agency in International Organizations*.

14. Johnson and Urpelainen, "International Bureaucrats and the Formation of Intergovernmental Organizations." The specific application here is the design of new IGOs, but the underlying model is a straightforward extension of the general model discussed below.

15. Koremenos, *Continent of International Law*, 85. As mentioned before, only 27 percent of agreements deal with distributive problems in this coding.

16. The framework also suggests a rationale for why transnational experts may influence policy even without explicit delegation (given that even without contracts experts can be influential), although the literature does not often make this point explicit.

17. See Johnson and Urpelainen, "International Bureaucrats and the Formation of Intergovernmental Organizations." Others explicitly analyze how having multiple principals makes it more difficult to hold agents accountable. See especially Nielson and Tierney, "Delegation to International Organizations." I will return to this issue later.

18. E.g., Singer, *Regulating Capital*.

19. In some models, this is a necessary condition for the agent to be willing to exert effort to acquire information.

20. Bendor and Meirowitz, "Spatial Models of Delegation."

21. Bendor, Glazer, and Hammond, "Theories of Delegation."

22. Bendor and Meirowitz, "Spatial Models of Delegation."

23. Johnson and Urpelainen, "International Bureaucrats and the Formation of Intergovernmental Organizations."

24. Hulme and Mahony, "Climate Change."

25. Gough and Shackley, "Respectable Politics of Climate Change."

26. Bourdieu, "Force of Law."

27. Dezalay and Garth, "Merchants of Law as Moral Entrepreneurs."

28. Slaughter, *New World Order*; Haas, "Do Regimes Matter?"

29. E.g., Pouliot, *International Pecking Orders*; Adler and Pouliot, "International Practices."

30. For a terrific overview, see Barrett, *Why Cooperate?*

31. Johnson, "Institutional Design and Bureaucrats' Impact on Political Control."

32. Gilligan and Krehbiel, "Asymmetric Information and Legislative Rules with a Heterogeneous Committee"; Bendor and Meirowitz, "Spatial Models of Delegation"; Bendor, Glazer, and Hammond, "Theories of Delegation."

33. Maggi and Morelli, "Self-Enforcing Voting in International Organizations."

34. Unless the experts are biased in opposite directions. Krishna and Morgan, "Model of Expertise."

35. E.g., Lyne, Nielson, and Tierney, "Controlling Coalitions"; Dreher, Sturm, and Vreeland, "Development Aid and International Politics"; Lim and Vreeland, "Regional Organizations and International Politics."

36. Rodrigues Vieira, "Who Joins Counter-hegemonic IGOs?"

37. Voeten, "Politics of International Judicial Appointments."

38. Johns, "Servant of Two Masters."

39. Downs, "Economic Theory of Political Action in a Democracy."

40. Barnett and Finnemore, *Rules for the World.*

41. See Farrell and Newman, "Domestic Institutions beyond the Nation-State."

42. Alter, "Agents or Trustees?"

43. Thompson, *Channels of Power*; Thompson, "Coercion through IOs," 2006.

44. Voeten, "Political Origins of the UN Security Council's Ability to Legitimize the Use of Force"; Chapman, "International Security Institutions, Domestic Politics, and Institutional Legitimacy"; Fang, "Informational Role of International Institutions and Domestic Politics."

45. Lebovic and Voeten, "Cost of Shame."

46. Lebovic and Voeten, "Politics of Shame."

47. Lebovic and Voeten, "Cost of Shame."

48. Edwards et al., "Sins of Commission?"; Voeten, "Does Participation in International Organizations Increase Cooperation?"

49. Farrell and Simcoe, "Choosing the Rules for Consensus Standardization."

50. See, for instance, Farrell and Saloner, "Coordination through Committees and Markets."

51. Johns, "Courts as Coordinators Endogenous Enforcement and Jurisdiction in International Adjudication."

52. Schneider and Slantchev, "Abiding by the Vote."

53. Hollyer, Rosendorff, and Vreeland, *Transparency, Democracy, and Autocracy.*

54. Abbott and Snidal, "Why States Act through Formal International Organizations."

55. Kydd, "Trust, Reassurance, and Cooperation."

56. Kinne, "IGO Membership, Network Convergence, and Credible Signaling in Militarized Disputes."

57. Hyde, "Catch Us if You Can."

58. Kelley, "More the Merrier?"

59. Lipscy, *Renegotiating the World Order.*

60. Simmons and Elkins, "Globalization of Liberalization."

61. For a more general argument about independence and impartiality, see Abbott and Snidal, "Why States Act through Formal International Organizations."

62. Budescu, Por, and Broomell, "Effective Communication of Uncertainty in the IPCC Reports."

63. Carrubba, Gabel, and Hankla, "Judicial Behavior under Political Constraints"; Larsson and Naurin, "Judicial Independence and Political Uncertainty."

64. E.g., Majone, "Nonmajoritarian Institutions and the Limits of Democratic Governance"; Alter, "Agents or Trustees?"; Thatcher and Stone Sweet, "Theory and Practice of Delegation to Non-majoritarian Institutions"; Stone Sweet and Brunell, "European Court of Justice, State Noncompliance, and the Politics of Override."

65. Alter, "Agents or Trustees?" Other seminar articles on the trustee perspective include Majone, "Nonmajoritarian Institutions and the Limits of Democratic Governance"; Thatcher and Stone Sweet, "Theory and Practice of Delegation to Non-majoritarian Institutions.".

66. Alter, "Agents or Trustees?," 39.

67. Alter, "Agents or Trustees?," 40.

68. Danner, "Enhancing the Legitimacy and Accountability of Prosecutorial Discretion at the International Criminal Court."

69. Kelemen, "Limits of Judicial Power Trade-Environment Disputes in the GATT/WTO and the EU."

70. Gambetta and Hamill, *Streetwise*.

71. Gambetta, "Can We Trust Trust?"

72. Swift, "Honesty and Ethics Rating of Clergy Slides to New Low."

73. Akerlof, "Market for 'Lemons.'"

74. McCubbins and Schwartz, "Congressional Oversight Overlooked."

75. Gambetta, "Inscrutable Markets."

76. Gambetta, "Inscrutable Markets."

77. Swift, "Honesty and Ethics Rating of Clergy Slides to New Low."

78. Voeten, "Public Opinion and the Legitimacy of International Courts."

79. Caldeira and Gibson, "Legitimacy of the Court of Justice in the European Union"; Gibson and Caldeira, "Legitimacy of Transnational Legal Institutions"; Gibson and Caldeira, "Changes in the Legitimacy of the European Court of Justice"; Voeten, "Public Opinion and the Legitimacy of International Courts."

80. Caldeira and Gibson, "Legitimacy of the Court of Justice in the European Union"; Gibson and Caldeira, "Legitimacy of Transnational Legal Institutions"; Gibson and Caldeira, "Changes in the Legitimacy of the European Court of Justice"; Voeten, "Public Opinion and the Legitimacy of International Courts."

81. Voeten, "Public Opinion and the Legitimacy of International Courts."

82. Gambetta, "Can We Trust Trust?"

Chapter 6

1. Pevehouse, Nordstrom, and Warnke, "Correlates of War 2 International Governmental Organizations Data Version 2.0."

2. Lupu, "Why Do States Join Some Universal Treaties but Not Others?"; Koremenos, "Contracting around International Uncertainty"; Donno, Metzger, and Russett, "Screening Out Risk."

3. Kinne, "Defense Cooperation Agreements and the Emergence of a Global Security Network."

4. Davis and Wilf, "Joining the Club."

5. Rodrigues Vieira, "Who Joins Counter-hegemonic IGOs?"

6. Ikenberry, *After Victory*; Ikenberry, "Liberal Internationalism 3.0"; Ruggie, "International Regimes, Transactions, and Change."

7. The data come from the Correlates of War IGO project version 3.0, coded according to the following criteria: (1) An IGO must consist of at least three members of the COW-defined state system; (2) an IGO must hold regular plenary sessions at least once every ten years; (3) an IGO must possess a permanent secretariat and corresponding headquarters. Pevehouse, Nordstrom, and Warnke, "Correlates of War 2 International Governmental Organizations Data Version 2.0."

8. Fukuyama, "End of History?"

9. Lipscy, *Renegotiating the World Order*.

10. Carnegie, "Here's What Will Happen if Iran Joins the WTO."

11. Lipscy, *Renegotiating the World Order*.

12. Bosco, *Rough Justice*; Rudolph, *Power and Principle*.

13. Voeten, "Resisting the Lonely Superpower."

14. Lupu, "Why Do States Join Some Universal Treaties but Not Others?"

15. Poole et al., "Scaling Roll Call Votes with W-NOMINATE in R."

16. The analysis focuses on the post–World War II period. However, the same model also fits the interwar period quite well: a one-dimensional model accounts for 87 percent of IGO membership choices.

17. Bearce and Bondanella, "Intergovernmental Organizations, Socialization, and Member-State Interest Convergence."

18. Bearce and Bondanella, "Intergovernmental Organizations, Socialization, and Member-State Interest Convergence."

19. Hooghe, "Several Roads Lead to International Norms, but Few Via International Socialization."

20. Lupu, "Why Do States Join Some Universal Treaties but Not Others?" These data run only until 2008.

21. UN ideal points are still substantively and statistically significant after controlling for the covariates included by Lupu.

22. Boehmer, Gartzke, and Nordstrom, "Do Intergovernmental Organizations Promote Peace?"

23. Boehmer, Gartzke, and Nordstrom, "Do Intergovernmental Organizations Promote Peace?"

24. Borzyskowski and Vabulas, "Hello, Goodbye."

25. Singer, "Reconstructing the Correlates of War Dataset on Material Capabilities of States, 1816–1985."

26. I use the official UN classification of regions.

27. A border state is defined as either having a land border or being separated by no more than twelve miles of sea. Correlates of War Project, "Colonial Contiguity Data, 1816–2016" (Version 3.1).

28. Mansfield and Pevehouse, "Democratization and International Organizations."

29. Marshall, Jaggers, and Gurr, "Polity IV Project."

30. Mansfield and Pevehouse, "Democratization and International Organizations."

31. Trade data come from Barbieri and Keshk, "Correlates of War Project Trade Data Set Codebook."

32. Gibler and Sarkees, "Measuring Alliances."

33. Donno, Metzger, and Russett, "Screening Out Risk."

34. Mansfield and Pevehouse, "Democratization and International Organizations."

35. Chiba, Johnson, and Leeds, "Careful Commitments."

36. Morrow, "Alliances"; Leeds, "Why Do States Sign Alliances?"

37. Mesquita, "Measuring Systemic Polarity"; Signorino and Ritter, "Tau-b or Not Tau-b."

38. Signorino and Ritter, "Tau-b or Not Tau-b."

39. Kruskal, "Multidimensional Scaling by Optimizing Goodness of Fit to a Non-metric Hypothesis."

40. Chiba, Johnson, and Leeds, "Careful Commitments."

41. Based on classical MDS on the weighted S-scores provided by Chiba, Johnson, and Leeds, "Careful Commitments."

42. Gibler and Wolford, "Alliances, Then Democracy."

43. Gibler and Sarkees, "Measuring Alliances."

44. Ingram, Robinson, and Busch, "Intergovernmental Network of World Trade"; Kinne, "IGO Membership, Network Convergence, and Credible Signaling in Militarized Disputes"; Kinne, "Multilateral Trade and Militarized Conflict"; Hafner-Burton and Montgomery, "Power Positions"; Beckfield, "Inequality in the World Polity"; Kinne, "Network Dynamics and the Evolution of International Cooperation"; Greenhill and Lupu, "Clubs of Clubs"; Greenhill, *Transmitting Rights*; Cao, "Networks of Intergovernmental Organizations and Convergence in Domestic Economic Policies"; Cao, "Global Networks and Domestic Policy Convergence"; Maoz et al., "Structural Equivalence and International Conflict"; Beckfield, "Social Structure of the World Polity."

45. Kinne, "IGO Membership, Network Convergence, and Credible Signaling in Militarized Disputes."

46. Goddard, "Embedded Revisionism."

47. Hafner-Burton, Kahler, and Montgomery, "Network Analysis for International Relations."

48. Pauls and Cranmer, "Affinity Communities in United Nations Voting."

49. E.g., Dorussen and Ward, "Intergovernmental Organizations and the Kantian Peace."

50. Greenhill, *Transmitting Rights*; Bearce and Bondanella, "Intergovernmental Organizations, Socialization, and Member-State Interest Convergence."

51. Greenhill and Lupu, "Clubs of Clubs".

Chapter 7

1. E.g., Oneal, Russett, and Berbaum, "Causes of Peace"; Russett, Oneal, and Davis, "Third Leg of the Kantian Tripod for Peace"; Oneal and Russett, "Kantian Peace"; Boehmer, Gartzke, and Nordstrom, "Do Intergovernmental Organizations Promote Peace?"; Pevehouse and Russett, "Democratic International Governmental Organiza-

tions Promote Peace"; Boehmer and Sacko, "Economic Affinity and Liberal Pacificity"; Bearce and Omori, "How Do Commercial Institutions Promote Peace?"; Mansfield, Pevehouse, and Bearce, "Preferential Trading Arrangements and Military Disputes"; Haftel, "From the Outside Looking In."

2. E.g., Pevehouse and Russett, "Democratic International Governmental Organizations Promote Peace."

3. E.g., Boehmer, Gartzke, and Nordstrom, "Do Intergovernmental Organizations Promote Peace?"

4. E.g., Hafner-Burton and Montgomery, "Power Positions"; Dorussen and Ward, "Intergovernmental Organizations and the Kantian Peace."

5. Mearsheimer, "False Promise of International Institutions."

6. Fearon, "Rationalist Explanations for War."

7. Fearon, "Rationalist Explanations for War."

8. See, for example, Johnson and Urpelainen, "International Bureaucrats and the Formation of Intergovernmental Organizations."

9. Abbott and Snidal, "Why States Act through Formal International Organizations."

10. Bolton and Farrell, "Decentralization, Duplication, and Delay."

11. Boehmer, Gartzke, and Nordstrom, "Do Intergovernmental Organizations Promote Peace?"

12. Drezner, "Power and Peril of International Regime Complexity."

13. Convention on the Prohibition of Chemical Weapons, Syrian Accession.

14. Carnegie and Carson, "Spotlight's Harsh Glare."

15. Boehmer, Gartzke, and Nordstrom, "Do Intergovernmental Organizations Promote Peace?"

16. Hafner-Burton and Montgomery, "Power or Plenty."

17. Martin, "Institutions and Cooperation."

18. Kydd, "Which Side Are You On?"; Kydd, "When Can Mediators Build Trust?"

19. Kydd, "Rationalist Approaches to Conflict Prevention and Resolution."

20. Lindley, *Promoting Peace with Information*.

21. Fortna, *Does Peacekeeping Work?*; Walter, "Designing Transitions from Civil War."

22. Dorussen and Ward, "Intergovernmental Organizations and the Kantian Peace."

23. Kinne, "IGO Membership, Network Convergence, and Credible Signaling in Militarized Disputes."

24. Kinne build heavily on Kydd's theory of how states can establish their trustworthiness through signaling and how trustworthiness may help prevent conflicts (Kydd, *Trust and Mistrust in International Relations*).

25. The literature is massive. Some overviews including various arguments are in Abbott and Snidal, "Why States Act through Formal International Organizations"; Johnston, *Social States*; Martin and Simmons, "Theories and Empirical Studies of International Institutions"; Simmons, "Treaty Compliance and Violation."

26. There is a very large literature on this with somewhat conflicting findings and theoretical justifications (e.g., Polachek and Xiang, "How Opportunity Costs Decrease the Probability of War in an Incomplete Information Game"; Gartzke, Li, and Boehmer,

"Investing in the Peace"; Russett, Oneal, and Davis, "Third Leg of the Kantian Tripod for Peace"; Schneider, Barbieri, and Gleditsch, *Globalization and Armed Conflict*.

27. Bearce and Bondanella, "Intergovernmental Organizations, Socialization, and Member-State Interest Convergence."

28. Gartzke, "Preferences and the Democratic Peace."

29. Adler and Barnett, *Security Communities*; Acharya, *Constructing a Security Community in Southeast Asia*; Risse-Kappen, *Cooperation among Democracies*.

30. Bearce, "Grasping the Commercial Institutional Peace"; Bearce and Omori, "How Do Commercial Institutions Promote Peace?"

31. Pevehouse and Russett, "Democratic International Governmental Organizations Promote Peace."

32. Knight, *Institutions and Social Conflict*.

33. Downs, Rocke, and Barsoom, "Managing the Evolution of Multilateralism"; Donno, Metzger, and Russett, "Screening Out Risk."

34. Statement by the president on the Trans-Pacific Partnership, www.whitehouse. gov/the-press-office/2015/10/05/statement-president-trans-pacific-partnership.

35. Peterson, "Insiders versus Outsiders."

36. Grieco, "Anarchy and the Limits of Cooperation."

37. Bhagwati, "Regionalism versus Multilateralism."

38. Carnegie, *Power Plays*.

39. Similar restrictions apply to some other free trade agreements.

40. Carnegie, "States Held Hostage"; Carnegie, *Power Plays*.

41. www.bscn.nl/sanctions-consulting/sanctions-list-countries.

42. www.tehrantimes.com/index_View.asp?code=248982.

43. Ikenberry, *After Victory*.

44. Russett, Oneal, and Davis, "Third Leg of the Kantian Tripod for Peace."

45. Doyle, "Kant, Liberal Legacies, and Foreign Affairs, Part 2."

46. Drezner, "Bargaining, Enforcement, and Multilateral Sanctions"; Bapat and Clifton Morgan, "Multilateral versus Unilateral Sanctions Reconsidered."

47. Drury, James, and Peksen, "Neo-Kantianism and Coercive Diplomacy."

48. Cao, "Networks of Intergovernmental Organizations and Convergence in Domestic Economic Policies."

49. Snyder, "Security Dilemma in Alliance Politics."

50. Mearsheimer, "False Promise of International Institutions."

51. Mearsheimer, "Why the Ukraine Crisis Is the West's Fault."

52. Leeds, "Alliance Reliability in Times of War."

53. Historically, 40 percent of all militarized interstate disputes include Russia (Soviet Union), the United States, the United Kingdom, or China. McDonald, "Great Powers, Hierarchy, and Endogenous Regimes."

54. Lemke and Reed, "Relevance of Politically Relevant Dyads."

55. Schultz, "What's in a Claim?"

56. Huth, Croco, and Appel, "Does International Law Promote the Peaceful Settlement of International Disputes?"

57. Signorino and Ritter, "Tau-b or Not Tau-b."

58. Voeten, "Clashes in the Assembly"; Bailey, Strezhnev, and Voeten, "Estimating Dynamic State Preferences from United Nations Voting Data."

59. Lupu, "Why Do States Join Some Universal Treaties but Not Others?"

60. Dorussen and Ward, "Intergovernmental Organizations and the Kantian Peace"; Hafner-Burton and Montgomery, "Power Positions"; Kinne, "IGO Membership, Network Convergence, and Credible Signaling in Militarized Disputes."

61. Kinne, "IGO Membership, Network Convergence, and Credible Signaling in Militarized Disputes." Euclidean distance is one often-used measure of structural similarity.

62. Signorino and Ritter, "Tau-b or Not Tau-b."

63. Hafner-Burton and Montgomery, "Power Positions."

64. Graciously shared by Jon Pevehouse.

65. Stinnett et al., "Correlates of War (Cow) Project Direct Contiguity Data, Version 3.0."

66. Carter and Signorino, "Back to the Future."

67. There is some debate in the literature on the wisdom of including such confounders, so I present results both with and without them (Ray, "Explaining Interstate Conflict and War"; Oneal and Russett, "Rule of Three, Let It Be?" For example, it is not entirely clear whether alliance should be thought of as a confounding or as an intervening variable. I bracket that debate and simply note that results are consistent with and without controls.

68. Gibler and Sarkees, "Measuring Alliances."

69. Barbieri, Keshk, and Pollins, "Trading Data."

70. Gartzke, "Preferences and the Democratic Peace"; Gartzke, "Kant We All Just Get Along?"; Reed et al., "War, Power, and Bargaining."

71. Green, Kim, and Yoon, "Dirty Pool."

72. Beck and Katz, "Throwing Out the Baby with the Bath Water."

73. An alternative is that the difference is due to the different sample sizes with fixed effects. I re-estimated the random effects model on the fixed effects sample and found the same result.

74. This coefficient is not significant in the post-1945 period with fixed dyad effects, which is already known in the literature (Green, Kim, and Yoon, "Dirty Pool").

75. Hensel et al., "Bones of Contention." I coded a territorial dispute if the salience was 1, 2, or 3.

76. Pevehouse and Russett, "Democratic International Governmental Organizations Promote Peace."

77. Boehmer, Gartzke, and Nordstrom, "Do Intergovernmental Organizations Promote Peace?"

78. Hafner-Burton and Montgomery, "Power Positions."

Chapter 8

1. E.g., Simmons, "Bargaining over BITs, Arbitrating Awards."

2. In late 2018, there had been over 1,300 cases according to the PITAD database, Pluricourts, University of Oslo.

3. Pelc, "What Explains the Low Success Rate of Investor-State Disputes?"

4. E.g., Jandhyala, Henisz, and Mansfield, "Three Waves of BITs"; Neumayer and

Spess, "Do Bilateral Investment Treaties Increase Foreign Direct Investment to Developing Countries?"

5. Ginsburg, "International Substitutes for Domestic Institutions."

6. Barbara Koremenos's extensive Continent of International Law database codes investment agreements as solving problems of uncertainty, commitment, and enforcement but not distribution (Koremenos, "Continent of International Law").

7. Ginsburg, "International Substitutes for Domestic Institutions."

8. St. John, *Rise of Investor-State Arbitration*; Poulsen, *Bounded Rationality and Economic Diplomacy*; Allee and Peinhardt, "Evaluating Three Explanations for the Design of Bilateral Investment Treaties"; Chilton, "Political Motivations of the United States' Bilateral Investment Treaty Program."

9. St. John, *Rise of Investor-State Arbitration*.

10. Allee and Peinhardt, "Evaluating Three Explanations for the Design of Bilateral Investment Treaties."

11. Poulsen, *Bounded Rationality and Economic Diplomacy*.

12. Lipson, *Standing Guard*; Maurer, *Empire Trap*.

13. Gasiorowski, "1953 Coup D'état in Iran."

14. Gertz, Jandhyala, and Poulsen, "Legalization, Diplomacy, and Development."

15. Maurer, *Empire Trap*.

16. Guzman, "Why LDCs Sign Treaties That Hurt Them."

17. Dawson and Weston, "Prompt, Adequate and Effective."

18. Factory at Chorzów, Germany v. Poland, Judgment, Claim for Indemnity, Merits, Judgment no. 13, 1928 Permanent Court of International Justice Series A no. 17, ICGJ 255, September 13, 1928.

19. O'Keefe, "United Nations and Permanent Sovereignty over Natural Resources."

20. American Law Institute, *Restatement of the Law*, § 102.

21. Verdier and Voeten, "How Does Customary International Law Change?"

22. Shea, *Calvo Clause*.

23. Bonnitcha, Poulsen, and Waibel, *Political Economy of the Investment Treaty Regime*.

24. Maurer, *Empire Trap*.

25. Cited in Maurer, *Empire Trap*, 336.

26. General Assembly Resolution 1803 (XVII) of December 14, 1962, "Permanent Sovereignty over Natural Resources."

27. Doyle, "Stalemate in the North-South Debate."

28. Weston, "Charter of Economic Rights and Duties of States and the Deprivation of Foreign-Owned Wealth International Law of Expropriation."

29. Report of the Ad Hoc Committee of the Sixth Special Session.

30. Guzman, "Why LDCs Sign Treaties That Hurt Them."

31. Salacuse, "BIT by BIT."

32. St. John, *Rise of Investor-State Arbitration*.

33. St. John, *Rise of Investor-State Arbitration*.

34. Vandevelde, "Of Politics and Markets."

35. Maurer, *Empire Trap*.

36. Vandevelde, "Bilateral Investment Treaty Program of the United States."

37. Vandevelde, "Of Politics and Markets."

38. St. John, *Rise of Investor-State Arbitration*, 197.

39. St. John, *Rise of Investor-State Arbitration*.

40. Vandevelde, "Political Economy," 628. Also quoted in Bonnitcha, Poulsen, and Waibel, *Political Economy of the Investment Treaty Regime*.

41. Zeng, "Understanding the Institutional Variation in China's Bilateral Investment Treaties (BITs)."

42. Chilton, "Political Motivations of the United States' Bilateral Investment Treaty Program."

43. Allee and Peinhardt, "Evaluating Three Explanations for the Design of Bilateral Investment Treaties."

44. Chilton, "Political Motivations of the United States' Bilateral Investment Treaty Program."

45. U.S. Bureau of Economic Analysis, "Foreign Direct Investment in the U.S."

46. Barbieri, Keshk, and Pollins, "Trading Data."

47. Based on Barbieri, Keshk, and Pollins, "Trading Data." The export dependence indicator is multiplied by 10 simply to make the scale comparable to the FDI measure.

48. Li and Resnick, "Reversal of Fortunes"; Jensen, "Democratic Governance and Multinational Corporations."

49. Carter and Signorino, "Back to the Future."

50. Hainmueller, Mummolo, and Xu, "How Much Should We Trust Estimates from Multiplicative Interaction Models?"

51. The nonlinear kernel estimator shows a similar result.

52. Guzman, "Why LDCs Sign Treaties That Hurt Them."

53. Langford, Behn, and Fauchald, "Backlash and State Strategies in International Investment Law."

54. Elkins, Guzman, and Simmons, "Competing for Capital."

55. Lee, "Liberal Reward?"

56. Haftel and Thompson, "When Do States Renegotiate Investment Agreements?"

57. Calvert, "Constructing Investor Rights?"

58. Cremades, "Resurgence of the Calvo Doctrine in Latin America"; Polanco Lazo, "No of Tokyo Revisited"; Koivumaeki, "Evading the Constraints of Globalization."

59. Results from the other models are qualitatively similar and available from the online appendix.

60. The other models test variations of this count variable, including lags and moving averages. Those do not affect the finding on the ideal point variables.

61. Mattes, Leeds, and Carroll, "Leadership Turnover and Foreign Policy Change."

Chapter 9

1. Borzyskowski and Vabulas, "Hello, Goodbye."

2. Copelovitch and Pevehouse, "International Organizations in a New Era of Populist Nationalism."

3. Mudde, "Populist Zeitgeist," 543.

4. Mudde, "Populist Zeitgeist."

5. I am going to use the term "court" liberally to include all international judicial institutions with binding legal authority, including investment arbitration and the WTO's Dispute Settlement Understanding.

6. Alter, *New Terrain of International Law.*

7. Waibel, *Backlash against Investment Arbitration*; Caron and Shirlow, "Dissecting Backlash."

8. Krueger, "Combat Zone."

9. Alter, "European Union's Legal System and Domestic Policy."

10. Sandholtz, Bei, and Caldwell, "Backlash and International Human Rights Courts."

11. Madsen, "Challenging Authority of the European Court of Human Rights."

12. Helfer, "Overlegalizing Human Rights."

13. Alter, Gathii, and Helfer, "Backlash against International Courts in West, East and Southern Africa."

14. Helfer and Showalter, "Opposing International Justice."

15. Hawkins and Jacoby, "Partial Compliance"; Hillebrecht, *Domestic Politics and International Human Rights Tribunals.*

16. Alter, Gathii, and Helfer, "Backlash against International Courts in West, East and Southern Africa."

17. Shaffer, Elsig, and Pollack, "U.S. Threats to the WTO Appellate Body."

18. Helfer, "Burdens and Benefits of Brighton."

19. Peinhardt and Wellhausen, "Withdrawing from Investment Treaties but Protecting Investment."

20. I exclude Brexit as the U.K. government did not endorse leaving the EU and it is not clear that Brexit was about the CJEU. However, there is a large literature that links the Brexit referendum with populism (e.g., Inglehart and Norris, "Trump, Brexit, and the Rise of Populism").

21. Alter, Gathii, and Helfer, "Backlash against International Courts in West, East and Southern Africa"; Alter and Helfer, *Authority of the Andean Tribunal of Justice in a Time of Regional Political Crisis.*

22. Helfer, "Populism and International Human Rights Institutions."

23. Posner, "Liberal Internationalism and the Populist Backlash Symposium."

24. Madsen, Cebulak, and Wiebusch, "Backlash against International Courts."

25. Sandholtz, Bei, and Caldwell, "Backlash and International Human Rights Courts"; Alter, Gathii, and Helfer, "Backlash against International Courts in West, East and Southern Africa."

26. Goldstein, *Legalization and World Politics.*

27. Sandholtz, Bei, and Caldwell, "Backlash and International Human Rights Courts"; Abebe and Ginsburg, "Dejudicialization of International Politics?"

28. Haftel and Thompson, "When Do States Renegotiate Investment Agreements?"

29. Hillebrecht, *Domestic Politics and International Human Rights Tribunals.*

30. *OAO Neftyanaya Kompaniya Yukos v. Russia*, Application No. 14902/04, Judgment (just satisfaction), July 31, 2014, http://hudoc.echr.coe.int/sites/eng/pages /search.aspx?i=001-145730.

31. Sims, "Vladimir Putin Signs Law Allowing Russia to Ignore International Human Rights Rulings."

32. Netesova and Taussig, "Putin's No Populist, but He Can Gain from Populist Movements Worldwide."

33. Zwart, "More Human Rights Than Court."

34. Haftel and Thompson, "When Do States Renegotiate Investment Agreements?"

35. McNulty, Watson, and Philo, "Human Rights and Prisoners' Rights."

36. Sandholtz, Bei, and Caldwell, "Backlash and International Human Rights Courts."

37. Moravcsik, "Origins of Human Rights Regimes"; Simmons, *Mobilizing for Human Rights*; Simmons and Danner, "Credible Commitments and the International Criminal Court"; Mansfield, Milner, and Rosendorff, "Why Democracies Cooperate More"; Jandhyala, Henisz, and Mansfield, "Three Waves of BITs."

38. Moravcsik, "Origins of Human Rights Regimes."

39. Jandhyala, Henisz, and Mansfield, "Three Waves of BITs."

40. Simmons, *Mobilizing for Human Rights*.

41. Moravcsik, "Origins of Human Rights Regimes"; Simmons and Danner, "Credible Commitments and the International Criminal Court."

42. Mudde, "Populist Zeitgeist," 543.

43. Hinich and Munger, *Ideology and the Theory of Political Choice*, 11.

44. Canovan, "Trust the People!"

45. Weyland, "Neoliberal Populism in Latin America and Eastern Europe"; Roberts, "Neoliberalism and the Transformation of Populism in Latin America."

46. Weyland, "Neoliberal Populism in Latin America and Eastern Europe."

47. Mudde and Kaltwasser, *Populism in Europe and the Americas*.

48. Müller, *What Is Populism?*

49. Mudde and Kaltwasser, "Exclusionary vs. Inclusionary Populism."

50. Müller, "Populist Constitutions."

51. Pelc, "What Explains the Low Success Rate of Investor-State Disputes?"

52. Alter and Helfer, "Nature or Nurture?"

53. Boone, "Electoral Populism Where Property Rights Are Weak."

54. French, "Understanding the Politics of Latin America's Plural Lefts (Chávez/Lula)."

55. Hayek, *Road to Serfdom*, 235.

56. Duranti, *Conservative Human Rights Revolution*.

57. Duranti, *Conservative Human Rights Revolution*, 7.

58. Moravcsik, "Origins of Human Rights Regimes."

59. Elster, "On Majoritarianism and Rights."

60. Hirschl, "Judicialization of Mega-Politics and the Rise of Political Courts," 98.

61. Hirschl, "Judicialization of Mega-Politics and the Rise of Political Courts," 99.

62. Cichowski, "Women's Rights, the European Court, and Supranational Constitutionalism"; Alter, Helfer, and McAllister, "New International Human Rights Court for West Africa."

63. Pelc, "What Explains the Low Success Rate of Investor-State Disputes?"

64. Alvarez, "Use (and Misuse) of European Human Rights Law in Investor-State Dispute Settlement."

65. Pelc, "What Explains the Low Success Rate of Investor-State Disputes?"

66. Stone Sweet and Brunell, "Trustee Courts and the Judicialization of International Regimes."

67. Ferejohn, "Judicializing Politics, Politicizing Law."

68. Hillebrecht, *Domestic Politics and International Human Rights Tribunals*; Hawkins and Jacoby, "Partial Compliance."

69. This objection does not necessarily translate to courts that primarily resolve interstate disputes, which cannot always be resolved through democratic politics.

70. Houle and Kenny, "Political and Economic Consequences of Populist Rule in Latin America."

71. Bugaric and Kuhelj, "Varieties of Populism in Europe."

72. Huber and Ruth, "Mind the Gap!"

73. Voeten, "Public Opinion and the Legitimacy of International Courts."

74. Boone, "Electoral Populism Where Property Rights Are Weak."

75. Boone, "Electoral Populism Where Property Rights Are Weak."

76. Alter, Gathii, and Helfer, "Backlash against International Courts in West, East and Southern Africa."

77. "Mugabe Says Zimbabwe Land Seizures Will Continue." Also quoted in Alter, Gathii, and Helfer, "Backlash against International Courts in West, East and Southern Africa."

78. Thomas, "Land Reform in Zimbabwe."

79. Meredith, *Mugabe*.

80. Madinah, "Did He Jump, or Was He Pushed?"

81. Alter, Gathii, and Helfer, "Backlash against International Courts in West, East and Southern Africa."

82. Amiott, "Environment, Equality, and Indigenous Peoples' Land Rights in the Inter-American Human Rights System."

83. Castaneda, "Latin America's Left Turn Essay."

84. Waibel, *Backlash against Investment Arbitration*.

85. Haftel and Thompson, "When Do States Renegotiate Investment Agreements?"

86. Vincentelli, "Uncertain Future of ICSID in Latin America."

87. Ellner, "Distinguishing Features of Latin America's New Left in Power."

88. Alter and Helfer, *Authority of the Andean Tribunal of Justice in a Time of Regional Political Crisis*. Correa also threatened to leave the Andean Community in 2015 over unfavorable Andean Tribunal of Justice rulings regarding free trade, although it is not yet clear how this dispute will turn out.

89. Malamud, "Venezuela's Withdrawal from the Andean Community of Nations and the Consequences for Regional Integration."

90. Torre, "Technocratic Populism in Ecuador."

91. Hawkins, "Is Chávez Populist?"

92. Driscoll and Nelson, "Judicial Selection and the Democratization of Justice."

93. Orecki, "Bye-Bye BITs?"

94. Sen, "India's Democracy at 70."

95. Peinhardt and Wellhausen, "Withdrawing from Investment Treaties but Protecting Investment."

96. Ewing, "Human Rights Act and Parliamentary Democracy."

97. Greenhill, "So What Have Our Judges Against Britain?"

98. "Judges Must Bow to the Will of Parliament."

99. Murray, "Perfect Storm."

100. McNulty, Watson, and Philo, "Human Rights and Prisoners' Rights."

101. McNulty, Watson, and Philo, "Human Rights and Prisoners' Rights."

102. Hough, "Prisoner Vote."

103. Voeten, "Public Opinion and the Legitimacy of International Courts," 418.

104. Ross, "Tories Vote to Scrap 'Undemocratic' Human Rights Act."

105. Asthana and Mason, "UK Must Leave European Convention on Human Rights, Says Theresa May."

106. "Abu Qatada Case Is Reason to Change Human Rights Laws, Says Justice Secretary."

107. "Grieve, Clarke and Green Were Last Protectors of Our Human Rights Laws."

108. Helfer, "Burdens and Benefits of Brighton."

109. Madsen, "Challenging Authority of the European Court of Human Rights."

110. "Thorny Human Rights Reform Put Off at OAS Meeting."

111. "Ecuadoran President Interviewed on Regional Human Rights Body."

112. "Correa Calls for New Inter-American Human Rights System."

113. Huneeus, "Courts Resisting Courts."

114. Shelton and Huneeus, "In Re Direct Action of Unconstitutionality Initiated Against the Declaration of Acceptance of the Jurisdiction of the Inter-American Court of Human Rights."

115. Shelton and Huneeus, "In Re Direct Action of Unconstitutionality Initiated Against the Declaration of Acceptance of the Jurisdiction of the Inter-American Court of Human Rights."

116. Ihonvbere and Mbaku, *Political Liberalization and Democratization in Africa.*

117. Saine, "Gambia's 'Elected Autocrat Poverty, Peripherality, and Political Instability,' 1994–2006."

118. Perfect, "Gambia under Yahya Jammeh."

119. Alter, Gathii, and Helfer, "Backlash against International Courts in West, East and Southern Africa."

120. Sandholtz, Bei, and Caldwell, "Backlash and International Human Rights Courts."

121. Guha, "Jacob Zuma."

122. Parpworth, "South African Constitutional Court."

123. Boehme, "'We Chose Africa.'"

124. Helfer, "Overlegalizing Human Rights."

125. Quoted in Mancini, "Crucifix Rage," 6.

126. Mancini, "Crucifix Rage."

127. The Lautsi case was filed by a Finnish immigrant (an atheist), but similar cases were pursued by Muslims.

128. *Lautsi and others v. Italy*, app. no. 30814/06, European Court of Human Rights, Grand Chamber, March 18, 2011.

129. Stiansen and Voeten, "Backlash and Judicial Restraint."

130. Langford and Behn, "Managing Backlash."

131. Lupu, "International Judicial Legitimacy."

Chapter 10

1. E.g., Barma, Ratner, and Weber, "World without the West"; Colgan and Keohane, "Liberal Order Is Rigged"; Ikenberry, "End of Liberal International Order?"; Nye, "Will the Liberal Order Survive."

2. Ruggie, "Multilateralism."

3. Fukuyama, "End of History?"

4. E.g., Hooghe, Lenz, and Marks, "Contested World Order"; Hobolt, "Brexit Vote"; Helfer, "Populism and International Human Rights Institutions."

5. Zürn, "Global Governance and Legitimacy Problems."

6. Simmons and Danner, "Credible Commitments and the International Criminal Court"; Simmons, *Mobilizing for Human Rights.*

7. Kriesi et al., "Globalization and the Transformation of the National Political Space."

8. Hooghe and Marks, "Cleavage Theory Meets Europe's Crises"; Norris, *Cultural Backlash.*

9. Milner, "Globalization, Development, and International Institutions."

10. Hooghe and Marks, "Cleavage Theory Meets Europe's Crises."

11. Tourinho, Stuenkel, and Brockmeier, "'Responsibility while Protecting.'"

12. Barma, Ratner, and Weber, "World without the West."

13. Lipscy, "Explaining Institutional Change"; Lipscy, *Renegotiating the World Order.*

14. Brack and Startin, "Introduction."

Abbott, Kenneth W., and Duncan Snidal. "Why States Act through Formal International Organizations." *Journal of Conflict Resolution* 42, no. 1 (February 1, 1998): 3–32.

Abebe, Daniel, and Tom Ginsburg. "The Dejudicialization of International Politics?" *International Studies Quarterly* 63, no. 3 (2019): 521–30.

"Abu Qatada Case Is Reason to Change Human Rights Laws, Says Justice Secretary." *Telegraph*, November 13, 2012.

Acharya, Amitav. *Constructing a Security Community in Southeast Asia: ASEAN and the Problem of Regional Order*. Routledge, 2014.

Adler, Emanuel, and Michael Barnett. *Security Communities*. Cambridge University Press, 1998.

Adler, Emanuel, and Vincent Pouliot. "International Practices." *International Theory* 3, no. 1 (February 2011): 1–36.

Ahiakpor, James C. W. "The Success and Failure of Dependency Theory: The Experience of Ghana." *International Organization* 39, no. 3 (1985): 535–52.

Akerlof, George A. "The Market for 'Lemons': Quality Uncertainty and the Market Mechanism." *Quarterly Journal of Economics* 84, no. 3 (August 1, 1970): 488–500.

Alesina, Alberto, and David Dollar. "Who Gives Foreign Aid to Whom and Why?" *Journal of Economic Growth* 5, no. 1 (March 1, 2000): 33–63.

Allee, Todd, and Clint Peinhardt. "Evaluating Three Explanations for the Design of Bilateral Investment Treaties." *World Politics* 66, no. 1 (January 2014): 47–87.

Alter, Karen J. "Agents or Trustees? International Courts in Their Political Context." *European Journal of International Relations* 14, no. 1 (March 1, 2008): 33–63.

———. "The European Union's Legal System and Domestic Policy: Spillover or Backlash?" *International Organization* 54, no. 3 (2000): 489–18.

———. *The New Terrain of International Law: Courts, Politics, Rights*. Princeton University Press, 2014.

———. "Who Are the 'Masters of the Treaty'? European Governments and the European Court of Justice." *International Organization* 52, no. 1 (1998): 121–47.

Alter, Karen J., James T. Gathii, and Laurence R. Helfer. "Backlash Against International Courts in West, East and Southern Africa: Causes and Consequences." *European Journal of International Law* 27, no. 2 (May 1, 2016): 293–328.

Alter, Karen J., and Laurence R. Helfer. *The Authority of the Andean Tribunal of Justice in a Time of Regional Political Crisis*. Oxford University Press, 2017.

———. "Nature or Nurture? Judicial Lawmaking in the European Court of Justice and the Andean Tribunal of Justice." *International Organization* 64, no. 4 (October 2010): 563–92.

Alter, Karen J., Laurence Helfer, and Jacqueline R. McAllister. "A New International

Human Rights Court for West Africa: The ECOWAS Community Court of Justice." *American Journal of International Law* 107, no. 4 (October 2013): 737–79.

Alter, Karen J., and Sophie Meunier-Aitsahalia. "Judicial Politics in the European Community European Integration and the Pathbreaking Cassis de Dijon Decision." *Comparative Political Studies* 26, no. 4 (January 1, 1994): 535–61.

Alvarez, José E. "The Use (and Misuse) of European Human Rights Law in Investor-State Dispute Settlement." SSRN Scholarly Paper, November 23, 2016. https://papers.ssrn.com/abstract=2875089.

American Law Institute. *Restatement of the Law (Third): The Foreign Relations Law of the United States*. American Law Institute Publishers, 1986.

Amiott, Jennifer A. "Environment, Equality, and Indigenous Peoples' Land Rights in the Inter-American Human Rights System." *Environmental Law* 32, no. 4 (2002): 873–903.

Arrow, Kenneth J. *Social Choice and Individual Values*. Yale University Press, 2012.

Asthana, Anushka, and Rowena Mason. "UK Must Leave European Convention on Human Rights, Says Theresa May." *Guardian*, April 25, 2016. www.theguardian.com/politics/2016/apr/25/uk-must-leave-european-convention-on-human-rights-theresa-may-eu-referendum.

Axelrod, Robert, and Robert O. Keohane. "Achieving Cooperation under Anarchy: Strategies and Institutions." *World Politics* 38, no. 1 (October 1985): 226–54.

Bailey, Michael A., Anton Strezhnev, and Erik Voeten. "Estimating Dynamic State Preferences from United Nations Voting Data." *Journal of Conflict Resolution* 61, no. 2 (February 1, 2017): 430–56.

Bailey, Michael A., and Erik Voeten. "A Two-Dimensional Analysis of Seventy Years of United Nations Voting." *Public Choice* 176, nos. 1–2 (2018): 33–55.

Bapat, Navin A., and T. Clifton Morgan. "Multilateral versus Unilateral Sanctions Reconsidered: A Test Using New Data." *International Studies Quarterly* 53, no. 4 (December 1, 2009): 1075–94.

Barbieri, Katherine, and Omar M. G. Keshk. 2016. "Correlates of War Project Trade Data Set Codebook." Version 4.0. http://correlatesofwar.org.

Barbieri, Katherine, Omar M. G. Keshk, and Brian M. Pollins. "Trading Data: Evaluating Our Assumptions and Coding Rules." *Conflict Management and Peace Science* 26, no. 5 (November 1, 2009): 471–91.

Barma, Naazneen, Ely Ratner, and Steven Weber. "A World without the West." *National Interest*, no. 90 (2007): 23–30.

Barnett, Michael, and Martha Finnemore. *Rules for the World: International Organizations in Global Politics*. Cornell University Press, 2004.

Barrett, Scott. *Why Cooperate? The Incentive to Supply Global Public Goods*. Oxford University Press, 2007.

Bearce, David H. "Grasping the Commercial Institutional Peace." *International Studies Quarterly* 47, no. 3 (2003): 347–70.

Bearce, David H., and Stacy Bondanella. "Intergovernmental Organizations, Socialization, and Member-State Interest Convergence." *International Organization* 61, no. 4 (2007): 703–33.

Bearce, David H., and Sawa Omori. "How Do Commercial Institutions Promote Peace?" *Journal of Peace Research* 42, no. 6 (November 1, 2005): 659–78.

Beck, Nathaniel, and Jonathan N. Katz. "Throwing Out the Baby with the Bath Water: A Comment on Green, Kim, and Yoon." *International Organization* 55, no. 2 (March 2001): 487–95.

Beck, Thorsten, George Clarke, Alberto Groff, Philip Keefer, and Patrick Walsh. "New Tools in Comparative Political Economy: The Database of Political Institutions." *World Bank Economic Review* 15, no. 1 (June 1, 2001): 165–76.

Beckfield, Jason. "Inequality in the World Polity: The Structure of International Organization." *American Sociological Review* 68, no. 3 (June 1, 2003): 401–24.

———. "The Social Structure of the World Polity." *American Journal of Sociology* 115, no. 4 (January 1, 2010): 1018–68.

Bendor, Jonathan, Amihai Glazer, and Thomas Hammond. "Theories of Delegation." *Annual Review of Political Science* 4, no. 1 (2001): 235–69.

Bendor, Jonathan, and Adam Meirowitz. "Spatial Models of Delegation." *American Political Science Review* 98, no. 2 (May 1, 2004): 293–310.

Bhagwati, Jagdish. "Regionalism versus Multilateralism." *World Economy* 15, no. 5 (September 1, 1992): 535–56.

Birchfield, Vicki. "Contesting the Hegemony of Market Ideology: Gramsci's 'Good Sense' and Polanyi's 'Double Movement.'" *Review of International Political Economy* 6, no. 1 (January 1, 1999): 27–54.

Boehme, Franziska. "'We Chose Africa': South Africa and the Regional Politics of Cooperation with the International Criminal Court." *International Journal of Transitional Justice* 11, no. 1 (March 1, 2017): 50–70.

Boehmer, Charles, Erik Gartzke, and Timothy Nordstrom. "Do Intergovernmental Organizations Promote Peace?" *World Politics* 57, no. 1 (2004): 1–38.

Boehmer, Charles R., and David Sacko. "Economic Affinity and Liberal Pacificity: Why Democracies Really Kant Fight: Political Community and Peace." Unpublished working paper, 2004.

Bolton, Patrick, and Mathias Dewatripont. *Contract Theory*. MIT Press, 2005.

Bolton, Patrick, and Joseph Farrell. "Decentralization, Duplication, and Delay." *Journal of Political Economy* 98, no. 4 (1990): 803–26.

Bonnitcha, Jonathan, Lauge N. Skovgaard Poulsen, and Michael Waibel. *The Political Economy of the Investment Treaty Regime*. 1st ed. Oxford University Press, 2017.

Boone, Catherine. "Electoral Populism Where Property Rights Are Weak: Land Politics in Contemporary Sub-Saharan Africa." *Comparative Politics* 41, no. 2 (2009): 183–201.

Borzyskowski, Inken von, and Felicity Vabulas. "Hello, Goodbye: When Do States Withdraw from International Organizations?" *Review of International Organizations* 14, no. 2 (June 1, 2019): 335–66.

Bosco, David. *Rough Justice: The International Criminal Court in a World of Power Politics*. Oxford University Press, 2013.

Bourdieu, Pierre. "The Force of Law: Toward a Sociology of the Juridical Field Essay." *Hastings Law Journal* 38 (1987): 805–13.

Bown, Chad P. "Unappreciated Hazards of the US-China Phase One Deal." PIIE, January 21, 2020. www.piie.com/blogs/trade-and-investment-policy-watch/unappreciated-hazards-us-china-phase-one-deal.

Brack, Nathalie, and Nicholas Startin. "Introduction: Euroscepticism, from the Margins to the Mainstream." *International Political Science Review* 36, no. 3 (June 1, 2015): 239–49.

Budescu, David V., Han-Hui Por, and Stephen B. Broomell. "Effective Communication of Uncertainty in the IPCC Reports." *Climatic Change* 113, no. 2 (July 1, 2012): 181–200.

Bugaric, Bojan, and Alenka Kuhelj. "Varieties of Populism in Europe: Is the Rule of Law in Danger?" *Hague Journal on the Rule of Law* 10, no. 1 (April 1, 2018): 21–33.

Burley, Anne-Marie, and Walter Mattli. "Europe Before the Court: A Political Theory of Legal Integration." *International Organization* 47, no. 1 (1993): 41–76.

Caldeira, Gregory A., and James L. Gibson. "The Legitimacy of the Court of Justice in the European Union: Models of Institutional Support." *American Political Science Review* 89, no. 2 (June 1, 1995): 356–76.

Calvert, Julia. "Constructing Investor Rights? Why Some States (Fail to) Terminate Bilateral Investment Treaties." *Review of International Political Economy* 25, no. 1 (January 2, 2018): 75–97.

Canovan, Margaret. "Trust the People! Populism and the Two Faces of Democracy." *Political Studies* 47, no. 1 (March 1, 1999): 2–16.

Cao, Xun. "Global Networks and Domestic Policy Convergence: A Network Explanation of Policy Changes." *World Politics* 64, no. 3 (July 2012): 375–425.

——. "Networks of Intergovernmental Organizations and Convergence in Domestic Economic Policies." *International Studies Quarterly* 53, no. 4 (December 1, 2009): 1095–1130.

Cardoso, Fernando Henrique. "The Consumption of Dependency Theory in the United States." *Latin American Research Review* 12, no. 3 (1977): 7–24.

Carnegie, Allison. "Here's What Will Happen if Iran Joins the WTO." *Washington Post*, October 24, 2015. www.washingtonpost.com/news/monkey-cage/wp/2015/10/24 /heres-what-will-happen-if-iran-joins-the-wto/.

——. *Power Plays: How International Institutions Reshape Coercive Diplomacy*. 1st ed. Cambridge University Press, 2015.

——. "States Held Hostage: Political Hold-Up Problems and the Effects of International Institutions." *American Political Science Review* 108, no. 1 (February 2014): 54–70.

Carnegie, Allison, and Austin Carson. "The Spotlight's Harsh Glare: Rethinking Publicity and International Order." *International Organization* 72, no. 3 (2018): 627–57.

Caron, David D., and Esme Shirlow. "Dissecting Backlash: The Unarticulated Causes of Backlash and Its Unintended Consequences." SSRN Scholarly Paper, June 29, 2016. https://papers.ssrn.com/abstract=2834000.

Carr, E. H. "The League of Peace and Freedom: An Episode in the Quest for Collective Security." *International Affairs* 14, no. 6 (November 1, 1935): 837–44.

Carrubba, Clifford J., Matthew Gabel, and Charles Hankla. "Judicial Behavior under Political Constraints: Evidence from the European Court of Justice." *American Political Science Review* 102, no. 4 (2008): 435–52.

Carter, David B., and Curtis S. Signorino. "Back to the Future: Modeling Time Dependence in Binary Data." *Political Analysis* 18, no. 3 (June 20, 2010): 271–92.

Carter, David B., and Randall W. Stone. "Democracy and Multilateralism: The Case of Vote Buying in the UN General Assembly." *International Organization* 69, no. 1 (January 2015): 1–33.

Castaneda, Jorge G. "Latin America's Left Turn Essay." *Foreign Affairs* 85 (2006): 28–44.

Chapman, Terrence L. "International Security Institutions, Domestic Politics, and Institutional Legitimacy." *Journal of Conflict Resolution* 51, no. 1 (February 1, 2007): 134–66.

Checkel, Jeffrey T. "International Institutions and Socialization in Europe: Introduction and Framework." *International Organization* 59, no. 4 (October 2005): 801–26.

Chiba, Daina, Jesse C. Johnson, and Brett Ashley Leeds. "Careful Commitments: Democratic States and Alliance Design." *Journal of Politics* 77, no. 4 (October 1, 2015): 968–82.

Chilton, Adam S. "The Political Motivations of the United States' Bilateral Investment Treaty Program." *Review of International Political Economy* 23, no. 4 (July 3, 2016): 614–42.

Chinn, Menzie D., and Hiro Ito. "What Matters for Financial Development? Capital Controls, Institutions, and Interactions." *Journal of Development Economics* 81, no. 1 (October 1, 2006): 163–92.

Cichowski, Rachel A. "Women's Rights, the European Court, and Supranational Constitutionalism." *Law & Society Review* 38, no. 3 (September 1, 2004): 489–512.

"Clinton's Words on China: Trade Is the Smart Thing." *New York Times*, March 9, 2000. www.nytimes.com/2000/03/09/world/clinton-s-words-on-china-trade-is-the-smart-thing.html.

Colgan, Jeff D., and Robert O. Keohane. "The Liberal Order Is Rigged: Fix It Now or Watch It Wither Essays." *Foreign Affairs* 96 (2017): 36–44.

Convention on the Prohibition of the Development, Production, Stockpiling and Use of Chemical Weapons and on Their Destruction, Syrian Accession. "Reference: C.N.592.2013.TREATIES-XXVI.3 (Depositary Notification)." Secretary-General of the United Nations, September 14, 2013.

Converse, Philip. "Ideology and Discontent." In *International Yearbook of Political Behavior Research*, vol. 5, edited by David Apter. Free Press, 1964.

Copelovitch, Mark, and Jon C. W. Pevehouse. "International Organizations in a New Era of Populist Nationalism." *Review of International Organizations* 14, no. 2 (June 1, 2019): 169–86.

"Correa Calls for New Inter-American Human Rights System." *EFE News Service*, October 10, 2016. http://global.factiva.com/redir/default.aspx?P=sa&an=WEFE0 00020161010ecaa000gp&cat=a&ep=ASE.

Cox, Gary W., and Matthew McCubbins. *Legislative Leviathan: Party Government in the House*. University of California Press, 1993.

Cox, Robert W. "Gramsci, Hegemony and International Relations : An Essay in Method." *Millennium* 12, no. 2 (June 1, 1983): 162–75.

———. "Ideologies and the New International Economic Order: Reflections on Some Recent Literature." *International Organization* 33, no. 2 (1979): 257–302.

Craig, Edward. *Routledge Encyclopedia of Philosophy: Questions to Sociobiology*. Taylor & Francis, 1998.

Crawford, Vincent P., and Joel Sobel. "Strategic Information Transmission." *Economet-rica* 50, no. 6 (1982): 1431–51.

Cremades, Bernardo M. "Resurgence of the Calvo Doctrine in Latin America." *Business Law International* 7 (2006): 53.

Danner, Allison Marston. "Enhancing the Legitimacy and Accountability of Prosecuto-rial Discretion at the International Criminal Court." *American Journal of Interna-tional Law* 97, no. 3 (July 1, 2003): 510–52.

Davis, Christina L., and Meredith Wilf. "Joining the Club: Accession to the GATT/WTO." *Journal of Politics* 79, no. 3 (May 10, 2017): 964–78.

Dawson, Frank G., and Burns H. Weston. "Prompt, Adequate and Effective: A Uni-versal Standard of Compensation." *Fordham Law Review* 30 (1962): 727–58.

Dewan, Torun, and Kenneth A. Shepsle. "Recent Economic Perspectives on Political Economy, Part II." *British Journal of Political Science* 38, no. 3 (July 1, 2008): 543–64.

Dezalay, Yves, and Bryant Garth. "Merchants of Law as Moral Entrepreneurs: Con-structing International Justice from the Competition for Transnational Business Disputes." *Law & Society Review* 29, no. 1 (1995): 27–64.

Dixit, Avinash, and John Londregan. "Ideology, Tactics, and Efficiency in Redistributive Politics." *Quarterly Journal of Economics* 113, no. 2 (May 1, 1998): 497–529.

Donno, Daniela. "Who Is Punished? Regional Intergovernmental Organizations and the Enforcement of Democratic Norms." *International Organization* 64, no. 4 (2010): 593–625.

Donno, Daniela, Shawna K. Metzger, and Bruce Russett. "Screening Out Risk: IGOs, Member State Selection, and Interstate Conflict, 1951–2000." *International Studies Quarterly* 59, no. 2 (2015): 251–63.

Dorussen, Han, and Hugh Ward. "Intergovernmental Organizations and the Kantian Peace: A Network Perspective." *Journal of Conflict Resolution* 52, no. 2 (April 1, 2008): 189–212.

Dougan, William R., and Michael C. Munger. "The Rationality of Ideology." *Journal of Law & Economics* 32, no. 1 (1989): 119–42.

Downs, Anthony. *An Economic Theory of Democracy.* Harper & Row, 1957.

———. "An Economic Theory of Political Action in a Democracy." *Journal of Political Economy* 65, no. 2 (1957): 135–50.

Downs, George, and Michael Jones. "Reputation, Compliance, and International Law." *Journal of Legal Studies* 31, no. 2 (January 1, 2002). http://chicagounbound.uchicago.edu/jls/vol31/iss2/15.

Downs, George W., David M. Rocke, and Peter N. Barsoom. "Is the Good News about Compliance Good News about Cooperation?" *International Organization* 50, no. 3 (1996): 379–406.

———. "Managing the Evolution of Multilateralism." *International Organization* 52, no. 2 (March 1998): 397–419.

Doyle, Michael W. "Kant, Liberal Legacies, and Foreign Affairs." *Philosophy & Public Affairs* 12, no. 3 (1983): 205–35.

———. "Kant, Liberal Legacies, and Foreign Affairs, Part 2." *Philosophy & Public Af-fairs* 12, no. 4 (October 1, 1983): 323–53.

——. "Stalemate in the North-South Debate: Strategies and the New International Economic Order." *World Politics* 35, no. 3 (1983): 426–64.

Dreher, Axel, and Martin Gassebner. "Does Political Proximity to the U.S. Cause Terror?" *Economics Letters* 99, no. 1 (April 2008): 27–29.

Dreher, Axel, and Nathan M. Jensen. "Country or Leader? Political Change and UN General Assembly Voting." *European Journal of Political Economy* 29 (March 2013): 183–96.

Dreher, Axel, Peter Nunnenkamp, and Rainer Thiele. "Does US Aid Buy UN General Assembly Votes? A Disaggregated Analysis." *Public Choice* 136, no. 1/2 (2008): 139–64.

Dreher, Axel, Jan-Egbert Sturm, and James Raymond Vreeland. "Development Aid and International Politics: Does Membership on the UN Security Council Influence World Bank Decisions?" *Journal of Development Economics* 88, no. 1 (January 2009): 1–18.

——. "Global Horse Trading: IMF Loans for Votes in the United Nations Security Council." *European Economic Review* 53, no. 7 (October 2009): 742–57.

Drezner, Daniel W. "Bargaining, Enforcement, and Multilateral Sanctions: When Is Cooperation Counterproductive?" *International Organization* 54, no. 1 (2000): 73–102.

——. "The Power and Peril of International Regime Complexity." *Perspectives on Politics* 7, no. 1 (March 1, 2009): 65–70.

Driscoll, Amanda, and Michael J. Nelson. "Judicial Selection and the Democratization of Justice: Lessons from the Bolivian Judicial Elections." *Journal of Law and Courts* 3, no. 1 (March 1, 2015): 115–48.

Drury, A. Cooper, Patrick James, and Dursun Peksen. "Neo-Kantianism and Coercive Diplomacy: The Complex Case of Economic Sanctions." *International Interactions* 40, no. 1 (January 1, 2014): 25–51.

Duranti, Marco. *The Conservative Human Rights Revolution: European Identity, Transnational Politics, and the Origins of the European Convention.* Oxford University Press, 2017.

"Ecuadoran President Interviewed on Regional Human Rights Body." *BBC Monitoring Americas*, June 8, 2012. http://global.factiva.com/redir/default.aspx?P=sa&an=B BCMAP0020120608e8680002t&cat=a&ep=ASE.

Edwards, Martin S., Kevin M. Scott, Susan Hannah Allen, and Kate Irvin. "Sins of Commission? Understanding Membership Patterns on the United Nations Human Rights Commission." *Political Research Quarterly* 61, no. 3 (March 4, 2008): 390–402.

Elkins, Zachary, Andrew T. Guzman, and Beth A. Simmons. "Competing for Capital: The Diffusion of Bilateral Investment Treaties, 1960–2000." *International Organization* 60, no. 4 (2006): 811–46.

Ellner, Steve. "The Distinguishing Features of Latin America's New Left in Power: The Chávez, Morales, and Correa Governments." *Latin American Perspectives* 39, no. 1 (January 1, 2012): 96–114.

Elsig, Manfred, and Mark A. Pollack. "Agents, Trustees, and International Courts: The Politics of Judicial Appointment at the World Trade Organization." *European Journal of International Relations* 20, no. 2 (June 1, 2014): 391–415.

Elster, Jon. "On Majoritarianism and Rights." *East European Constitutional Review* 1 (1992): 19.

Epstein, David, and Sharyn O'Halloran. "Administrative Procedures, Information, and Agency Discretion." *American Journal of Political Science* 38, no. 3 (August 1994): 697–722.

European Court of Human Rights. "Lautsi and Others v. Italy." 2011. http://hudoc .echr.coe.int.

Ewing, K. D. "The Human Rights Act and Parliamentary Democracy." *Modern Law Review* 62, no. 1 (January 1, 1999): 79–99.

Fang, Songying. "The Informational Role of International Institutions and Domestic Politics." *American Journal of Political Science* 52, no. 2 (April 1, 2008): 304–21.

Farrell, Henry, and Abraham L. Newman. "Domestic Institutions beyond the Nation-State: Charting the New Interdependence Approach." *World Politics* 66, no. 2 (April 2014): 331–63.

———. "The New Politics of Interdependence Cross-National Layering in Trans-Atlantic Regulatory Disputes." *Comparative Political Studies* 48, no. 4 (2015): 497–526.

Farrell, Joseph, and Garth Saloner. "Coordination through Committees and Markets." *Rand Journal of Economics* 19, no. 2 (Summer 1988): 235–52.

Farrell, Joseph, and Timothy Simcoe. "Choosing the Rules for Consensus Standardization." *Rand Journal of Economics* 43, no. 2 (2012): 235–52.

Fearon, James D. "Bargaining, Enforcement, and International Cooperation." *International Organization* 52, no. 2 (1998): 269–305.

———. "Rationalist Explanations for War." *International Organization* 49, no. 3 (1995): 379–414.

Fearon, James D., and Alexander Wendt. "Rationalism and Constructivism in International Relations Theory." In *Handbook of International Relations*, edited by Walter Carlsnaes, Thomas Risse, and Beth A. Simmons, 52–72. Sage, 2002.

Ferejohn, John. "Judicializing Politics, Politicizing Law." *Law and Contemporary Problems* 65 (2002): 41–68.

Finnemore, Martha. "Norms, Culture, and World Politics: Insights from Sociology's Institutionalism." *International Organization* 50, no. 2 (March 1996): 325–47.

Finnemore, Martha, and Kathryn Sikkink. "International Norm Dynamics and Political Change." *International Organization* 52, no. 4 (1998): 887–917.

Fioretos, Orfeo. "Historical Institutionalism in International Relations." *International Organization* 65, no. 2 (April 2011): 367–99.

Fordham, Benjamin O. "Economic Interests, Party, and Ideology in Early Cold War Era U.S. Foreign Policy." *International Organization* 52, no. 2 (1998): 359–96.

Fortna, Page. *Does Peacekeeping Work? Shaping Belligerents' Choices after Civil War.* Princeton University Press, 2008.

Freeden, Michael. "Is Nationalism a Distinct Ideology?" *Political Studies* 46, no. 4 (September 1, 1998): 748–65.

French, Howard. "China in Africa: All Trade, with No Political Baggage." *New York Times*, August 8, 2004.

French, John D. "Understanding the Politics of Latin America's Plural Lefts (Chávez/

Lula): Social Democracy, Populism and Convergence on the Path to a Post-neoliberal World." *Third World Quarterly* 30, no. 2 (2009): 349–69.

Fukuyama, Francis. "The End of History?" *National Interest*, no. 16 (1989): 3–18.

Gaddis, John Lewis. "The Cold War, the Long Peace, and the Future." *Diplomatic History* 16, no. 2 (1992): 234–46.

Gailmard, Sean, and John W. Patty. "Formal Models of Bureaucracy." *Annual Review of Political Science* 15, no. 1 (2012): 353–77.

Gallagher, Kevin P. "Understanding Developing Country Resistance to the Doha Round." *Review of International Political Economy* 15, no. 1 (December 13, 2007): 62–85.

Gambetta, Diego. "Can We Trust Trust?" In *Trust: Making and Breaking Cooperative Relations*, 216–35. Blackwell, 1988.

———. "Inscrutable Markets." *Rationality and Society* 6, no. 3 (July 1, 1994): 353–68.

Gambetta, Diego, and Heather Hamill. *Streetwise: How Taxi Drivers Establish Customer's Trustworthiness*. Russell Sage Foundation, 2005.

Garrett, Geoffrey. "Capital Mobility, Trade, and the Domestic Politics of Economic Policy." *International Organization* 49, no. 4 (October 1995): 657–87.

Gartzke, Erik. "The Capitalist Peace." *American Journal of Political Science* 51, no. 1 (2007): 166–91.

———. "Kant We All Just Get Along? Opportunity, Willingness, and the Origins of the Democratic Peace." *American Journal of Political Science* 42, no. 1 (1998): 1–27.

———. "Preferences and the Democratic Peace." *International Studies Quarterly* 44, no. 2 (2000): 191–212.

Gartzke, Erik, Quan Li, and Charles Boehmer. "Investing in the Peace: Economic Interdependence and International Conflict." *International Organization* 55, no. 2 (2001): 391–438.

Gasiorowski, Mark J. "The 1953 Coup D'état in Iran." *International Journal of Middle East Studies* 19, no. 3 (1987): 261–86.

Gerring, John. "Ideology: A Definitional Analysis." *Political Research Quarterly* 50, no. 4 (1997): 957–94.

Gertz, Geoffrey, Srividya Jandhyala, and Lauge N. Skovgaard Poulsen. "Legalization, Diplomacy, and Development: Do Investment Treaties De-politicize Investment Disputes?" *World Development* 107 (July 1, 2018): 239–52.

Gibler, Douglas M., and Meredith Reid Sarkees. "Measuring Alliances: The Correlates of War Formal Interstate Alliance Dataset, 1816–2000." *Journal of Peace Research* 41, no. 2 (March 1, 2004): 211–22.

Gibler, Douglas M., and Scott Wolford. "Alliances, Then Democracy: An Examination of the Relationship between Regime Type and Alliance Formation." *Journal of Conflict Resolution* 50, no. 1 (February 1, 2006): 129–53.

Gibson, James L., and Gregory A. Caldeira. "Changes in the Legitimacy of the European Court of Justice: A Post-Maastricht Analysis." *British Journal of Political Science* 28, no. 1 (January 1, 1998): 63–91.

———. "The Legitimacy of Transnational Legal Institutions: Compliance, Support, and the European Court of Justice." *American Journal of Political Science* 39, no. 2 (May 1, 1995): 459–89.

Gill, Stephen R., and David Law. "Global Hegemony and the Structural Power of Capital." *International Studies Quarterly* 33, no. 4 (December 1, 1989): 475–99.

Gilligan, Thomas W., and Keith Krehbiel. "Asymmetric Information and Legislative Rules with a Heterogeneous Committee." *American Journal of Political Science* 33, no. 2 (May 1, 1989): 459–90.

———. "Collective Decision-making and Standing Committees: An Informational Rationale for Restrictive Amendment Procedures." *Journal of Law, Economics & Organization* 3 (1987): 287–335.

Gillingham, John. *Coal, Steel, and the Rebirth of Europe, 1945–1955: The Germans and French from Ruhr Conflict to Economic Community.* Cambridge University Press, 2004.

Gilpin, Robert. *The Political Economy of International Relations.* Princeton University Press, 2016.

Ginsburg, Tom. "International Substitutes for Domestic Institutions: Bilateral Investment Treaties and Governance." *International Review of Law and Economics* 25, no. 1 (March 2005): 107–23.

Girod, Desha M., and Jennifer L. Tobin. "Take the Money and Run: The Determinants of Compliance with Aid Agreements." *International Organization* 70, no. 1 (January 2016): 209–39.

Gladstone, Rick. "Trump Administration Defends Cuba Embargo at U.N., Reversing Obama." *New York Times*, November 1, 2017. www.nytimes.com/2017/11/01/world/americas/cuba-un-us-embargo.html.

Glaser, Charles L., Andrew H. Kydd, Mark L. Haas, John M. Owen, and Sebastian Rosato. "Correspondence: Can Great Powers Discern Intentions?" *International Security* 40, no. 3 (January 1, 2016): 197–215.

Goddard, Stacie E. "Embedded Revisionism: Networks, Institutions, and Challenges to World Order." *International Organization* 72, no. 4 (2018): 763–97.

Goldstein, Judith, ed. *Legalization and World Politics.* MIT Press, 2001.

———. "The Political Economy of Trade: Institutions of Protection." *American Political Science Review* 80, no. 1 (1986): 161–84.

Goldstein, Judith, and Robert Owen Keohane. *Ideas and Foreign Policy: Beliefs, Institutions, and Political Change.* Cornell University Press, 1993.

Gough, Clair, and Simon Shackley. "The Respectable Politics of Climate Change: The Epistemic Communities and NGOs." *International Affairs* 77, no. 2 (2001): 329–46.

Gowa, Joanne. *Allies, Adversaries, and International Trade.* Princeton University Press, 1995.

Gowa, Joanne, and Edward D. Mansfield. "Power Politics and International Trade." *American Political Science Review* 87, no. 2 (1993): 408–20.

Gray, Julia. *The Company States Keep.* Cambridge University Press, 2013.

———. "International Organization as a Seal of Approval: European Union Accession and Investor Risk." *American Journal of Political Science* 53, no. 4 (October 1, 2009): 931–49.

Green, Donald P., Soo Yeon Kim, and David H. Yoon. "Dirty Pool." *International Organization* 55, no. 2 (March 2001): 441–68.

Greenhill, Brian. *Transmitting Rights: International Organizations and the Diffusion of Human Rights Practices*. Oxford University Press, 2015.

Greenhill, Brian, and Yonatan Lupu. "Clubs of Clubs: Fragmentation in the Network of Intergovernmental Organizations." *International Studies Quarterly* 61, no. 1 (March 1, 2017): 181–95.

Greenhill, Michael Clarke. "So What Have Our Judges Against Britain?—Another Devastating Verdict on Asylum Laws Denies Elected. . . ." *Daily Mail*, February 20, 2003. http://global.factiva.com/redir/default.aspx?P=sa&an=daim0000200 30306dz2k0020b&cat=a&ep=ASE.

Greif, Avner, and Christopher Kingston. "Institutions: Rules or Equilibria?" In *Political Economy of Institutions, Democracy and Voting*, edited by Norman Schofield and Gonzalo Caballero, 13–43. Springer, 2011.

Grieco, Joseph M. "Anarchy and the Limits of Cooperation: A Realist Critique of the Newest Liberal Institutionalism." *International Organization* 42, no. 3 (June 1988): 485–507.

"Grieve, Clarke and Green Were Last Protectors of Our Human Rights Laws." *Guardian*, July 15, 2014. www.theguardian.com/law/2014/jul/15/grieve-clarke-green -human-rights-conservatives-europe.

Grossman, Gene M., and Elhanan Helpman. "Protection for Sale." *American Economic Review* 84, no. 4 (September 1994): 833–50.

Gruber, Lloyd. *Ruling the World: Power Politics and the Rise of Supranational Institutions*. Princeton University Press, 2000.

Guha, Keshava D. "Jacob Zuma: Assessing His First Three Years." *Harvard International Review* 34, no. 3 (Winter 2013): 6–7.

Guzman, Andrew T. "Why LDCs Sign Treaties That Hurt Them: Explaining the Popularity of Bilateral Investment Treaties." *Virginia Journal of International Law* 38 (1998): 639.

Haas, Ernst B. *Beyond the Nation-State: Functionalism and International Organization*. Stanford University Press, 1964.

———. *The Obsolescence of Regional Integration Theory*. Institute of International Studies, University of California, 1975.

———. "Turbulent Fields and the Theory of Regional Integration." *International Organization* 30, no. 2 (1976): 173–212.

Haas, Mark L. "Ideological Polarity and Balancing in Great Power Politics." *Security Studies* 23, no. 4 (October 2, 2014): 715–53.

———. "Ideology and Alliances: British and French External Balancing Decisions in the 1930s." *Security Studies* 12, no. 4 (January 1, 2003): 34–79.

Haas, Peter M. "Do Regimes Matter? Epistemic Communities and Mediterranean Pollution Control." *International Organization* 43, no. 3 (1989): 377–403.

Hafner-Burton, Emilie M. "Trading Human Rights: How Preferential Trade Agreements Influence Government Repression." *International Organization* 59, no. 3 (August 9, 2005): 593–629.

Hafner-Burton, Emilie M., Miles Kahler, and Alexander H. Montgomery. "Network Analysis for International Relations." *International Organization* 63, no. 3 (2009): 559–92.

Hafner-Burton, Emilie M., and Alexander H. Montgomery. "Power or Plenty: How Do International Trade Institutions Affect Economic Sanctions?" *Journal of Conflict Resolution* 52, no. 2 (April 1, 2008): 213–42.

———. "Power Positions: International Organizations, Social Networks, and Conflict." *Journal of Conflict Resolution* 50, no. 1 (February 1, 2006): 3–27.

Haftel, Yoram Z. "Commerce and Institutions: Trade, Scope, and the Design of Regional Economic Organizations." *Review of International Organizations* 8, no. 3 (January 11, 2013): 389–414.

———. "From the Outside Looking In: The Effect of Trading Blocs on Trade Disputes in the GATT/WTO." *International Studies Quarterly* 48, no. 1 (2004): 121–42.

Haftel, Yoram Z., and Alexander Thompson. "When Do States Renegotiate Investment Agreements? The Impact of Arbitration." *Review of International Organizations* 13 (2018): 25–48.

Hainmueller, Jens, Jonathan Mummolo, and Yiqing Xu. "How Much Should We Trust Estimates from Multiplicative Interaction Models? Simple Tools to Improve Empirical Practice." *Political Analysis* 27, no. 2 (April 2019): 163–92.

Hall, Rodney Bruce. "Moral Authority as a Power Resource." *International Organization* 51, no. 4 (1997): 591–622.

Hanania, Richard. "Are Liberal Governments More Cooperative? Voting Trends at the UN in Five Anglophone Democracies." *Journal of Conflict Resolution* 63, no. 6 (2019): 1403–32.

Hardin, Russell. *Indeterminacy and Society*. Princeton University Press, 2006.

Hawkins, Darren, and Wade Jacoby. "Partial Compliance: A Comparison of the European and Inter-American Courts of Human Rights." *Journal of International Law and International Relations* 6 (2011): 35–85.

Hawkins, Darren G., David A. Lake, Daniel L. Nielson, and Michael J. Tierney. *Delegation and Agency in International Organizations*. Cambridge University Press, 2006.

Hawkins, Kirk A. "Is Chávez Populist? Measuring Populist Discourse in Comparative Perspective." *Comparative Political Studies* 42, no. 8 (August 1, 2009): 1040–67.

Hayek, Friedrich von. *Road to Serfdom*. Institute of Economic Affairs, 1994.

Helfer, Laurence R. "The Burdens and Benefits of Brighton." European Society of International Law, 2012. http://esil-sedi.eu/node/138.

———. "Overlegalizing Human Rights: International Relations Theory and the Commonwealth Caribbean Backlash Against Human Rights Regimes." *Columbia Law Review* 102, no. 7 (November 1, 2002): 1832–1911.

———. "Populism and International Human Rights Institutions: A Survival Guide." SSRN Scholarly Paper, June 26, 2018. https://papers.ssrn.com/abstract=320 2633.

Helfer, Laurence R., and Anne E. Showalter. "Opposing International Justice: Kenya's Integrated Backlash Strategy Against the ICC." *International Criminal Law Review* 17, no. 1 (February 19, 2017): 1–46.

Helleiner, Eric. "Economic Liberalism and Its Critics: The Past as Prologue?" *Review of International Political Economy* 10, no. 4 (November 1, 2003): 685–96.

Hemmer, Christopher, and Peter J. Katzenstein. "Why Is There No NATO in Asia?

Collective Identity, Regionalism, and the Origins of Multilateralism." *International Organization* 56, no. 3 (2002): 575–607.

Hensel, Paul R., Sara McLaughlin Mitchell, Thomas E. Sowers, and Clayton L. Thyne. "Bones of Contention: Comparing Territorial, Maritime, and River Issues." *Journal of Conflict Resolution* 52, no. 1 (February 1, 2008): 117–43.

Hillebrecht, Courtney. *Domestic Politics and International Human Rights Tribunals: The Problem of Compliance.* Cambridge University Press, 2014.

Hinich, Melvin J. "Equilibrium in Spatial Voting: The Median Voter Result Is an Artifact." *Journal of Economic Theory* 16, no. 2 (December 1, 1977): 208–19.

Hinich, Melvin J., and Michael C. Munger. *Ideology and the Theory of Political Choice.* University of Michigan Press, 1996.

Hirschl, Ran. "The Judicialization of Mega-Politics and the Rise of Political Courts." *Annual Review of Political Science* 11, no. 1 (2008): 93–118.

Hix, Simon. "Parliamentary Behavior with Two Principals: Preferences, Parties, and Voting in the European Parliament." *American Journal of Political Science* 46, no. 3 (2002): 688–98.

Hobolt, Sara B. "The Brexit Vote: A Divided Nation, a Divided Continent." *Journal of European Public Policy* 23, no. 9 (October 20, 2016): 1259–77.

Hollyer, James R., B. Peter Rosendorff, and James Raymond Vreeland. *Transparency, Democracy, and Autocracy: Economic Transparency and Political (In)Stability.* Cambridge University Press, 2018.

Hooghe, Liesbet. *Measuring International Authority: A Postfunctionalist Theory of Governance.* Oxford University Press, 2017.

——. "Several Roads Lead to International Norms, but Few Via International Socialization: A Case Study of the European Commission." *International Organization* 59, no. 4 (October 2005): 861–98.

Hooghe, Liesbet, Tobias Lenz, and Gary Marks. "Contested World Order: The Delegitimation of International Governance." *Review of International Organizations* 14 (2019): 731–43.

——. *A Theory of International Organization.* Oxford University Press, 2019.

Hooghe, Liesbet, and Gary Marks. "Cleavage Theory Meets Europe's Crises: Lipset, Rokkan, and the Transnational Cleavage." *Journal of European Public Policy* 25, no. 1 (January 2, 2018): 109–35.

——. "A Postfunctionalist Theory of European Integration: From Permissive Consensus to Constraining Dissensus." *British Journal of Political Science* 39, no. 1 (January 2009): 1–23.

Hooghe, Liesbet, Gary Marks, and Carole J. Wilson. "Does Left/Right Structure Party Positions on European Integration?" *Comparative Political Studies* 35, no. 8 (October 1, 2002): 965–89.

Hough, Andrew. "Prisoner Vote: What MPs Said in Heated Debate." *Telegraph*, February 11, 2011. www.telegraph.co.uk/news/politics/8317485/Prisoner-vote-what-MPs-said-in-heated-debate.html.

Houle, Christian, and Paul D. Kenny. "The Political and Economic Consequences of Populist Rule in Latin America." *Government and Opposition* 53, no. 2 (April 2018): 256–87.

Huber, John D. "Values and Partisanship in Left-Right Orientations: Measuring Ideology." *European Journal of Political Research* 17, no. 5 (September 1, 1989): 599–621.

Huber, Robert A., and Saskia P. Ruth. "Mind the Gap! Populism, Participation and Representation in Europe." *Swiss Political Science Review* 23, no. 4 (December 1, 2017): 462–84.

Hulme, Mike, and Martin Mahony. "Climate Change: What Do We Know about the IPCC?" *Progress in Physical Geography: Earth and Environment* 34, no. 5 (October 1, 2010): 705–18.

Huneeus, Alexandra. "Courts Resisting Courts: Lessons from the Inter-American Court's Struggle to Enforce Human Rights." *Cornell International Law Journal* 44 (2011): 493.

Hurrell, Andrew. *On Global Order: Power, Values, and the Constitution of International Society.* Oxford University Press, 2007.

Huth, Paul K., Sarah E. Croco, and Benjamin J. Appel. "Bringing Law to the Table: Legal Claims, Focal Points, and the Settlement of Territorial Disputes since 1945." *American Journal of Political Science* 57, no. 1 (2013): 90–103.

———. "Does International Law Promote the Peaceful Settlement of International Disputes? Evidence from the Study of Territorial Conflicts since 1945." *American Political Science Review* 105, no. 2 (2011): 415–36.

Hyde, Susan D. "Catch Us if You Can: Election Monitoring and International Norm Diffusion." *American Journal of Political Science* 55, no. 2 (2011): 356–69.

Ihonvbere, Julius Omozuanvbo, and John Mukum Mbaku. *Political Liberalization and Democratization in Africa: Lessons from Country Experiences.* Greenwood, 2003.

Ikenberry, G. John. *After Victory: Institutions, Strategic Restraint, and the Rebuilding of Order after Major Wars.* Princeton University Press, 2009.

———. "Constitutional Politics in International Relations." *European Journal of International Relations* 4, no. 2 (June 1, 1998):147–77.

———. "The End of Liberal International Order?" *International Affairs* 94, no. 1 (January 1, 2018): 7–23.

———. "Institutions, Strategic Restraint, and the Persistence of American Postwar Order." *International Security* 23, no. 3 (January 1, 1999): 43–78.

———. "Liberal Internationalism 3.0: America and the Dilemmas of Liberal World Order." *Perspectives on Politics* 7, no. 1 (2009): 71–87.

Inglehart, Ronald F., and Pippa Norris. "Trump, Brexit, and the Rise of Populism: Economic Have-Nots and Cultural Backlash." 2016. https://ssrn.com/abstract=2818659.

Ingram, Paul, Jeffrey Robinson, and Marc L. Busch. "The Intergovernmental Network of World Trade: IGO Connectedness, Governance, and Embeddedness." *American Journal of Sociology* 111, no. 3 (2005): 824–58.

Jahn, Beate. "Liberal Internationalism: From Ideology to Empirical Theory—and Back Again." *International Theory* 1, no. 3 (November 2009): 409–38.

Jandhyala, Srividya, Witold J. Henisz, and Edward D. Mansfield. "Three Waves of BITs: The Global Diffusion of Foreign Investment Policy." *Journal of Conflict Resolution* 55, no. 6 (December 1, 2011): 1047–73.

Jensen, Nathan M. "Democratic Governance and Multinational Corporations: Political Regimes and Inflows of Foreign Direct Investment." *International Organization* 57, no. 3 (2003): 587–616.

Johns, Leslie. "Courts as Coordinators Endogenous Enforcement and Jurisdiction in International Adjudication." *Journal of Conflict Resolution* 56, no. 2 (April 1, 2012): 257–89.

———. "A Servant of Two Masters: Communication and the Selection of International Bureaucrats." *International Organization* 61, no. 2 (2007): 245–75.

Johnson, Tana. "Institutional Design and Bureaucrats' Impact on Political Control." *Journal of Politics* 75, no. 1 (January 1, 2013): 183–97.

Johnson, Tana Lynn, and Johannes Urpelainen. "International Bureaucrats and the Formation of Intergovernmental Organizations: Institutional Design Discretion Sweetens the Pot." *International Organization* 68, no. 1 (January 2014): 177–209.

Johnston, Alastair I. *Social States: China in International Institutions, 1980–2000.* Princeton University Press, 2008.

Jost, John T., Christopher M. Federico, and Jaime L. Napier. "Political Ideology: Its Structure, Functions, and Elective Affinities." *Annual Review of Psychology* 60, no. 1 (2009): 307–37.

"Judges Must Bow to the Will of Parliament." *Telegraph*, August 10, 2005.

Kaczmarek, Sarah C., and Abraham L. Newman. "The Long Arm of the Law: Extraterritoriality and the National Implementation of Foreign Bribery Legislation." *International Organization* 65, no. 4 (2011): 745–70.

Kagan, Robert. "The Twilight of the Liberal World Order." *Brookings*, January 24, 2017. www.brookings.edu/research/the-twilight-of-the-liberal-world-order/.

Kahler, Miles. "Rationality in International Relations." *International Organization* 52, no. 4 (1998): 919–41.

———. "Who Is Liberal Now? Rising Powers and Global Norms." In *Why Govern? Rethinking Demand and Progress in Global Governance*, edited by Amitav Acharya, 55–73. Cambridge University Press, 2016.

Kahler, Miles, and Andrew MacIntyre. *Integrating Regions: Asia in Comparative Context.* Stanford University Press, 2013.

Kasa, Sjur, Anne T. Gullberg, and Gørild Heggelund. "The Group of 77 in the International Climate Negotiations: Recent Developments and Future Directions." *International Environmental Agreements: Politics, Law and Economics* 8, no. 2 (December 12, 2007): 113–27.

Keck, M. E., and K. Sikkink. *Activists beyond Borders: Advocacy Networks in International Politics.* Cambridge University Press, 1998.

Kelemen, R. Daniel. "The Limits of Judicial Power Trade-Environment Disputes in the GATT/WTO and the EU." *Comparative Political Studies* 34, no. 6 (August 1, 2001): 622–50.

Kelley, Judith. "Assessing the Complex Evolution of Norms: The Rise of International Election Monitoring." *International Organization* 62, no. 2 (2008): 221–55.

———. "The More the Merrier? The Effects of Having Multiple International Election Monitoring Organizations." *Perspectives on Politics* 7, no. 1 (2009): 59–64.

Kentikelenis, Alexander E., and Sarah Babb. "The Making of Neoliberal Globalization:

Norm Substitution and the Politics of Clandestine Institutional Change." *American Journal of Sociology* 124, no. 6 (May 1, 2019): 1720–62.

Keohane, Robert O. *After Hegemony: Cooperation and Discord in the World Political Economy*. Princeton University Press, 1984.

———. "Institutionalization in the United Nations General Assembly." *International Organization* 23, no. 4 (1969): 859–96.

Keohane, Robert O., and Joseph S. Nye. *Power and Interdependence: World Politics in Transition*. Little, Brown, 1977.

Kim, Diana. "A 'Surreptitious Introduction': Opium Smuggling and Colonial State Formation in Late 19th Century Bengal and Burma." In *The Legitimacy of Power: New Perspectives on the History of Political Economy*, edited by Sophus Reinert and Robert Fredona, 233–52. Palgrave Macmillan, 2018.

Kim, Soo Yeon, and Bruce Russett. "The New Politics of Voting Alignments in the United Nations General Assembly." *International Organization* 50, no. 4 (October 1996): 629–52.

Kinne, Brandon J. "Defense Cooperation Agreements and the Emergence of a Global Security Network." *International Organization* 72, no. 4 (2018): 799–837.

———. "IGO Membership, Network Convergence, and Credible Signaling in Militarized Disputes." *Journal of Peace Research* 50, no. 6 (November 1, 2013): 659–76.

———. "Multilateral Trade and Militarized Conflict: Centrality, Openness, and Asymmetry in the Global Trade Network." *Journal of Politics* 74, no. 1 (2012): 308–22.

———. "Network Dynamics and the Evolution of International Cooperation." *American Political Science Review* 107, no. 4 (November 2013): 766–85.

Knight, Jack. *Institutions and Social Conflict*. Cambridge University Press, 1992.

Koivumaeki, Riitta-Ilona. "Evading the Constraints of Globalization: Oil and Gas Nationalization in Venezuela and Bolivia." *Comparative Politics* 48, no. 1 (2015): 107–25.

Kono, Daniel Y. "Making Anarchy Work: International Legal Institutions and Trade Cooperation." *Journal of Politics* 69, no. 3 (August 1, 2007): 746–59.

Koremenos, Barbara. "The Continent of International Law." *Journal of Conflict Resolution* 57, no. 4 (August 1, 2013): 653–81.

———. *The Continent of International Law: Explaining Agreement Design*. Cambridge University Press, 2016.

———. "Contracting around International Uncertainty." *American Political Science Review* 99, no. 4 (2005): 549–65.

Koremenos, Barbara, Charles Lipson, and Duncan Snidal. "The Rational Design of International Institutions." *International Organization* 55, no. 4 (2001): 761–99.

Kramer, Mark. "Ideology and the Cold War." *Review of International Studies* 25, no. 4 (October 1999): 539–76.

Krasner, Stephen D. *International Regimes*. Cornell University Press, 1983.

———. "State Power and the Structure of International Trade." *World Politics* 28, no. 3 (1976): 317–47.

———. "The Tokyo Round: Particularistic Interests and Prospects for Stability in the Global Trading System." *International Studies Quarterly* 23, no. 4 (December 1, 1979): 491–531.

Kratochwil, Friedrich V. *Rules, Norms, and Decisions: On the Conditions of Practical and Legal Reasoning in International Relations and Domestic Affairs.* Cambridge University Press, 1991.

Krehbiel, Keith. *Pivotal Politics: A Theory of U.S. Lawmaking.* University of Chicago Press, 2010.

Kriesi, Hanspeter, Edgar Grande, Romain Lachat, Martin Dolezal, Simon Bornschier, and Timotheos Frey. "Globalization and the Transformation of the National Political Space: Six European Countries Compared." *European Journal of Political Research* 45, no. 6 (October 1, 2006): 921–56.

Krishna, Vijay, and John Morgan. "A Model of Expertise." *Quarterly Journal of Economics* 116, no. 2 (May 1, 2001): 747–75.

Krueger, Dana. "Combat Zone: Mondev International, Ltd. v. United States and the Backlash Against NAFTA Chapter 11 Note." *Boston University International Law Journal* 21 (2003): 399–426.

Kruskal, J. B. "Multidimensional Scaling by Optimizing Goodness of Fit to a Nonmetric Hypothesis." *Psychometrika* 29, no. 1 (March 1, 1964): 1–27.

Kydd, Andrew H. "Rationalist Approaches to Conflict Prevention and Resolution." *Annual Review of Political Science* 13, no. 1 (2010): 101–21.

———. *Trust and Mistrust in International Relations.* Princeton University Press, 2005.

———. "Trust, Reassurance, and Cooperation." *International Organization* 54, no. 2 (April 1, 2000): 325–57.

———. "When Can Mediators Build Trust?" *American Political Science Review* 100, no. 3 (2006): 449–62.

———. "Which Side Are You On? Bias, Credibility, and Mediation." *American Journal of Political Science* 47, no. 4 (October 1, 2003): 597–611.

Lacher, Hannes. "Embedded Liberalism, Disembedded Markets: Reconceptualising the Pax Americana." *New Political Economy* 4, no. 3 (November 1, 1999): 343–60.

Langford, Malcolm, and Daniel Behn. "Managing Backlash: The Evolving Investment Treaty Arbitrator?" *European Journal of International Law* 29, no. 2 (2018): 551–80.

Langford, Malcolm, Daniel Behn, and Ole Kristian Fauchald. "Backlash and State Strategies in International Investment Law." SSRN Scholarly Paper, May 30, 2017. https://papers.ssrn.com/abstract=2704344.

Larsson, Olof, and Daniel Naurin. "Judicial Independence and Political Uncertainty: How the Risk of Override Affects the Court of Justice of the EU." *International Organization* 70, no. 2 (April 2016): 377–408.

Lebovic, James H., and Erik Voeten. "The Cost of Shame: International Organizations and Foreign Aid in the Punishing of Human Rights Violators." *Journal of Peace Research* 46, no. 1 (January 1, 2009): 79–97.

———. "The Politics of Shame: The Condemnation of Country Human Rights Practices in the UNCHR." *International Studies Quarterly* 50, no. 4 (December 1, 2006): 861–88.

Lee, Haillie. "A Liberal Reward? How Do State Foreign Policy Preferences Condition Investors' Perception of BITs Compliance?" Working paper, 2019.

Leeds, Brett Ashley. "Alliance Reliability in Times of War: Explaining State Decisions to Violate Treaties." *International Organization* 57, no. 4 (September 2003): 801–27.

Leeds, Brett Ashley. "Why Do States Sign Alliances?" In *Emerging Trends in the Social and Behavioral Sciences*, 1–14. John Wiley, 2015.

Leffler, Melvyn P. "The Cold War: What Do 'We Now Know'?" *American Historical Review* 104, no. 2 (April 1, 1999): 501–24.

———. *For the Soul of Mankind: The United States, the Soviet Union, and the Cold War*. Macmillan, 2007.

———. *A Preponderance of Power: National Security, the Truman Administration, and the Cold War*. Stanford University Press, 1992.

Le Melle, Tilden J. "Race in International Relations." *International Studies Perspectives* 10, no. 1 (2009): 77–83.

Lemke, Douglas, and William Reed. "The Relevance of Politically Relevant Dyads." *Journal of Conflict Resolution* 45, no. 1 (February 1, 2001): 126–44.

Li, Quan, and Adam Resnick. "Reversal of Fortunes: Democratic Institutions and Foreign Direct Investment Inflows to Developing Countries." *International Organization* 57, no. 1 (2003): 175–211.

Liao, Steven, and Daniel McDowell. "No Reservations: International Order and Demand for the Renminbi as a Reserve Currency." *International Studies Quarterly* 60, no. 2 (June 1, 2016): 272–93.

Lijphart, Arend. "The Analysis of Bloc Voting in the General Assembly: A Critique and a Proposal." *American Political Science Review* 57, no. 4 (December 1963): 902–17.

Lim, Daniel Yew Mao, and James Raymond Vreeland. "Regional Organizations and International Politics: Japanese Influence over the Asian Development Bank and the UN Security Council." *World Politics* 65, no. 1 (January 2013): 34–72.

Lindley, Dan. *Promoting Peace with Information: Transparency as a Tool of Security Regimes*. Princeton University Press, 2007.

Lipscy, Phillip Y. "Explaining Institutional Change: Policy Areas, Outside Options, and the Bretton Woods Institutions." *American Journal of Political Science* 59, no. 2 (February 1, 2015): 341–56.

———. *Renegotiating the World Order: Institutional Change in International Relations*. Cambridge University Press, 2016.

Lipson, Charles. *Standing Guard: Protecting Foreign Capital in the Nineteenth and Twentieth Centuries*. University of California Press, 1985.

Lupu, Yonatan. "International Judicial Legitimacy: Lessons from National Courts." *Theoretical Inquiries in Law* 14, no. 2 (2013): 437–54.

———. "Why Do States Join Some Universal Treaties but Not Others? An Analysis of Treaty Commitment Preferences." *Journal of Conflict Resolution* 60, no. 7 (2016): 1219–50.

Lyne, Mona M., Daniel L. Nielson, and Michael J. Tierney. "Controlling Coalitions: Social Lending at the Multilateral Development Banks." *Review of International Organizations* 4, no. 4 (September 10, 2009): 407–33.

Madinah, T. "Did He Jump, or Was He Pushed?" *New African*, no. 394 (2001): 8.

Madsen, Mikael Rask. "The Challenging Authority of the European Court of Human

Rights: From Cold War Legal Diplomacy to the Brighton Declaration and Backlash." *Law and Contemporary Problems* 79, no. 1 (2016): 141–78.

Madsen, Mikael Rask, Pola Cebulak, and Micha Wiebusch. "Backlash Against International Courts: Explaining the Forms and Patterns of Resistance to International Courts." *International Journal of Law in Context* 14, no. 2 (June 2018): 197–220.

Maggi, Giovanni, and Massimo Morelli. "Self-Enforcing Voting in International Organizations." *American Economic Review* 96, no. 4 (2006): 1137–58.

Majone, Giandomenico. "Nonmajoritarian Institutions and the Limits of Democratic Governance: A Political Transaction-Cost Approach." *Journal of Institutional and Theoretical Economics* 157, no. 1 (2001): 57–78.

Malamud, Carlos. "Venezuela's Withdrawal from the Andean Community of Nations and the Consequences for Regional Integration." Royal Institute, 2006.

Mancini, Susanna. "The Crucifix Rage: Supranational Constitutionalism Bumps Against the Counter-Majoritarian Difficulty." *European Constitutional Law Review* 6, no. 1 (February 2010): 6–27.

Mansfield, Edward D., Helen V. Milner, and B. Peter Rosendorff. "Why Democracies Cooperate More: Electoral Control and International Trade Agreements." *International Organization* 56, no. 3 (July 2002): 477–513.

Mansfield, Edward D., and Jon C. Pevehouse. "Democratization and International Organizations." *International Organization* 60, no. 1 (January 1, 2006): 137–67.

Mansfield, Edward D., Jon C. Pevehouse, and David H. Bearce. "Preferential Trading Arrangements and Military Disputes." *Security Studies* 9, nos. 1–2 (1999): 92–118.

Maoz, Zeev, Ranan D. Kuperman, Lesley Terris, and Ilan Talmud. "Structural Equivalence and International Conflict: A Social Networks Analysis." *Journal of Conflict Resolution* 50, no. 5 (October 1, 2006): 664–89.

March, James G., and Johan P. Olsen. "The Institutional Dynamics of International Political Orders." *International Organization* 52, no. 4 (1998): 943–69.

Marinov, Nikolay, and Hein Goemans. "Coups and Democracy." *British Journal of Political Science* 44, no. 4 (October 2014): 799–825.

Marks, Gary W., and Marco R. Steenbergen. *European Integration and Political Conflict*. Cambridge University Press, 2004.

Marks, Gary, Carole J. Wilson, and Leonard Ray. "National Political Parties and European Integration." *American Journal of Political Science* 46, no. 3 (2002): 585–94.

Marshall, Monty G., Keith Jaggers, and Ted Robert Gurr. "Polity IV Project." Center for International Development and Conflict Management at the University of Maryland College Park, 2002.

Martin, Lisa L. "Institutions and Cooperation: Sanctions during the Falkland Islands Conflict." *International Security* 16, no. 4 (1992): 143–78.

——. "Interests, Power, and Multilateralism." *International Organization* 46, no. 4 (1992): 765–92.

Martin, Lisa L., and Beth A. Simmons. "Theories and Empirical Studies of International Institutions." *International Organization* 52, no. 4 (1998): 729–57.

Mattes, Michaela, Brett Ashley Leeds, and Royce Carroll. "Leadership Turnover and

Foreign Policy Change: Societal Interests, Domestic Institutions, and Voting in the United Nations." *International Studies Quarterly* 59, no. 2 (June 1, 2015): 280–90.

Maurer, Noel. *The Empire Trap: The Rise and Fall of U.S. Intervention to Protect American Property Overseas, 1893–2013*. Princeton University Press, 2013.

Mazower, Mark. *Governing the World: The History of an Idea, 1815 to the Present*. Penguin, 2012.

McAdams, Richard H., and Janice Nadler. "Coordinating in the Shadow of the Law: Two Contextualized Tests of the Focal Point Theory of Legal Compliance." *Law & Society Review* 42, no. 4 (2008): 865–98.

McCubbins, Mathew D., and Thomas Schwartz. "Congressional Oversight Overlooked: Police Patrols versus Fire Alarms." *American Journal of Political Science* 28, no. 1 (1984): 165–79.

McDonald, Patrick J. "Great Powers, Hierarchy, and Endogenous Regimes: Rethinking the Domestic Causes of Peace." *International Organization* 69, no. 3 (2015): 557–88.

McKelvey, Richard D. "Intransitivities in Multidimensional Voting Models and Some Implications for Agenda Control." *Journal of Economic Theory* 12, no. 3 (June 1976): 472–82.

McNamara, Kathleen R. *The Currency of Ideas: Monetary Politics in the European Union*. Cornell University Press, 1998.

McNulty, Des, Nick Watson, and Gregory Philo. "Human Rights and Prisoners' Rights: The British Press and the Shaping of Public Debate." *Howard Journal of Criminal Justice* 53, no. 4 (September 1, 2014): 360–76.

Mearsheimer, John J. "Back to the Future: Instability in Europe after the Cold War." *International Security* 15, no. 1 (1990): 5–56.

———. "Bound to Fail: The Rise and Fall of the Liberal International Order." *International Security* 43, no. 4 (April 1, 2019): 7–50.

———. "The False Promise of International Institutions." *International Security* 19, no. 3 (1994): 5–49. https://doi.org/10.2307/2539078.

———. *The Tragedy of Great Power Politics*. Norton, 2001.

———. "Why the Ukraine Crisis Is the West's Fault: The Liberal Delusions That Provoked Putin." *Foreign Affairs* 93 (2014): 77–89.

Meredith, Martin. *Mugabe: Power, Plunder and the Struggle for Zimbabwe*. New ed. Public Affairs, 2007.

Mesquita, Bruce Bueno de. "Measuring Systemic Polarity." *Journal of Conflict Resolution* 19, no. 2 (June 1, 1975): 187–216.

Meyer, John W., John Boli, Thomas George M., and Francisco O. Ramirez. "World Society and the Nation-State." *American Journal of Sociology* 103, no. 1 (July 1, 1997): 144–81.

Milner, Helen V. "Globalization, Development, and International Institutions: Normative and Positive Perspectives." *Perspectives on Politics* 3, no. 4 (December 2005): 833–54.

Milner, Helen V., and Benjamin Judkins. "Partisanship, Trade Policy, and Globalization: Is There a Left-Right Divide on Trade Policy?" *International Studies Quarterly* 48, no. 1 (March 1, 2004): 95–120.

Milward, Alan. *The European Rescue of the Nation State*. Routledge, 1999.

———. *The Reconstruction of Western Europe, 1945–51*. Routledge, 1984.

Mitrany, David. *A Working Peace System: An Argument for the Functional Development of International Organization*. Oxford University Press, 1944.

Moe, Terry M. "Political Institutions: The Neglected Side of the Story." *Journal of Law, Economics, and Organization* 6 (1990): 213–53.

Moravcsik, Andrew. *The Choice for Europe: Social Purpose and State Power from Messina to Maastricht*. Routledge, 1998.

———. "The Origins of Human Rights Regimes: Democratic Delegation in Postwar Europe." *International Organization* 54, no. 2 (April 1, 2000): 217–52.

———. "Preferences and Power in the European Community: A Liberal Intergovernmentalist Approach." *Journal of Common Market Studies* 31, no. 4 (1993): 473–524.

———. "Taking Preferences Seriously: A Liberal Theory of International Politics." *International Organization* 51, no. 4 (October 1, 1997): 513–53.

Morgan, T. Clifton. "Issue Linkages in International Crisis Bargaining." *American Journal of Political Science* 34, no. 2 (1990): 311–33.

Morrow, James D. "Alliances: Why Write Them Down?" *Annual Review of Political Science* 3, no. 1 (2000): 63–83.

———. "Modeling the Forms of International Cooperation: Distribution versus Information." *International Organization* 48, no. 3 (1994): 387–423.

———. "A Spatial Model of International Conflict." *American Political Science Review* 80, no. 4 (December 1986): 1131–50.

Mudde, Cas. "The Populist Zeitgeist." *Government and Opposition* 39, no. 4 (2004): 542–63.

Mudde, Cas, and Cristóbal Rovira Kaltwasser. "Exclusionary vs. Inclusionary Populism: Comparing Contemporary Europe and Latin America." *Government and Opposition* 48, no. 2 (April 2013): 147–74.

———. *Populism in Europe and the Americas: Threat Or Corrective for Democracy?* Cambridge University Press, 2012.

"Mugabe Says Zimbabwe Land Seizures Will Continue." *Mail and Guardian*, February 28, 2009. http://mg.co.za/article/2009-02-28-mugabe-says-zimbabwe-land -seizures-will-continue.

Müller, Jan-Werner. "Populist Constitutions—A Contradiction in Terms?" *International Journal of Constitutional Law Blog*, April 23, 2017. www.iconnectblog. com/2017/04/populist-constitutions-a-contradiction-in-terms/.

———. *What Is Populism?* University of Pennsylvania Press, 2016.

Murray, C. R. G. "A Perfect Storm: Parliament and Prisoner Disenfranchisement." *Parliamentary Affairs* 66, no. 3 (July 1, 2013): 511–39.

Narlikar, Amrita, and Diana Tussie. "The G20 at the Cancun Ministerial: Developing Countries and Their Evolving Coalitions in the WTO." *World Economy* 27, no. 7 (July 1, 2004): 947–66.

Netesova, Yulia, and Torrey Taussig. "Putin's No Populist, but He Can Gain from Populist Movements Worldwide." *Brookings*, March 30, 2017. www.brookings.edu/blog /order-from-chaos/2017/03/30/putins-no-populist-but-he-can-gain-from -populist-movements-worldwide/.

Neumayer, Eric. "Distance, Power and Ideology: Diplomatic Representation in a World of Nation-States." *Area* 40, no. 2 (2008): 228–36.

Neumayer, Eric, and Laura Spess. "Do Bilateral Investment Treaties Increase Foreign Direct Investment to Developing Countries?" *World Development* 33, no. 10 (October 2005): 1567–85.

Newman, Abraham L. "Building Transnational Civil Liberties: Transgovernmental Entrepreneurs and the European Data Privacy Directive." *International Organization* 62, no. 1 (January 1, 2008): 103–30.

Nielson, Daniel L., and Michael J. Tierney. "Delegation to International Organizations: Agency Theory and World Bank Environmental Reform." *International Organization* 57, no. 2 (April 1, 2003): 241–76.

Norris, Pippa. *Cultural Backlash: Trump, Brexit, and Authoritarian Populism*. Cambridge University Press, 2019.

Nye, Joseph S., Jr. "Will the Liberal Order Survive: The History of an Idea Out of Order." *Foreign Affairs* 96 (2017): 10–16.

O'Keefe, P. J. "The United Nations and Permanent Sovereignty over Natural Resources." *Journal of World Trade Law* 8 (1974): 239–82.

Oneal, John R., and Bruce Russett. "The Kantian Peace: The Pacific Benefits of Democracy, Interdependence, and International Organizations, 1885–1992." *World Politics* 52, no. 1 (1999): 1–37.

———. "Rule of Three, Let It Be? When More Really Is Better." *Conflict Management and Peace Science* 22, no. 4 (December 1, 2005): 293–310.

Oneal, John R., Bruce Russett, and Michael L. Berbaum. "Causes of Peace: Democracy, Interdependence, and International Organizations, 1885–1992." *International Studies Quarterly* 47, no. 3 (2003): 371–93.

Orecki, Marcin. "Bye-Bye BITs? Poland Reviews Its Investment Policy." *Kluwer Arbitration Blog*, January 31, 2017.

Owen, John M. *Liberal Peace, Liberal War: American Politics and International Security*. Cornell University Press, 2000.

———. "When Do Ideologies Produce Alliances? The Holy Roman Empire, 1517–1555." *International Studies Quarterly* 49, no. 1 (March 1, 2005): 73–100.

Oye, Kenneth A. *Cooperation under Anarchy*. Princeton University Press, 1986.

Parpworth, Neil. "The South African Constitutional Court: Upholding the Rule of Law and the Separation of Powers." *Journal of African Law* 61, no. 2 (June 2017): 273–87.

Pauls, Scott D., and Skyler J. Cranmer. "Affinity Communities in United Nations Voting: Implications for Democracy, Cooperation, and Conflict." *Physica A: Statistical Mechanics and Its Applications* 484 (October 15, 2017): 428–39.

Pedersen, Susan. "Back to the League of Nations." *American Historical Review* 112, no. 4 (October 1, 2007): 1091–1117.

Peinhardt, Clint, and Rachel L. Wellhausen. "Withdrawing from Investment Treaties but Protecting Investment." *Global Policy* 7, no. 4 (November 1, 2016): 571–76.

Pelc, Krzysztof. "What Explains the Low Success Rate of Investor-State Disputes?" *International Organization* 71, no. 3 (2017): 559–83.

Perfect, David. "The Gambia under Yahya Jammeh: An Assessment." *Round Table* 99, no. 406 (February 1, 2010): 53–63.

Peterson, Timothy M. "Insiders versus Outsiders: Preferential Trade Agreements, Trade Distortions, and Militarized Conflict." *Journal of Conflict Resolution* 59, no. 4 (June 1, 2015): 698–727.

Pevehouse, Jon, Timothy Nordstrom, and Kevin Warnke. "The Correlates of War 2 International Governmental Organizations Data Version 2.0." *Conflict Management and Peace Science* 21, no. 2 (January 1, 2004): 101–19.

Pevehouse, Jon, and Bruce Russett. "Democratic International Governmental Organizations Promote Peace." *International Organization* 60, no. 4 (2006): 969–1000.

Pierson, Paul. "Increasing Returns, Path Dependence, and the Study of Politics." *American Political Science Review* 94, no. 2 (June 2000): 251–67.

Poast, Paul, and Johannes Urpelainen. "How International Organizations Support Democratization: Preventing Authoritarian Reversals or Promoting Consolidation?" *World Politics* 67, no. 1 (2015): 72–113.

Polachek, Solomon, and Jun Xiang. "How Opportunity Costs Decrease the Probability of War in an Incomplete Information Game." *International Organization* 64, no. 1 (January 2010): 133–44.

Polanco Lazo, Rodrigo. "The No of Tokyo Revisited: Or How Developed Countries Learned to Start Worrying and Love the Calvo Doctrine." *ICSID Review—Foreign Investment Law Journal* 30, no. 1 (February 1, 2015): 172–93.

Pollack, Mark A. "Delegation, Agency, and Agenda Setting in the European Community." *International Organization* 51, no. 1 (December 1997): 99–134.

Poole, Keith T., Jeffrey B. Lewis, James Lo, and Royce Carroll. "Scaling Roll Call Votes with W-NOMINATE in R." SSRN Scholarly Paper, September 30, 2008. http://papers.ssrn.com/abstract=1276082.

Poole, Keith T., and Howard Rosenthal. *Congress: A Political-Economic History of Roll Call Voting*. Oxford University Press, 2000.

——. "D-Nominate after 10 Years: A Comparative Update to Congress: A Political-Economic History of Roll-Call Voting." *Legislative Studies Quarterly* 26, no. 1 (February 2001): 5–29.

——. "A Spatial Model for Legislative Roll Call Analysis." *American Journal of Political Science* 29, no. 2 (1985): 357–84.

Posner, Elliot. "Making Rules for Global Finance: Transatlantic Regulatory Cooperation at the Turn of the Millennium." *International Organization* 63, no. 4 (2009): 665–99.

Posner, Eric A. "Liberal Internationalism and the Populist Backlash Symposium: The Forefront of International Law." *Arizona State Law Journal* 49 (2017): 795–820.

Pouliot, Vincent. *International Pecking Orders: The Politics and Practice of Multilateral Diplomacy*. Cambridge University Press, 2016.

Poulsen, Lauge N. Skovgaard. *Bounded Rationality and Economic Diplomacy: The Politics of Investment Treaties in Developing Countries*. Cambridge University Press, 2015.

Rathbun, Brian. *Partisan Interventions*. Cornell University Press, 2004.

——. "Politics and Paradigm Preferences: The Implicit Ideology of International Relations Scholars." *International Studies Quarterly* 56, no. 3 (September 1, 2012): 607–22.

Rauh, Christian, and Michael Zürn. "Authority, Politicization, and Alternative Justifications: Endogenous Legitimation Dynamics in Global Economic Governance1."
Review of International Political Economy 27, no. 3 (2020): 583–611.

Ravenhill, John. "The 'New East Asian Regionalism': A Political Domino Effect." *Review of International Political Economy* 17, no. 2 (2010): 178–208.

Ray, James Lee. "Explaining Interstate Conflict and War: What Should Be Controlled
For?" *Conflict Management and Peace Science* 20, no. 2 (September 1, 2003):
1–31.

Reed, William, David H. Clark, Timothy Nordstrom, and Wonjae Hwang. "War, Power,
and Bargaining." *Journal of Politics* 70, no. 4 (2008): 1203–16.

Report of the Ad Hoc Committee of the Sixth Special Session, General Assembly.
"2229th Plenary Meeting, A/PV.2229." May 1, 1974.

Reus-Smit, Christian. "The Constitutional Structure of International Society and the
Nature of Fundamental Institutions." *International Organization* 51, no. 4 (1997):
555–89.

Riker, William H. *The Art of Political Manipulation.* Yale University Press, 1986.

Risse, Thomas, and Kathryn Sikkink. *The Persistent Power of Human Rights: From
Commitment to Compliance.* Cambridge University Press, 2013.

Risse-Kappen, Thomas. *Cooperation among Democracies: The European Influence on
U.S. Foreign Policy.* Princeton University Press, 1997.

Roberts, Kenneth M. "Neoliberalism and the Transformation of Populism in Latin
America: The Peruvian Case." *World Politics* 48, no. 1 (October 1995): 82–116.

Rodrigues Vieira, Vinícius. "Who Joins Counter-hegemonic IGOs? Early and Late
Members of the China-Led Asian Infrastructure Investment Bank." *Research &
Politics* 5, no. 2 (April 1, 2018).

Rodrik, Dani. *The Globalization Paradox: Democracy and the Future of the World
Economy.* Norton, 2011.

Romer, Thomas, and Howard Rosenthal. "Political Resource Allocation, Controlled
Agendas, and the Status Quo." *Public Choice* 33, no. 4 (December 1978): 27–43.

Rosato, Sebastian. "The Inscrutable Intentions of Great Powers." *International Security* 39, no. 3 (January 1, 2015): 48–88.

Rosenboim, Or. *The Emergence of Globalism: Visions of World Order in Britain and
the United States, 1939–1950.* Princeton University Press, 2017.

Ross, Tim. "Tories Vote to Scrap 'Undemocratic' Human Rights Act." *Telegraph*, December 4, 2012. www.telegraph.co.uk/news/politics/9722668/Tories-vote-to
-scrap-undemocratic-Human-Rights-Act.html.

Rudolph, Christopher. *Power and Principle: The Politics of International Criminal
Courts.* Cornell University Press, 2017.

Rudra, Nita, and Jennifer Tobin. "When Does Globalization Help the Poor?" *Annual
Review of Political Science* 20, no. 1 (2017): 287–307.

Ruggie, John Gerard. "International Regimes, Transactions, and Change: Embedded
Liberalism in the Postwar Economic Order." *International Organization* 36, no. 2
(March 1982): 379–415.

———. "Multilateralism: The Anatomy of an Institution." *International Organization*
46, no. 3 (June 1992): 561–98.

Russett, Bruce, John R. Oneal, and David R. Davis. "The Third Leg of the Kantian

Tripod for Peace: International Organizations and Militarized Disputes, 1950–85." *International Organization* 52, no. 3 (1998): 441–67.

Saine, Abdoulaye. "The Gambia's 'Elected Autocrat Poverty, Peripherality, and Political Instability,' 1994–2006: A Political Economy Assessment." *Armed Forces & Society* 34, no. 3 (April 1, 2008): 450–73.

Saint-Simon, Henri de. *Declaration of Principles.* 1817.

Salacuse, Jeswald W. "BIT by BIT: The Growth of Bilateral Investment Treaties and Their Impact on Foreign Investment in Developing Countries." *International Lawyer* 24, no. 3 (1990): 655–75.

Sandholtz, Wayne, Yining Bei, and Kayla Caldwell. "Backlash and International Human Rights Courts." Paper prepared for the Contracting Human Rights Workshop at the University of California, Santa Barbara, January 26–28, 2017.

Schelling, Thomas C. *The Strategy of Conflict.* Harvard University Press, 1960.

Schneider, Christina J., and Branislav L. Slantchev. "Abiding by the Vote: Between-Groups Conflict in International Collective Action." *International Organization* 67, no. 4 (October 2013): 759–96.

Schneider, Gerald, Katherine Barbieri, and Nils Petter Gleditsch. *Globalization and Armed Conflict.* Rowman & Littlefield, 2003.

Schultz, Kenneth A. "What's in a Claim? De Jure versus De Facto Borders in Interstate Territorial Disputes." *Journal of Conflict Resolution* 58, no. 6 (2014): 1059–84.

Schweller, Randall L. "The Problem of International Order Revisited: A Review Essay." *International Security* 26, no. 1 (July 1, 2001): 161–86.

Sell, Susan, and Christopher May. "Moments in Law: Contestation and Settlement in the History of Intellectual Property." *Review of International Political Economy* 8, no. 3 (January 1, 2001): 467–500.

Sen, Ronojoy. "India's Democracy at 70: The Disputed Role of the Courts." *Journal of Democracy* 28, no. 3 (July 6, 2017): 96–105.

Shaffer, Gregory, Manfred Elsig, and Mark A. Pollack. "U.S. Threats to the WTO Appellate Body." SSRN Scholarly Paper, December 13, 2017. https://papers.ssrn.com/abstract=3087524.

Shea, Donald. *The Calvo Clause: A Problem of Inter-American and International Law and Diplomacy.* University of Minnesota Press, 1955.

Shelton, Dinah, and Alexandra Huneeus. "In Re Direct Action of Unconstitutionality Initiated Against the Declaration of Acceptance of the Jurisdiction of the Inter-American Court of Human Rights." *American Journal of International Law* 109, no. 4 (2015): 866–72.

Shepsle, Kenneth A. "Institutional Arrangements and Equilibrium in Multidimensional Voting Models." *American Journal of Political Science* 23, no. 1 (February 1, 1979): 27–59.

Shepsle, Kenneth A., and Barry R. Weingast. "Structure-Induced Equilibrium and Legislative Choice." *Public Choice* 37, no. 3 (January 1, 1981): 503–19.

———. "Why So Much Stability? Majority Voting, Legislative Institutions, and Gordon Tullock." *Public Choice* 152, nos. 1–2 (July 1, 2012): 83–95.

Signorino, Curtis S., and Jeffrey M. Ritter. "Tau-b or Not Tau-b: Measuring the Similarity of Foreign Policy Positions." *International Studies Quarterly* 43, no. 1 (March 1, 1999): 115–44.

Simmons, Beth A. "Bargaining over BITs, Arbitrating Awards: The Regime for Protection and Promotion of International Investment." *World Politics* 66, no. 1 (January 2014): 12–46.

———. *Mobilizing for Human Rights: International Law in Domestic Politics*. Cambridge University Press, 2009.

———. "Treaty Compliance and Violation." *Annual Review of Political Science* 13, no. 1 (2010): 273–96.

Simmons, Beth A., and Allison Danner. "Credible Commitments and the International Criminal Court." *International Organization* 64, no. 2 (April 19, 2010): 225–56.

Simmons, Beth A., Frank Dobbin, and Geoffrey Garrett. "Introduction: The International Diffusion of Liberalism." *International Organization* 60, no. 4 (2006): 781–810.

Simmons, Beth A., and Zachary Elkins. "The Globalization of Liberalization: Policy Diffusion in the International Political Economy." *American Political Science Review* 98, no. 1 (2004): 171–89.

Sims, Alexandra. "Vladimir Putin Signs Law Allowing Russia to Ignore International Human Rights Rulings." *Independent*, December 15, 2015.

Singer, David Andrew. *Regulating Capital: Setting Standards for the International Financial System*. Cornell University Press, 2007.

Singer, J. David. "Reconstructing the Correlates of War Dataset on Material Capabilities of States, 1816–1985." *International Interactions* 14, no. 2 (May 1, 1988): 115–32.

Slaughter, Anne-Marie. *A New World Order*. Princeton University Press, 2009.

Snyder, Glenn H. "The Security Dilemma in Alliance Politics." *World Politics* 36, no. 4 (July 1984): 461–95.

Stein, Arthur A. "Coordination and Collaboration: Regimes in an Anarchic World." *International Organization* 36, no. 2 (1982): 299–324.

Stiansen, Øyvind, and Erik Voeten. "Backlash and Judicial Restraint: Evidence from the European Court of Human Rights." SSRN Scholarly Paper, March 30, 2018. https://papers.ssrn.com/abstract=3166110.

Stinnett, Douglas M., Jaroslav Tir, Paul F. Diehl, Philip Schafer, and Charles Gochman. "The Correlates of War (Cow) Project Direct Contiguity Data, Version 3.0." *Conflict Management and Peace Science* 19, no. 2 (September 1, 2002): 59–67.

St. John, Taylor. *The Rise of Investor-State Arbitration: Politics, Law, and Unintended Consequences*. Oxford University Press, 2018.

Stone, Randall W. *Controlling Institutions: International Organizations and the Global Economy*. Cambridge University Press, 2011.

———. "Informal Governance in International Organizations: Introduction to the Special Issue." *Review of International Organizations* 8, no. 2 (June 2013): 121–36.

Stone Sweet, Alec, and Thomas Brunell. "The European Court of Justice, State Noncompliance, and the Politics of Override." *American Political Science Review* 106, no. 1 (February 2012): 204–13.

———. "Trustee Courts and the Judicialization of International Regimes." *Journal of Law and Courts* 1, no. 1 (March 2013): 61–88.

Stuenkel, Oliver. "The BRICS and the Future of R2P." *Global Responsibility to Protect* 6, no. 1 (January 1, 2014): 3–28.

Sweeney, Kevin J. "The Severity of Interstate Disputes: Are Dyadic Capability Preponderances Really More Pacific?" *Journal of Conflict Resolution* 47, no. 6 (December 1, 2003): 728–50.

Sweet, Alec Stone, and Thomas L. Brunell. "Constructing a Supranational Constitution: Dispute Resolution and Governance in the European Community." *American Political Science Review* 92, no. 1 (March 1, 1998): 63–81.

Sweet, Alec Stone, and Wayne Sandholtz. "European Integration and Supranational Governance." *Journal of European Public Policy* 4, no. 3 (September 1, 1997): 297–317.

Swift, Art. "Honesty and Ethics Rating of Clergy Slides to New Low: Nurses Again Top List; Lobbyists Are Worst." Gallup, December 16, 2013. www.gallup.com/poll /166298/honesty-ethics-rating-clergy-slides-new-low.aspx?utm_source=tagrss &utm_medium=rss&utm_campaign=syndication&utm_reader=feedly.

Tallberg, Jonas, and Michael Zürn. "The Legitimacy and Legitimation of International Organizations: Introduction and Framework." *Review of International Organizations* 14 (2019): 581–606.

Thacker, Strom C. "The High Politics of IMF Lending." *World Politics* 52, no. 1 (1999): 38–75.

Thatcher, Mark, and Alec Stone Sweet. "Theory and Practice of Delegation to Non-majoritarian Institutions." *West European Politics* 25, no. 1 (2002): 1–22.

Thomas, Neil H. "Land Reform in Zimbabwe." *Third World Quarterly* 24, no. 4 (2003): 691–712.

Thompson, Alexander. *Channels of Power: The UN Security Council and U.S. Statecraft in Iraq.* Cornell University Press, 2010.

———. "Coercion through IOs: The Security Council and the Logic of Information Transmission." *International Organization* 60, no. 1 (2006): 1–34.

"Thorny Human Rights Reform Put Off at OAS Meeting." Reuters, June 6, 2012. http:// global.factiva.com/redir/default.aspx?P=sa&an=LBA0000020120606e8660004 y&cat=a&ep=ASE.

Tillman, Erik R. "Authoritarianism and Citizen Attitudes towards European Integration." *European Union Politics* 14, no. 4 (December 1, 2013): 566–89.

Tobin, Jennifer L., and Marc L. Busch. "A BIT Is Better Than a Lot: Bilateral Investment Treaties and Preferential Trade Agreements." *World Politics* 62, no. 1 (2010): 1–42.

Torre, Carlos de la. "Technocratic Populism in Ecuador." *Journal of Democracy* 24, no. 3 (July 11, 2013): 33–46.

Tourinho, Marcos. "The Co-constitution of Order." *International Organization* (forthcoming).

Tourinho, Marcos, Oliver Stuenkel, and Sarah Brockmeier. "'Responsibility while Protecting': Reforming R2P Implementation." *Global Society* 30, no. 1 (January 2, 2016): 134–50.

Tsebelis, George, and Geoffrey Garrett. "Legislative Politics in the European Union." *European Union Politics* 1, no. 1 (February 1, 2000): 9–36.

U.S. Bureau of Economic Analysis. "Foreign Direct Investment in the U.S.: Balance of Payments and Direct Investment Position Data." March 19, 2020. www.bea.gov /international/di1fdibal.

Vandevelde, Kenneth J. "The Bilateral Investment Treaty Program of the United States." *Cornell International Law Journal* 21 (1988): 201–76.

———. "Of Politics and Markets: The Shifting Ideology of the BITs." *International Tax and Business Law* 11 (1993): 159–76.

———. "The Political Economy of a Bilateral Investment Treaty." *American Journal of International Law* 92, no. 4 (1998): 621–41.

Verdier, Pierre-Hugues, and Erik Voeten. "How Does Customary International Law Change? The Case of State Immunity." *International Studies Quarterly* 59, no. 2 (June 1, 2015): 209–22.

Vincentelli, Ignacio A. "The Uncertain Future of ICSID in Latin America." *Law and Business Review of the Americas* 16 (2010): 409–56.

Voeten, Erik. "Clashes in the Assembly." *International Organization* 54, no. 2 (2000): 185–215

———. "Data and Analyses of Voting in the UN General Assembly." SSRN Scholarly Paper, July 17, 2012. http://papers.ssrn.com/abstract=2111149.

———. "Does Participation in International Organizations Increase Cooperation?" *Review of International Organizations* 9, no. 3 (September 21, 2013): 285–308.

———. "Making Sense of the Design of International Institutions." *Annual Review of Political Science* 22, no. 1 (2019): 147–63.

———. "Outside Options and the Logic of Security Council Action." *American Political Science Review* 95, no. 4 (December 1, 2001): 845–58.

———. "The Political Origins of the UN Security Council's Ability to Legitimize the Use of Force." *International Organization* 59, no. 3 (July 2005): 527–57.

———. "The Politics of International Judicial Appointments: Evidence from the European Court of Human Rights." *International Organization* 61, no. 4 (October 2007): 669–701.

———. "Populism and Backlashes Against International Courts." SSRN Scholarly Paper, February 2, 2019. https://papers.ssrn.com/abstract=3255764.

———. "Public Opinion and the Legitimacy of International Courts." *Theoretical Inquiries in Law* 14, no. 2 (2013): 411–36.

———. "Resisting the Lonely Superpower: Responses of States in the United Nations to U.S. Dominance." *Journal of Politics* 66, no. 3 (2004): 729–54.

Waibel, Michael, ed. *The Backlash Against Investment Arbitration: Perceptions and Reality*. Wolters Kluwer, 2010.

Walt, Stephen. "The Collapse of the Liberal World Order." *Foreign Policy*, 2016. https:// foreignpolicy.com/2016/06/26/the-collapse-of-the-liberal-world-order-european -union-brexit-donald-trump/.

Walter, Barbara F. "Designing Transitions from Civil War: Demobilization, Democratization, and Commitments to Peace." *International Security* 24, no. 1 (July 1, 1999): 127–55.

Waltz, Kenneth N. *Theory of International Politics*. Waveland, 2010.

Wang, T. Y. "U.S. Foreign Aid and UN Voting: An Analysis of Important Issues." *International Studies Quarterly* 43, no. 1 (March 1, 1999): 199–210.

Ward, Hugh, and Han Dorussen. "Standing alongside Your Friends: Network Centrality and Providing Troops to UN Peacekeeping Operations." *Journal of Peace Research* 53, no. 3 (May 1, 2016): 392–408.

Weber, Cynthia. *International Relations Theory: A Critical Introduction*. Routledge, 2013.

Weissmann, Jordan. "Waking the Sleeping Dragon." *Slate*, September 28, 2016. www .slate.com/articles/business/the_next_20/2016/09/when_china_joined_the _wto_it_kick_started_the_chinese_economy_and_roused.html.

Wendt, Alexander. "Collective Identity Formation and the International State." *American Political Science Review* 88, no. 2 (1994): 384–96.

———. "Constructing International Politics." *International Security* 20, no. 1 (1995): 71–81.

———. *Social Theory of International Politics*. Cambridge University Press, 1999.

Weston, Burns H. "The Charter of Economic Rights and Duties of States and the Deprivation of Foreign-Owned Wealth International Law of Expropriation." *American Journal of International Law* 75 (1981): 437–75.

Weyland, Kurt. "Neoliberal Populism in Latin America and Eastern Europe." *Comparative Politics* 31, no. 4 (1999): 379–401.

Wolford, Scott. *The Politics of Military Coalitions*. Cambridge University Press, 2015.

Xi Jinping. "Working Together to Forge a New Partnership of Win-Win Cooperation and Create a Community of Shared Future for Mankind Statement." Statement at the General Debate of the 70th Session of the UN General Assembly, New York, September 28, 2015.

Zeng, Ka. "Understanding the Institutional Variation in China's Bilateral Investment Treaties (BITs): The Complex Interplay of Domestic and International Influences." *Journal of Contemporary China* 25, no. 97 (January 2, 2016): 112–29.

Zürn, Michael. "Global Governance and Legitimacy Problems." *Government and Opposition* 39, no. 2 (2004): 260–87.

———. "The Politicization of World Politics and Its Effects: Eight Propositions." *European Political Science Review* 6, no. 1 (February 2014): 47–71.

Zürn, Michael, Martin Binder, and Matthias Ecker-Ehrhardt. "International Authority and Its Politicization." *International Theory* 4, no. 1 (March 2012): 69–106.

Zwart, Tom. "More Human Rights Than Court: Why the Legitimacy of the European Court of Human Rights Is in Need of Repair and How It Can Be Done." In *The European Court of Human Rights and Its Discontents*, edited by Spyridon Flogaitis, Tom Zwart, and Julie Fraser, 71–95. Edward Elgar, 2013.

INDEX

Page numbers in italics refer to figures

A NOTE ON THE TYPE

{⸎⸎⸎}

THIS BOOK has been composed in Miller, a Scotch Roman typeface designed by Matthew Carter and first released by Font Bureau in 1997. It resembles Monticello, the typeface developed for The Papers of Thomas Jefferson in the 1940s by C. H. Griffith and P. J. Conkwright and reinterpreted in digital form by Carter in 2003.

Pleasant Jefferson ("P. J.") Conkwright (1905–1986) was Typographer at Princeton University Press from 1939 to 1970. He was an acclaimed book designer and AIGA Medalist.

The ornament used throughout this book was designed by Pierre Simon Fournier (1712–1768) and was a favorite of Conkwright's, used in his design of the *Princeton University Library Chronicle*.

Lightning Source UK Ltd.
Milton Keynes UK
UKHW041000110121
376696UK00009BA/19